Norway:
Society and Culture

Editors
Eva Maagerø and Birte Simonsen

Norway:
Society and Culture

2. edition

Portal

© 2008 by Portal Books (Portal forlag), Kristiansand, Norway

2. edition

ISBN 978-82-92712-18-4

Distributed world-wide by fax +47 38 02 65 21, e-mail post@portalforlag.no or web-site www.portalforlag.no

Address:
Portal Books
Skippergaten 2
4611 Kristiansand
NORWAY

If you have comments about the contents of this book, or if you want to contact any of the authors, please get in touch with: post@portalforlag.no

Cover design: Marit Toppe Berg
Production manager: Steinsbu Design
Printing: OZGraf SA

Contents

Our Views on Norway

What does the word Norway make us think of? A wealthy oil nation, midnight sun and skiing, polar bears in the streets, a lot of languages and dialects and the noisiest students in the world – what is myth, and what is true?

In this book different authors with different backgrounds take you on a tour through Norwegian society and culture: history, literature, language, economy, politics, art, music, religion, and education. The aim is to present Norway through multiple voices and let the reader add his or her own knowledge, experiences and perspectives. One word in particular seems to link the authors texts together: equality. The concept of equality functions as a platform for understanding social and political conditions in Norway, and the different chapters try to explain how and why. The book consists of one opening chapter and then four parts: *History, Society, Culture* and *Facts about Norway.*

In the opening chapter *Andreas Aase* reflects on what it means to be a Norwegian. Does a Norwegian value system in fact exist? What environmental and historical factors have influenced our culture? How may egalitarian values be traced and explained? In addition to equality, Aase elaborates on two other values; moderation and nearness to nature.

The first part about Norwegian history starts with a chapter presenting an overview of the history of Norway, written by *Silve-Linn* and *Lars Aase.* This chapter provides the background for understanding all the other chapters in the book, and presents the reader with the most important historical lines and developments in Norwegian society.

Olav Arild Abrahamsen in his chapter asks why Norway is a wealthy nation. Is it because we have oil in the North Sea? Or would Norway have been a wealthy nation also without the oil? He takes us through 200 years of Norwegian history, discussing the economic modernization of the country in a long-term perspective.

Helje Kringlebotn Sødal and *Levi Geir Eidhamar* in the next chapter explore the significance of Christianity in Norway, from both a historical and a present-day perspective. Are people in Norway still religious, or has Norway become a secularized society, like many European societies?

The 17th of May is Norway's national day. It attracts much interest from all kind of visitors to Norway, especially in the way it is celebrated. It is a symbol both of freedom and democracy and of happiness and the future represented by children in processions all over the country. *Knut Mykland* gives a presentation of the 17th of May in a historical and national perspective.

The first article of part 2, Society, is about Norway as a welfare state. The notion of "a welfare state" is often connected to the Scandinavian region. *Olav Helge Angell* presents the structure of the welfare state in a Norwegian context, its formal organisation, its financing and its future challenges.

Compulsory, equal education has been a pillar of Norwegian society. *Arvid Hansen* in his chapter describes the development of the Norwegian school system through reflections about its organisation, curriculum, values, aims and the teacher's role. He relates school development and the school system to the values of equality and nature.

In the next two chapters *Kjetil Børhaug* presents important features of Norwegian politics in a national and a global context. Both national and international issues are discussed, and the reader obtains a better understanding of the domestic political life in Norway, of values which have been crucial in the development of Norway as a modern state, and of the role Norway plays in Europe and the world.

What is meant by the concept of equality? To what extent is Norwegian society "impregnated" by this value? *Pål Repstad* in his chapter discusses the concept of equality from different perspectives. He explicitly argues in favour of egalitarian values, and he asks whether equality has come to an end in modern Norway.

Eva Maagerø and *Birte Simonsen* present in their chapter the situation of minorities in Norway. In spite of its small population, our country has experienced the need to integrate both different national minorities and immigrants from all over the world. The Sámi population, one of the world's indigenous peoples, has a special status in Norwegian society with their own parliament and school curriculum in addition to their own language and culture.

Some people suggest that equality between adults and children has developed to an extreme extent, while others argue that Norwegian educational institutions train children for democracy. *Ann Christin E. Nilsen* describes in the last chapter of part 2 what Norwegian parents and society think about the upbringing of children.

The first chapter of the third part; culture, is about language. Norway's rather small population has two official Norwegian languages. Is it possible to look at this situation too from the viewpoint of equality? *Eva Maagerø* introduces the language situation and presents its historical and political background. She also discusses the status of dialects in Norway and the lack of an oral standard language.

Ibsen and Hamsun are well known all over the world. What about other Norwegian authors and other stories and poems? *Elise Seip Tønnessen* presents central Norwegian literature, and shows how literature plays a role in the building of a Norwegian identity. In a chapter about myths and tales she also takes us back to the stories of the Nordic gods and other mythological stories which have been, and still are, of great importance in Norwegian culture.

Norwegian children's literature has received much attention both in the Nordic countries and in Europe in recent decades. In the next chapter *Elise Seip Tønnessen* gives an overview of the most important literature for children. Some of the titles which are mentioned are translated into English, German or other languages.

Lisbet Skregelid in her chapter provides a brief overview of Norwegian art. She takes us back in history and presents a selection of works by Norwegian artists. She also describes trends in contemporary art, and presents modern works, which can be studied in museums and galleries today.

The last chapter of part 4 is about Norwegian music and is written by *Arvid Vollsnes*. It gives a broad introduction to different kinds of music in Norway, classical music, jazz, folk music and popular music. In the presentation, the development of music is closely related to the general development of Norwegian history and culture.

In the last part of the book, part 4, *Silve-Linn* and *Lars Aase* present facts about Norway: its geography, population and culture. Statistics and comparisons are used in order to illustrate differences and similarities between Norway and other countries of the world.

We hope readers will enjoy this textual journey through Norwegian history, society and culture that offers insights into our past and dreams about the future.

Eva Maagerø
Birte Simonsen

Mehamn
Honningsvåg Kjøllefjord Berlevåg
Båtsfjord
Vardø
Hammerfest Vadsø
Hasvik Skåidi
Tana bru
Okafjord Alta Kirkenes
Skjervøy FINNMARK Lakselv
Bjerkvik Storslett Karasjok
Tromsø TROMS
Gryllefjord Skibotn
Andenes Finnsnes Kautokeino
Andselv
Sortland Harstad
Stokmarknes
Svolvær Lødingen Narvik
Leknes
Stamsund
Reine Skutvika
Sørland
Røstlandet NORDLAND
Bodø Fauske
Sulitjelma
Ørnes
Mo i Rana
Sandnessjøen
Mosjøen
Brønnøysund Trofors
Majavatn
Rørvik
Namsos
NORD-TRØNDELAG
Steinkjer
Levanger
Kristiansund Orkanger Trondheim
MØRE OG
ROMSDAL Molde
SØR-TRØNDELAG
Sunndalsøra
Ålesund Røros
Sykkylven Åndalsnes Oppdal
Ørsta Geiranger
Volda Styn Tynset
Florø
Dombås
Lom
SOGN OG
FJORDANE Ferde
Øvre Årdal OPPLAND Koppang
Sogndal
Lillehammer HEDMARK
Fagernes
Voss Gjøvik Elverum
Bergen Gol Beitostølen Hamar
Geilo
Kinsarvik
HORDALAND Odda BUSKERUD Aldsvoll Kongsvinger
Leirvik Rjukan
Haukeligrend Hønefoss Oslo
Sauda Kongsberg OSLO
Haugesund Oslo Drammen
TELEMARK AKERSHUS
Seljord Notodden Moss
ROGALAND Ulefoss Horten ØSTFOLD
Stavanger Ålle Tønsberg Sarpsborg
Skien
Sandnes Pors- Sande Fredrikstad
Tonstad grunn fjord Halden
AUST- Kragerø
Egersund AGDER Evje Risør VESTFOLD
VEST- Tvedestrand
Flekkefjord AGDER Arendal
Grimstad
Farsund Lillesand
Mandal Kristiansand

It may seem like a contradiction when a nation that stresses democratic and egalitarian values is a monar-chy. However, the Norwegian royal family has become popular in Norway. One of the reasons is that to a large extent they have lived according to what are considered to be true Norwegian values: equality, mod-eration and nearness to nature. The most popular photo of King Olav V was taken on the underground in Oslo during the oil crisis in 1973. He is travelling together with ordinary people, and wants to pay for his own ticket (equality). He is wearing an old, worn-out anorak (moderation), and he is on his way to a nearby skiing area (nearness to nature).

Chapter 1

In Search of Norwegian Values

By Andreas Aase

Once upon a time, the nations of the world were invited to write a book about the elephant. The Germans, being both punctual and thorough, published a twelve volume work, before the deadline, entitled *A Short Introduction to the Life of Elephants*. In succession, the French published *The Elephant and L'amour*, the Danish *101 Ways to Cook an Elephant*, the British *The Elephant and the Empire*, and the Americans *How I Shot an Elephant*. Last, but not least, the Norwegians published their contribution: *Norway: Its Land and its People.*

This joke illustrates what many seem to think is a distinct Norwegian endeavour: a self-centred discussion about Norway and Norwegian culture. Living in a small and relatively new nation, located on the edge of the European continent, Norwegians seem to be in acute need of defining their values and their identity. And they have been given plenty of opportunities to do so. Four occasions stand out: the two referendums in 1972 and 1994 when the Norwegian population voted against joining the European Union, the Olympic winter games in Lillehammer in 1994, and the centenary of the dissolution of the union with Sweden in 2005.

After the Olympics in 1994, Norwegian writer Inge Eidsvåg introduced three values he thought the majority of the population would recognize as theirs: equality, moderation and nearness to nature. The purpose of this chapter is to examine the content, the historical background and the present day relevance of these three values.

Equality

Norway has been considered as a country where egalitarian values have had greater success than elsewhere. This means that Norwegians have been receptive to trends emphasizing factors such as codetermination, integration and economic equalisation. Visitors to Norway are often surprised by the relatively small differences in income between rich and poor, the generous grants supplied by the state to students and families with children, and the extent to which children with special needs have been integrated in our schools, which are just a few examples.

Political scientist Bernt Hagtvet made this comment in *Aftenposten* in April 2004: "The quest for equality is distinctly Norwegian. If you go to Britain, you discover the immense amount of energy people use in order to create distance between each other." In Norway he finds an easy-going atmosphere between members of different classes in society, between those who govern and those governed. Hagtvet elaborates: "I can send an e-mail to our prime minister if I want to. Norway is the most transparent society in Europe. This is a triumph."

How, then, do historians explain this Norwegian preference for egalitarian values? I will give two explanations. First of all, in a very long-term historical perspective, Norway stands out in European history as a country where feudalism never had any real success. With certain exceptions (the expansive farmlands in the east and parts of Trøndelag) Norwegian rural society has been characterised by considerable social equality, and so differs from rural Europe as a whole. The Norwegian author Bjørnstjerne Bjørnson (1832-1910) wrote that "Norway is a country of houses and cottages, but no castles". This absence of an aristocratic upper class can partially be explained against the geographical background. In most parts of the country, natural elements do not provide the opportunity for farming on a large scale. Flying over Norway, you will see mountains, lakes, fjords, glaciers, forests and small islands. The lack of arable land is striking. Today, less than 3 % of Norway is cultivated.

Consequently, in a long-term historical perspective, Norway has been sparsely populated, and it has been difficult for rich farmers to mobilize poor farmers to work on their fields and to pay land taxes in ways characteristic of feudal societies elsewhere in Europe. The typical rural pattern in Norway is one small farmstead being very much like the next. These decisive geographical factors have contributed to the fact that Norwegian economic life has invariably been based on small units. Consequently, by European standards, Norway lacks an influential, conservative upper class. A British female student in my class once commented: "I'm a socialist, and my aim is to tear down the class system in Britain. It seems that

In most European countries there has been an aristocratic upper class wealthy enough to build castles like this one in Germany. The Norwegian writer Bjørnstjerne Bjørnson wrote that "Norway is a country of houses and cottages, but no castles".

likeminded Norwegians have a much easier job. They don't have a rigid class system to tear down."

There have, of course, been differences between people in Norway, as in most societies. From about 1300-1800 there was a small class of lesser nobility in the countryside, and along the coast during the last 400 years, shipowners have managed to make immense fortunes in international trade. In church, the social hierarchy of everyday life was reflected in where you were seated, well into the 19th century: The upper class at the front, the "free" farmers in the middle, and the smallholders at the back. It seems, however, to be a matter of scale: In a comparative perspective, the differences were greater elsewhere in Europe.

A second possible explanation for the success of an egalitarian value system is the emergence of several popular movements in the 19th century. It started around the turn of the century with the preachings of a farmer called Hans Nielsen Hauge (1771-1824). Contrary to the law, which stated that laymen were not allowed to organize religious meetings without the consent of the local minister, Hauge travelled up and down the country, discussing religious matters with people and preaching the gospel to ordinary men and women. He was also an energetic financial entrepreneur, organizing mills, printing shops and sawmills. He had no formal education, he had no gown and no authorization from the king. Consequently, he was sent to prison on several occasions. More important, when people met to sing, pray and listen to Hauge's religious messages, the rich and the poor, men and women, the farmer and the smallholder sat next to each other. 200 000 copies of his writing were printed and read all over the country. This is probably a world record considering that Norway had a population of 900 000 at the time. Historian Berge Furre claims that Hauge's work has had a lasting impact on Norwegian history, stressing such values as equal status and giving people the opportunity to be master of their own life. These were values that fitted perfectly with the ideals from the American and French revolutions at the time: Liberty, equality and fraternity. Hauge was not a socialist, but he disliked the capitalist tendency to show off wealth. The aim of economic enterprise was not maximum profits and material opulence. His aim was to eradicate poverty and live a devout life as a Christian. Too much and too little were equally immoral. During the 19th century, the tradition of segregating people in church according to social status was changed.

Several popular movements left their mark on Norwegian values during the 19th century, and some may be considered a protest against the senior state officials (*embetsmenn*) that dominated political life at the time. Søren Jaabæk (1814-94) organized farmers all over Norway in associations where the rural population was trained to discuss, make speeches and to fight for their rights. Jaabæk himself worked hard in the Storting (the Norwegian national assembly) in order to increase the political influence of the farmers. Outside the Storting, Marcus Thrane (1817-90) organized the emerging working class in 414 associations with 30 000 members. This movement was sparked by urban dissatisfaction, and spread like wildfire to the surrounding rural areas. The fight for universal suffrage was given the highest priority. Like Hans Nielsen Hauge, Marcus Thrane was imprisoned for several years. The fight for equality, religious, political and economic, was still seen as a provocation in the mid 19th century. The awakening of the laymen, the farmers and the workers, however, had a lasting influence on the formation of Norwegian values.

The growth of the welfare state after 1945 has also been a factor promoting equality in Norway. The Norwegian state has been very active in introducing measures aiming at equalizing access to material goods and benefits. An elaborate and generous social security system was introduced after World War II. Child benefit (1946), sickness benefit (1956) and old age pensions (1957) were among the most important reforms made available for all. Young families were given subsidized loans in order to build apartments and houses, and students have been offered scholarships and low interest rates on loans. The aim of the welfare state has been to fight what was considered the five main evils in society: poverty, illness, unemployment, ignorance and bad housing conditions. In other words: Each member of Norwegian society should have equal access to work, education, health care and a house to live in. You will find an introduction to the Norwegian welfare state in chapter 8.

Equality has become an increasingly controversial value in Norway during the last 25-30 years. Some argue that egalitarianism suppresses the quest for freedom; e.g. the ability to do things your own way, to move boundaries, to achieve your true potential. Others argue that Norway is becoming more diverse. We are in a process of integrating immigrant minorities, and in this situation all talk about equality will only cause alienation and resentment. It is, according to these critics, vital that we do not develop a segregated society with "Norwegians" and "immigrants". A more detailed discussion about whether Norway may be considered an egalitarian country today, and whether equality is a desirable value or not, is found in chapter 10.

Moderation

One approach to understanding a social system is to explore the way people prepare and eat their meals. In many countries, people put a lot of energy and consideration into the preparation of meals. In Norway, simplicity and moderation in preparing food have been a virtue.

Returning to Norway on a charter flight from the Azores in 2004, I observed a group of Norwegian tourists eating their lunch. We had been given the choice between making our own packed lunch (matpakke) at the hotel or buying a $5 sandwich on board the aircraft. Most of the tourists around me had chosen to wrap their food in sandwich paper in the hotel, and then eat it hours later. They were wealthy and over 50. They could afford to fly for hours, to the middle of the Atlantic Ocean, for a week of sunshine. Most of them would have an expensive car and a spacious house

The tradition of eating packed lunch (matpakke) is strong in Norway. Ideally, it contains a few slices of brown bread with butter and a slice of cheese. People drink milk with it and also have a piece of fruit or vegetable.

back home. But buying a $5 sandwich was unthinkable. An obvious conclusion would be: the relationship between Norwegians and what they eat is not a matter of economy, it's a question of ethics and morality.

Historically, Norway has not been a land of milk and honey. The natural surroundings have not provided for a life of material abundance. Consequently, moderation and thrift became a virtue. It may be difficult to observe these values in Norway today if you look at the houses in which people live or at the cars they buy. But it is still possible to see it in the ways we eat. It has been said that shipowner Fred Olsen, one of the wealthiest people in Norway, makes his own matpakke with crispbread and Norwegian brown cheese (brunost) every day.

The ideal content of a matpakke is a few slices of brown bread with butter and a slice of white, mild cheese or Norwegian brown cheese. The cheese is cut with a true Norwegian invention, a symbol of moderation: the cheese slicer. The purpose of this invention is to cut as little cheese as possible, an invention that has never been successful in France. A matpakke is cheap, ascetic and believed to be healthy.

The tradition of the matpakke is not very old. It dates back to the 1930s when parents in Oslo were encouraged to give their children nutritious

The cheese slicer is a true Norwegian invention. Its purpose is to slice the cheese as thinly as possible.

bread, milk, raw vegetables and maybe a piece of fruit in a *matpakke*. In 1991, a survey showed that 95 % of all children in elementary school brought a *matpakke* to school every day. When children are older, as many as 30 % throw it in the dustbin and buy buns and Coke instead. Later in a person's life-cycle, however, grown-ups make a *matpakke* for their children, and it is still a widespread tradition to bring a *matpakke* to work. Norwegians spend less time than other Europeans on meals, and the tradition of the *matpakke* contributes to this. Even in neighbouring countries like Finland, Denmark and Sweden people usually have a long break in the middle of the day to eat a warm lunch. A famous Norwegian chef, Trond Moi, claims that in France, people drive to lunch on their scooter, and then eat a three-course lunch, while in Norway, people drive to lunch in a Mercedes, and then eat their *matpakke*.

Eating a *matpakke* is something every Norwegian should do. You often meet this moralistic attitude among teachers claiming that there is a close correspondence between eating a *matpakke* and having good manners. If you eat bread and cheese during the week, then you can go wild and have unhealthy white bread, Coke and sweets at week-ends. On Saturdays and Sundays, Norwegians tend to forget the value of moderation in several spheres of life: They consume excessive quantities of alcohol, and some even spend money on taking a taxi.

A *matpakke* is not only eaten in schools and in work-places. It is also a central factor in Norwegian outdoor life, which brings us over to our last value: Nearness to nature.

Nearness to nature

Long Litt Woon is a Malaysian social anthropologist who immigrated to Norway in 1976. One of the things hard for her to understand in the beginning was the emphasis Norwegians placed on going for walks in the country. She recalls first of all the embarrassing feeling of dressing up in an old-fashioned outfit, and then the surprise she experienced when she discovered how Norwegians went about walking in the country. In an interview in 2005, she remembers how exhausting it was: "We climbed a mountain, and when we reached the peak, there was barely time for an orange, a bar of chocolate and a few photographs. Then it was time to go home. The funny thing was that there was not much conversation made. It was not a social event. Everyone seemed happy to walk alone. Now I realise that it is not the destination of the trip that's important to Norwegians; they focus on the walk itself."

Walking in the country is for most Norwegians a pleasure and a duty. You need a good excuse to sit inside on a Sunday when the sun is shining and all your neighbours are out in the woods cooking hot-dogs on a bonfire or skiing down the slopes. Leisure time is highly valued in Norway. And leisure time should be spent sensibly. The outdoors is looked upon as the place to relax and recharge your batteries. Walks in the country compensate for the daily routines in the city, and national parks, barren mountain plateaus and spectacular fjords even serve as symbols of the nation itself. Norway has a law from 1957 which guarantees the public the right of access to the countryside. This means that anyone may use private property for hiking, swimming and gathering berries, flowers and mushrooms of all kinds as long as the area is not under cultivation.

According to most surveys, 80 % of the Norwegian population go cross-country skiing and hiking. However, this does not mean that everyone goes for a walk in the country on a weekly basis. During Easter, between 13-20 % of the total population go skiing in the mountains. But surveys indicate

Walking in the country is for most Norwegians is a pleasure and a duty. Here is a family on their way carrying rucksacks, sleeping-bags and mattresses. The plan is to sleep outdoors even though if it is autumn up in the mountains.

that 70-80 % of the Norwegian population wish they could spend more time on outdoor activities. This is a high figure compared to other desired goals, for example spending more time with their family (50 %), spending more time with friends (56 %), making more money (18 %) or spending more time in shopping centres (5 %).

Signs indicate that an increasing number of people are starting to live according to their values. In 1970, there were 190 000 holiday homes in Norway. In January 2008, the number had risen to 383 000, and anyone who reads newspapers will realise that there is an explosion in the building of cabins. The main difference from earlier times is that most cabins today have electricity and running water. Many are located next to a skiing resort with machine-made ski tracks and restaurants. A new trend is to build luxury apartments in the mountains with an outdoor Jacuzzi and a panoramic view of the mountains. This is a provocation to traditionalists, who think that cabins should be located "in the middle of nowhere", where the charm is to fetch water from a nearby lake, to put logs on the fire, to make your own ski-tracks in virgin snow, and to eat your *matpakke* under the blue sky.

Signs like this are common in many places in the world. In Norway, however, a law was passed in 1957 allowing anyone access to use private property as long as the area is not under cultivation. This means that everybody may use the countryside for hiking, skiing, swimming or gathering berries.

Anthropologist Ernst Gellner claims that a national value system is only possible in a modern society with universal schooling and a strong state to maintain a national educational system. There has been a strong and long-term emphasis on educating pupils to value and use the outdoors in Norway. It started in the 19th century during the nation-building process. Norway was a colony under Denmark until 1814 and farmers and fishermen living in different parts of the country had few values in common. The leaders in the nation-building process lived in the cities, were educated, decided the content of the school curriculum, and found the true Norwegian character in the inland valleys, as far away as you could get from Denmark. The farmer, living close to nature, was to become the incarnation of Norway. Literature, music and painting in the 19th century were often inspired by life in rural areas, and taught to children in schools. According to this tradition, the original Norway was located out in the countryside, not in the cities. Norwegian heroes in the 20th century were people like Fritjof Nansen (1861-1930), Roald Amundsen (1872-1928), Thor Heyerdahl (1914-2002) and Monica Kristensen Solås (1950 –) who challenged the forces of nature, skiing to the North and South Poles and crossing the oceans on wooden rafts.

Here is Roald Amundsen skiing in a fur coat. Together with his team, he was the first person to reach the South Pole in 1911.

One consequence of this emphasis on values connected to nature has been a certain scepticism towards cultural expression connected to city-life, such as non-figurative art, ballet and opera. Norwegians lack a firmly rooted urban culture. Even today, it is difficult to find urban dwellers with 3-4 generations of urban ancestors. But things change. Today, 75 % of the Norwegian population live in the cities. A well-founded prophecy would be that urban culture will increasingly permeate Norwegian values in the future.

In the Norwegian national curricula during the last few decades, it has been emphasised that education should support the tradition of an active outdoor life. For the youngest children, there has been a rapid growth in the establishment of kindergartens where the children spend most of the day outdoors in all kinds of weather (*naturbarnehager*). Let's take a closer look at this new trend. The first *naturbarnehager* appeared in the late 1980s. Today, there are between 100 and 200. The government has been a bit worried that children in *naturbarnehager* will suffer from the fact that that they spend 5-8 hours outside in the forest every day of the week in cold and wet

In most Norwegian elementary schools and kindergartens, the children spend lots of time on outdoor activities. Some parents choose to send their children to so-called "naturbarnehager" where they spend most of their time outdoors in all kinds of weather. Here is a group of children from Kristiansand playing with bows and arrows on an island on a rainy day.

weather conditions. As a consequence, the government in Oslo published a set of guidelines in 2001 emphasising that all *naturbarnehager* need premises similar to ordinary kindergartens. Parents and employees, on the other hand, do not seem worried. They are motivated by a Norwegian value system that emphasises children spending time outdoors. It is assumed that it is good for children to go for walks in the woods. Parents give several reasons why this is desirable: 1. Children learn to respect and enjoy nature. 2. They learn about plants and animals. 3. They learn to enjoy going for walks in the country. Many seem to think that a happy childhood is closely connected to spending a lot of time outdoors.

Who, then, are the parents that send children to *naturbarnehager*? As a general rule, it is parents with a high income, higher education and who themselves like to spend time on outdoor activities. This corresponds with research showing that it is the urban upper and middle classes who are the proponents of walks in the country in general.

Modifications

How will Norwegians reading this chapter react? In my opinion, a majority will nod approvingly. But I also realise that there are some modifications necessary.

An obvious question is: Are values like equality, moderation and nearness to nature distinctly Norwegian? The answer is of course no. The Scandinavian countries share an egalitarian value system. The feeling of anxiety when a person is challenged to stand out from the crowd, the social pressure to reach an understanding, the ideology of equality – all this has been described by sociologists as typical of most rural societies. The Norwegian cheese slicer, a symbol of moderation, has never been a success in France, but has been introduced with a certain success in countries with a Protestant Calvinist value system, like Holland. Consequently, equality, moderation and nearness to nature are not exclusively Norwegian values. The hypothesis underpinning this article is that these are values that permeate Norwegian society to a larger extent than elsewhere. But they are in no way unique to Norway.

Secondly, we have to remind ourselves – Norway consists of many social systems: some connected to geography, some to class – we have families, counties, relatively poor and wealthy suburbs, small fishing communities and so on. As a citizen of Norway, a person is a member of several social systems, and hence has been taught different values and in some cases contradicting values. Consequently, not all Norwegians will recognise equality, moderation and nearness to nature as their values. An increasing number of people look upon themselves as mainly urban, they think liberty is a more important value than equality, and they have no moral qualms about spending money in restaurants and cafés.

A third point to be made is: People do not always live according to prescribed values. Many sociological surveys ask people about their attitudes. And there is no doubt that equality, moderation (when it comes to eating) and nearness to nature are considered important values by many Norwegians. But some critics will argue that it is not what people say that matters, but how they live. There is no doubt that more Norwegians *think* equality, moderation and nearness to nature are important values than those that actually *live* accordingly. The relationship between theory and practice, ethics and morality is complicated. But in my opinion, it would be a mistake to conclude that because people do not live up to their ideals,

After the dissolution of the union with Sweden in 1905, a refrerendum approved the choice of a Danish prince as King of Norway. King Haakon VII and his family really made an effort to become Norwegian in the following decades. For example, they went skiing and took part in other outdoor activities. In the photograph above the royal family is practising skiing in Oslo in 1906: Crown Prince Olav in front is followed by Queen Maud and King Haakon.

the ideals are meaningless and not relevant when we try to understand a social system. Over time, they have exerted a powerful, if often indirect, influence on how everyday affairs are conducted, and they still do.

Lastly, values are taught by parents, teachers, politicians and clergy to the younger generation. Normally, however, each member of a social system chooses to live their lives according to their own will. They are critical and selective. Consequently – values change. Does this mean that the values described in this chapter are the values of the older generation? Teenagers living today will think differently about equality, a *matpakke* and walks in the forests when in the future they teach their children about what is a virtuous life. Cultural change has always been, and always will be, an integrated part of all societies. The purpose of this article has not been to specify a Norwegian value system. My aim has been to select three values Norwegians have emphasised in the past which, I hope, make it easier to understand Norwegian society today. What the next generation of Norwegians will make their priorities is a different matter.

Most of you who read this book are not Norwegians. You are probably visitors to Norway as students or tourists. You might be working here for a year or two. Please do not use this article (or this book) as a key which will unlock the truth about Norway. Use it as a set of hypotheses or points for consideration if you like. Hopefully, you will be able to visit Norway long enough to find your own answers to these questions: What are the characteristics of Norwegian society? Does a Norwegian value system in fact exist? And finally, when the German magazine *Der Spiegel* tried to find out what characterized German culture, their conclusion was: Germans like to discuss what it means to be a German. So maybe it is a myth that Norwegians are more self-centred than other people. Most people are!

Part 1

History

Chapter 2

The History of Norway: A Long-Term Perspective

By Silve-Linn and Lars Aase

Hunting, gathering and agriculture

12 000 years ago, Norway was covered with ice. 2000 years later the glacial retreat was complete, and plants and animals conquered the open land-scape. For the first time, humans were able to settle along the Norwegian coastline. They lived as hunters and gatherers, catching fish in the rivers and lakes, picking berries in the forests and chasing animals over cliffs.

Agriculture was introduced around 4000 BC. This laid the material foundations for a more advanced social and political structure. Wealth and power became more centralized, and wealthy tribal leaders were able to seize control of other clans. The rise of local, powerful chieftains would eventually make way for the Viking Age starting in the 8th century, ultimately leading to the unification of Norway.

The Evolution of Norway as a State (872-1319)

Early signs of unification

The unification of the Norwegian territories laid the basis for the future evolution of a Norwegian state and people. From the ninth century we have evidence of a form of cultural unity in the geographical area that later evolved into the modern state of Norway. Ottar (about 890), a chief-tain in northern Norway, told the English king about the land of the Norse people in what is the first known written description of Norway. At this

The Oseberg ship: An original Viking ship from the 9th century. It was excavated in Vestfold in 1904, and is presently located at Bygdøy, Oslo.

time the Norwegians spoke a language distinctly different from people in neighbouring areas. The Norwegian Vikings were also connected through a common, pagan religion based on Norse heathenism. Their area stretched from the Oslo fjord to the southern part of the county of Troms, which means most of modern Norway.

Geographically, uniting Norway was quite a challenge. An extremely long coastline, indented fjords, scattered islands, high mountains and barren plateaus divide the country. Yet the challenges were possible to overcome. The coast became the main travel route, and the Norsemen developed strong, swift wooden ships that could sail along the coast and across the seas. The evolving economy was based on trading goods and exchanging gifts with one another. Politically, Norway was fragmented and unstable at this time. Small kingdoms were ruled by chieftains; political, religious and military leaders that owned the largest land areas.

It was in this setting that the unification of Norway took its first steps in the last three decades of the ninth century. The entire unification process would take more than three hundred years to complete. The pioneer of the unification idea is known as Harald Fairhair. He was able to control large areas in the southern part of Norway from approximately 872 to 933. During his reign, there were problems along the entire west coast. Viking clans attacked and plundered trading ships sailing from the city of Trondheim and the areas north of it, down the coast to reach the trading centres in eastern Norway. To conquer these chieftains Harald allied himself with the powerful Earls of Lade in Trondheim, who also had interests in the trade. The final battle of this campaign was the Battle of Hafrsfjord, which is dated at the end of the ninth century, possibly around 872. Harald Fairhair may also have exercised power in other parts of Norway. However, due to the great distances and severely limited administrative forces, it is likely that the actual power might have been limited to local chieftains paying tribute or in other ways claiming a formal loyalty. Instead of establishing a central administration, Harald travelled around with his warriors, the Hird. The local inhabitants were required to provide the king and his men with the supplies they needed or wanted.

The Fairhair dynasty controlled a kingdom with its main seat in the coastal districts of western Norway until the eleventh century. They also tried to gain control of other parts of the country, but were unable to remain in power for longer periods of time. The Earls of Lade had turned their backs on the crown, taking control of the fertile grounds in Trøndelag. In the areas surrounding the Oslo fjord, the Danes tried to gain control and exercised shifting authority. This made it difficult to consolidate the entire Norwegian territory before the year 1000.

The Viking Journeys

Vikings ravaging the British monastery of Lindisfarne in year 793 marks the start of the Viking era. The Vikings plundered all over the British Isles, continental Europe, and Russia; but they also had less violent reasons for their journeys. Trade and the search for colonies were also important factors. Viking traders brought goods all the way from northern Russia, around the Norwegian coast, to Denmark and Germany. The Viking search for new land led to settlements on the Orkney, Faroe and Shetland Islands, as well as in Iceland, Greenland and Newfoundland. Wealth accumulated by trade, swift and strong ships, combined with knowledge of surrounding peoples and lands made the journeys possible. Population growth within the Norwegian territory and political instability on the continent were contributing factors in explaining why the Vikings looked outwards for land and wealth.

Unification and christening

Olav Haraldsson stands out as the man, king, and eventually saint that consolidated the Norwegian territories and unified the country of Norway. He was a Viking warrior, having served in an army in England under Danish authority. In 1015, he returned to Norway with the aim of becoming king. At this time, Norway was divided between the king of Sweden, the king of Denmark, and the Earls of Lade. Olav's timing was impeccable – the Danish king had his hands full with raids in England, making it easier for Olav to conquer the Earls of Lade. Until 1028, Olav was the first king who managed to consolidate his power and remain in power throughout the entire country. Because he offered the most powerful clans income from his personal estate and assured them some local authority, they swore allegiance to him as the king of Norway. One of the reasons why he was able to succeed was the great fortune he had been able to acquire as a Viking warrior. Another reason was his ruthless campaign to convert the Norwegians to Christianity. By using violence, he forced subjects into accepting Christianity. When Christianity eventually prevailed, it gave the throne a new legitimacy based not only on personal power and loyalty, but on a power given to the throne by a higher, divine force. However, Olav's commitment to christianising Norway also gave him powerful enemies; some of the chieftains were concerned they might lose the power and positions they held as religious authorities.

King Knut, or Canute the Great of Denmark, claimed supremacy and came to Norway with his army in 1028. Olav had lost support in Norway, and escaped to Sweden to gather men for his army. The armies met at the Battle of Stiklestad in 1030, where Olav died. His death seems to have changed the attitudes of many people. He was canonized shortly after his death, and legends of his healing powers made their way into the mix of heathen and Christian religion practised by the people. Five years after Olav's death, his family regained the throne. His son Magnus the Good became the legitimate king, supported by the people. In many ways, 1035 is the year the Norwegian unification was finalized. During the next hundred years the Norwegian kings formed an offensive alliance with the aristocracy. A unified Norway entered international affairs by attacking the British Isles, involving themselves in Danish conflicts, and embarking on prestigious expeditions to the Middle East.

Civil war makes way for a new order

Only a hundred years after St. Olav finalized the unification, Norway was thrown into 110 years of ravaging civil war. Rights of succession to the throne seem to have been the main reason for conflict. The law of succession was very unclear and did not guarantee rights to the descendants of the previous king. This made it possible for anyone with a certain amount of power, resources and support to claim their right to succeed in the battle for the throne. Another reason for the civil war was that the Church was playing a more independent role in society, and the civil war helped the Church gain more power and influence.

The law of royal succession was eventually rewritten in 1163, strengthening the king's position. The local aristocracy realized that their way to power would be through supporting the throne and the Church. A sort of co-dependency emerged amongst the different power groups – the Church gave the king his legitimacy, the king gave the Church protection and security, and the aristocracy needed the king to secure their old position while they helped the king exercise power in more remote areas and on a local level.

In the following centuries, the king extended his legislative power. His position was further secured through the practice of the succession laws. The *leidang* tax, which since the eighth century had secured the king additional income during times of war, was now extended to include times of peace as well. Perhaps most importantly, King Magnus the Lawmender enacted a unified set of laws for the entire kingdom in 1274. This law was adopted throughout the country by inclusion at the local *ting*, the local place where people gathered to settle conflicts. The fact that the law was adopted at every local *ting*, can be seen as a sign that the king's subjects respected his power and that the king must have cooperated with the local authorities in order to find consensus for the law.

In medieval Norway, the Church emerged as a powerful player in society. Around 1300, the Church owned 40% of the land – in comparison, the king owned 7%, the local aristocracy 20%, and peasants owned 33%. The Church collected its own taxes, and exercised judicial authority in cases related to religious practices. How much the Church actually affected the everyday lives of its subjects is difficult to establish. However, as a political and economic player in state affairs, there can be no doubt that the Church had a powerful position.

The Age of Unions (1319-1905)

The geography of Norway makes the country unsuitable for large-scale farming. There are few vast, open fields – with the exception of a few places in the east and in Trøndelag. This has been a contributory factor in explaining why Norwegian peasants generally have held a stronger position in society than their equals on the European continent, and in comparison why the Norwegian aristocracies never acquired the same fortunes as those in the rest of Europe. There are no castles in Norway – in contrast to, for instance, France and Germany.

While geography might have been on the farmers' side, it also made the country more vulnerable to attacks from foreign powers. There were no large aristocracies with standing armies ready to defend the vast borders of Norway. This might have been one of the contributory factors in what has been called "The Age of Unions". If we use a wide definition of the term, Norway was in a union with either Denmark or Sweden from 1319 to 1905. In 1319, the king of Norway died, leaving no direct descendants. His daughter's son was the king of Sweden, and a union was formed based on the two countries having a common king. To a great extent, Norway was self-governed during those years and the *Riksråd*, or Norwegian council, was the highest political instance until its cessation in 1536.

The Black Death

In 1349, a British ship arrived in Bergen. The ship brought the Black Death with it, probably instigating the worst disaster in Norwegian history. Around half of the population died in a mere couple of years. The plague spread all across the country and left enormous cultivated areas deserted. The areas that were least devastated by the plague were the remote coastal areas in the western and northern parts of the country. The following decades brought new, minor outbreaks and, eventually, estimates suggest that about two thirds of the population were wiped out by the Black Death. It is hard to imagine the disastrous effect the plague had on the economy and on the survivors. Not a single person could have survived the plague without having been affected drastically by the loss of loved ones.

Ironically, the long term effects for the survivors and the coming generations were very good. Areas of fertile, cultivated land had been deserted, and there was a very low population density. However, the survivors were

German traders etablished themselves at The Wharf in Bergen in 1360.

able to cultivate the most fertile lands and there were enough resources to support livestock and grow grain. The coastal areas that had not been affected quite as hard as the rest of the country based their livelihoods on fishing, and as a result fishing now became a substantially more important industry. In addition, the state, the Church and the aristocracy had been severely weakened. These groups had based their power and wealth on taxation and lending out land to peasants. When so many peasants died, leaving great areas of arable land unused, the base for taxation disappeared and rent levels fell dramatically. In effect, the peasants had been weakened in numbers, but came out stronger economically.

When the Black Death came to Norway, the country was still in a monarchic union with Sweden. The plague severely weakened the state and the administration, leaving an opportunity for foreigners to take control of Norwegian trade. German traders had been present in Norway for more than a century, specializing in buying dried fish. In 1360, these German traders, known as the Hanseatic League, established an office at Bryggen, The Wharf, in Bergen. The Hanseatic traders wanted to establish total control over the valuable fish trade. The League was based in the coastal areas of northern Germany and had a larger capital base and a stronger organization than its Norwegian competitors. During the following 150 years, the Hanseatic League achieved a monopoly on Norwegian foreign trade and exercised total control of fish exports and grain imports, which Norway was dependent upon. The German traders also established minor offices in eastern Norway, but Bergen was their main base with more than 1 000 permanent and, to some extent, self-governing German inhabitants. The Hanseatic League maintained their position in Norway until approximately 1500. Their hegemony ended partly because the Danish-Norwegian state grew stronger and became able to control the trade itself, and partly because English and Dutch traders presented strong competition in the markets.

From union member to province

The political development in Norway during the age of unions can partly be seen in the context of the developments in trade. In 1397, the Scandinavian countries joined to form the Kalmar union. The Swedish queen had managed to convince the national councils in Denmark and Sweden that she was the rightful successor to their thrones, but the countries also wanted to join forces in trying to regain control of their own foreign trade. However, they did not achieve much success, as all the countries were bound to the Hanseatic League through massive amounts of loans. The Kalmar union lasted for fifty years, until Sweden broke out and left Norway in a union with Denmark that would last until 1814.

The Norway-Denmark union began with each country having equal political power and position, but throughout the 16th century this changed dramatically. The Reformation in Germany reached Denmark, where the Danish king established a Lutheran state church. The leader of the Norwegian council, the *Riksråd*, was the Catholic archbishop Olaf, who would not accept a Lutheran state church in a Danish-Norwegian union. Consequently, the Danish king abolished the council, and declared Norway a Danish province. Norway was then subordinate to Danish rule until 1660, when absolute monarchy was established in the union. This led to a shift in favour of Norway, making the two countries slightly more politically equal. However, this did not last long; throughout the 1700s until the split in 1814, the Danish king and administration actively promoted policies in favour of Denmark at Norway's expense.

An expanding economy and an emerging elite

Norway was a Danish province for almost three centuries (1536-1814). During this time, the economy and the population grew and many new industries emerged. Fishing had been an important source of food and income for several centuries, and in the 16th century forestry emerged as another important industry. The population growth on the European continent created a demand for wood for houses and ships, and as firewood. There were vast forests in the eastern parts of Europe, but it was more cost efficient to transport wood across the sea from Norway. New technology allowed sawmills to exploit energy from water, which resulted in a large forestry expansion in the southern parts of Norway. In the beginning, peasants sold wood directly to foreign traders. New urban settlements emerged at the mouths of the rivers where the wood was gathered after being floated from the inland to the coast, and Norwegian townsmen took control of the trade, making great fortunes for themselves. Eventually the Danish king started to worry about deforestation leading to a shortage of wood for his military fleet. Consequently, he imposed regulations to limit forestry-related trade, making it easier for him to keep the trade under his own control by allowing only towns to export wood.

The 16th century also saw the birth of the Norwegian mining industry, but it was not until the following century the industry truly expanded. Mining created a demand for workers both in the mines and in the areas surrounding the mines. The Danish king was engaged in several armed conflicts with Sweden, and realized that mining might be a source of income that could be used to strengthen the army. Several steps were taken to encourage the mining industry, experts were brought in from Germany, and by 1660 the first mines started bringing in a decent profit.

Shipping is another example of an emerging and eventually very profitable industry. The long coastline of Norway has many natural harbours and protected waters. It also had long traditions of seafaring and trading, and capital holders were willing to invest in the shipping industry. The king encouraged shipping by promising economic support to the production of merchant ships, if in return he would be allowed to use them as warships in cases of military conflicts. Such conflicts on the European continent had favourable effects for the shipping fleet, as the Danish-Norwegian union was a neutral party and was allowed free passage on the seas. The years between 1690 and 1710 stand as the first golden age for Norwegian

Røros is an old mining town. Copper was discovered during the 18th century and the mine was running for 333 years; until 1977.

shipping, an industry that would experience a second boom towards the end of the 18th century.

The expanding trade and growing industries in Norway were closely linked to the growth of towns. New towns emerged, and more people moved to the urban settlements. The king supported their growth and urban trade by giving the towns an export trade monopoly that encompassed almost all trade. There were only eight towns in Norway in 1660. The number rose to 23 in 1814. A new order in society emerged. Town-based merchants became somewhat of an urban elite. Many were foreign traders that immigrated and established their businesses in Norwegian towns. It is estimated that between 25 to 40% of the urban population were engaged in mercantile activities, including large capital holders and smaller-scale craftsmen.

The long road towards independence

Norway went through several changes during the years of union with Denmark. The country had increased its population and its wealth. Socially, society had become more stratified, showing signs of an emerging social elite with the resources available in order to build a future independent state. Throughout the entire union with Denmark, the king had built a strong administration, especially aimed at collecting taxes imposed by the throne. The king also encouraged Norwegian industry, promoting growth and strengthening the state. However, as the 18th century progressed, the two countries were treated differently in economic matters. Taxes paid by Norwegian peasants were spent on projects in Denmark, and Norwegians were taxed more heavily than the Danes. A gradual centralization of power in Copenhagen took place, causing frustration among the upper classes and civil servants in Norway, who wanted Norway to have its own political and administrative bodies.

The Norwegian upper classes were also influenced by romanticism and budding patriotism. The idea of Norway as a separate unit and Norwegians as a separate people with a unique culture and history gradually gained support. However, this early patriotism did not include language, as Danish was the official language spoken and written by the upper classes. The main emphasis was on Norwegian nature, and how living so close to and being dependent on nature created a certain toughness and strength of character in the Norwegian people. It also focused on the Norwegian way of living, and how the Norwegian peasants historically had been more autonomous than their Danish peers. The dissatisfaction with Danish rule grew stronger, as did the patriotic feelings amongst the upper classes in power. The conditions necessary for Norway to break out of the union were present, but the spark to set off the independence process was lacking. International affairs at the time might have produced just that.

At the beginning of the 19th century, the Napoleonic wars ravaged Europe. Denmark-Norway wanted to stay out of the conflict, but the Danish king found himself caught in what seemed an impossible clinch between the French and the British. He chose to side with the French, with disastrous results for the people of Norway. Famine and disease ravaged the Norwegian people, and dismay with Danish rule spread to all layers of society. Napoleon lost the war in 1813, and as a result Denmark was forced to renounce its supremacy of Norway at the signing of the Treaty of Kiel in January 1814.

1814: The forgotten land

According to the Treaty of Kiel, Norway was to enter into a union with Sweden. But the Swedes were deeply engaged in events following the war on the continent, and Norway was "forgotten" throughout the spring of 1814. The Norwegian upper classes, civil servants, military officers, wealthy land owners and members of the aristocracy, did not waste any time. The independence movement finally had the chance to influence the course of Norway's history. Elections were arranged and held, resulting in the appointment of an electoral college which subsequently appointed 112 representatives. These representatives formed a body whose task was to write a Norwegian constitution. On April 10th, they gathered at Eidsvoll. They overcame great personal and fundamental differences, and eventually presented and ratified the Constitution of Norway, which was signed on May 17th.

The Swedish army returned from the continent a few weeks later, demanding that the Treaty of Kiel should be effectuated. After brief armed exchanges between the Norwegian peasant army and the Swedish soldiers in the border areas in the south of Norway, a compromise was reached. Norway was to enter into a personal monarchic union with Sweden, accepting the Swedish king as its own. In return, Norway would be granted political independence as a state of its own. In September, a Norwegian parliament, the Storting, was elected. One of the first assignments for the Storting was to make the changes necessary so the Constitution would be in accordance with the Swedish-Norwegian union. This process followed the guidelines given in the Constitution, and gave the Storting an opportunity to add changes that consolidated its own position and reduce the power of the king. While still entrenched in a union, Norway had moved a long way towards independence.

State of the civil servants

Norway's governing system from 1814 to 1884 has been called a "State of the Civil Servants". Other European countries were ruled by monarchs and aristocracy, but Norway had no aristocracy to speak of, and the last remains of aristocratic privileges were brought to an end by law in 1821. The civil servants were highly educated men: clergy, jurists, military officers. The civil servants and their families became a powerful, class conscious group – the country's elite. The king of the Swedish-Norwegian union, Carl Johan, appointed the Norwegian government – and all government officials were civil servants. The rest of the population consisted mostly of peasants, and they elected civil servants as their representatives into parliament, the Storting. This started to change in the 1830s, when the farmers started electing representatives from their peers. The differences between the farmers and the civil servants can be seen as a driving force behind the political events throughout the rest of the century. The King and the civil servants in government tried to limit the power of the Storting, and the farmers in the Storting worked against that agenda.

The first nationwide electoral association was founded in the 1860s by Søren Jaabæk. *The Society of Farmers' Friends* numbered approximately 25 000 members, with the goal of helping more farmers to be elected into the Storting. By 1868, farmers represented the majority in the Storting. The following year, the Storting went from meeting every third year to assembling annually. The opposition against the government of the Civil Servants was growing, and there was more to come. Jaabæk and his farmer supporters joined forces with a group of radical academics led by Johan Sverdrup, eventually founding the first political party in Norway – the Liberals. Jaabæk and Sverdrup were ready to take on the civil servants' government and started a campaign to concentrate power in the hands of the people, represented by the Storting. The following years were filled with conflicts between the government and the Storting, between the king and the farmers. The conflicts escalated, eventually reaching their climax in 1884. King Oscar II attempted to stage a coup d'état, but the plans were revealed. This left him with no choice other than to ask Johan Sverdrup to form a government. Sverdrup had the majority of the Storting with him, and 1884 stands as the year parliamentarism was brought to Norway, even though it took several more years for it to find its true form. Parliamentarism has been the ruling practice in Norway since 1884, but it was not formally added to the Constitution until 2007.

Population growth and migration

Throughout the 1800s, Norway experienced an immense population growth. The causes for this growth are many and multi-faceted. Nationwide hygiene improvements and better nutrition – herring and potatoes became something of a national staple – led to decreasing death rates and a drastically declining infant mortality rate. Better disease control included the smallpox vaccine and district medical officers, and the overall improvements in immune defence caused by better hygiene and nutrition.

Table 2.1

Population growth and percentage of population in urban areas		
1801	882 951	8.8
1815	904 777	9.8
1855	1 467 398	16.9
1900	2 217 971	35.7
2007	4 692 174	78.0

Source: Statistics Norway

Until the 1850s, the rural areas of Norway were able to absorb most of the population growth. Farms were divided, new land was cleared, agriculture was able to produce more, and the growing urban areas were in need of workers. Around 1850, however, there was not much land left to clear and resources were getting scarcer. The largest city, Kristiania (now Oslo), experienced a population increase from 9 000 in 1800 to more than 40 000 fifty years later. Many people migrated within the country, but emigrants leaving for the United States comprised the greatest wave of migration, unsurpassed in Norwegian history. More than 800 000 Norwegians left their home country in the years between 1860 and 1930 to start a new life in the United States.

Industry, farming and the economy

Non-farming related production prior to the 1840s consisted mostly of small-scale production based on manpower. In 1843, Britain lifted its industry export embargo and a steep rise in industrial production followed in Norway. The first industries were textile production, with factories in Kristiania and Bergen, located near rivers generating water power. Iron, metal, and forestry industries followed, and exports rose in the 1870s. After the turn of the century, water power was used to generate electricity, and another great industrial production wave followed. The Storting followed the European pattern of economic liberalism and passed laws that eased domestic trade, encouraged entrepreneurship, and abolished privileges that had previously been held by specific trade groups. The growing industrial activity provided work for young people, including women and children. The low wages paid to these workers might have been a contributory factor in providing the surplus needed to reinvest capital and causing further economic growth.

The Norwegian farmers had been mostly self-sufficient until the mid-1800s. Around this time, the agricultural sector restructured itself towards a market based economy. Farm work was usually labor intensive, especially during seasonal peaks of sowing and reaping. Throughout the century, developments in farming technology helped a less labor intensive farming production system to emerge. These changes included the use of iron ploughs, horse-drawn rakes, sowing drills, reapers and threshing machines. The farmers needed capital to acquire this new technology, and so the Storting founded the Kingdom of Norway's Mortgage Bank in 1851. This provided low cost, long-term mortgage loans for the rural industries. Women in the rural areas had long traditions of doing a great deal of work on the farms, and the division of labor between men and women in rural areas may have played an important role in making the changes in the agricultural economy relatively smooth. Families were able to combine sources of income by working their farm as well as taking part-time or seasonal work in other industries.

1850 to 1880 represented a golden age for Norwegian shipping. In 1880, more than 60 000 seamen were employed on what was the third largest merchant shipping fleet in the world. World trade was increasing, and Britain was highly dependant on ships, many of which were provided by Norwegian shipping companies. The transition from sailing ships to steamships caused a dramatic decrease in this industry in Norway, but eventually Norway was able to catch up again and at the beginning of the 1900s, Norway was once again a major shipping nation.

Infrastructure and communication

Norway's geography has always presented an infrastructural challenge. The modernization of Norway during the 19th century also included a rather rapid modernization and expansion of communication networks. The length of the road network more than doubled in a fifty year period. Steamships started regular passenger and cargo routes, and the first railway was finished in 1854 – followed by a rapid railway expansion connecting the largest towns in Norway by the 1890s. The telegraph was introduced in 1855, providing better communication methods as well as a new job opportunity for both men and women. . The postal service was unified and highly improved, and the first telephone lines opened in 1880. Behind this expansion was the state, trying to create favorable conditions for economic growth.

Organizations and interest groups

The 1880s and 1890s saw an increase in the number of workers organizations being established. Issues regarding labor and workers interests were the basis of many of them. In 1899, the Norwegian Federation of Trade Unions was established as a result of several similar, smaller organizations merging. By 1912, the organization numbered 53 000 members. Today this union, known by its Norwegian acronym LO, is the largest workers' union in the country. The Norwegian Labour Party was established in 1889, based on a socialist doctrine, demanding shorter working days and universal suffrage. Women's interest groups also grew in number, although the largest groups suffered from inner disagreements and were not able to present a completely unified front. Still, women's rights were improving slowly but surely. In 1882, women were allowed to receive their diploma for finishing upper secondary school. In 1884, women were allowed to enroll at the University, and in 1913 all women acquired the right to vote.

1905: A nation is born

As the twentieth century grew closer, many Norwegians started expressing their discontent with the Swedish-Norwegian union. Economically, the union did not seem to be of much importance to Norway. Norwegians engaged in international trade, but lacked public representatives to defend their own interests internationally. Nationalism – one people, one country – was on the rise in Europe, and a cultural awakening romanticizing " things Norwegian" had been growing stronger during the past century. Norway had been the first country in Europe to introduce universal suffrage for men, and the first country with a parliamentary system of government. It seemed inevitable and overdue that Norwegians should be given the opportunity to govern themselves. The Liberal Party tried to negotiate an agreement with Sweden, but the attempt failed. In 1895, Sweden threatened to go to war against Norway. In the following years, Norway engaged in something of an arms race – preparing for a war of independence. In 1905, the union issue was on the verge of turning into actual war. When the King refused to sign a bill from the Storting, the government resigned. On June 7th, the Storting replied by announcing that the King no longer functioned as the Norwegian king, and that the union was suspended. Conservative forces in Sweden wanted to go to war, and Norwegian soldiers manned the border forts. Negotiations took place, resulting in the union's dissolution and the destruction of a majority of the Norwegian border forts in order to minimize the military threat. Many Norwegians wanted a republic, but feared the possible repercussions from strong monarchies on the European continent. In order to avoid this, the Storting asked the Danish prince Carl to become King. He would only agree if a referendum on the subect was held. The result of the referendum showed that 80 % of the Norwegians wanted Carl to become their new King. In November 1905, Carl and his family arrived in Kristiania – now using the names King Haakon VII, Queen Maud, and Crown Prince Olav. Norway was, once more, a fully independent nation.

Independent Norway (1905 - today)

From independence to a neutral ally

While the 19th century in many ways was a century of national unification, during the 30 years following independence Norway was a more disunited society. The economic growth continued, and for some people, this led to wealth and lifestyles that would have been impossible to even think of just a few decades before. Yet, social inequality and poverty were unavoidable results of the rapid changes Norwegian society had gone through. The Labour Party and the Liberal Party expressed concerns and wanted to improve conditions for the less fortunate. Stronger labour unions and other pressure groups demanded safer working conditions, and we see that early signs of the future Norwegian welfare state are starting to emerge at the beginning of the twentieth century. However, there is nothing in the early welfare improvements that were taking place that could have prepared us for the welfare state Norwegians have today.

With regard to international relations, the new Norwegian nation decided to persue neutrality. As World War I approached, this seemed a difficult task. Many Norwegians sympathized with the British, and were closely connected to Britain through trade, industry, or personal connections. 25 % of all Norwegian exports went to British ports. On the other hand, one third of all imports (mostly machinery) came from Germany. But the relationship with Britain seems to have been the strongest. When Britain made demands, Norway followed them. This is why Norway was "the neutral ally". Norwegian ships transported goods that were crucial for Britain in the war. The war years were unstable and uncertain for Norwegians, with some people profiting from the war and others left economically ruined. During the war, 900 Norwegian ships, or half the fleet, were sunk and 2000 seamen lost their lives.

Between the wars

The political instability that characterized Europe and the United States during the years following World War I also prevailed in Norway – for instance, Norway had nine different minority governments from 1918 to 1935. There were three major economic crises that caused many bankruptcies. Unemployment rates rose to new heights, but those who held jobs were able to buy more goods than before and spend more money on entertainment – perhaps we could say that the 1920s showed the early signs of the consumption-focused culture so clearly obvious in the modern world.

A specific workers culture also emerged – with ties across national borders, united by a red flag and common cultural activities. The Labour Party was radicalized and gained broad support among the people, who wanted an eight-hour working day and improved workers rights. The Labour Party joined the international communist organization Komintern, and remained a member for four years. After winning some battles against the employers and their federation, such as the implementation of the eight- hour day, the Labour Party was split and ended up taking a less revolutionary line.

The political left was strongly divided, ranging from those closer to the center and those still supporting a communist line, hoping for a Soviet-style revolution. But the right side of the political spectrum also had its extremist movements. These included several small organizations; most important is Vidkun Quisling's party, National Unity. This pro-Nazi party was formed in 1933 and aimed at introducing dictatorship based on Hitler's model. National Unity only received 2.2 % of the votes in 1933. Still, the political movements on the extreme right were able to exercise a certain influence on some of the larger political parties.

In 1928, the first Labour government took office. The government held its position for a mere nineteen days. The conservative parties in the Storting could not accept a government whose political platform aimed at introducing "a socialist order" in Norway, and the Labour government had to resign. It must have seemed clear that in order to make any viable changes, worker-related interests had to be united and fortified. In 1933, Labour's election program was ready: "The whole nation at work!" The program was based on making deep changes in the economy in order to solve the economic and unemployment problems facing the Norwegian people. The Labour Party won a majority in the elections, but lacked seven seats in the Storting in order to form a government. However, in 1935, the Labour party was able to take office – and a 30-year period of Labour governments followed.

Some of the policies implemented by the new government were aimed at bridging the gaps between those who had everything and those who had lost everything. The economic crises of the previous years, which had caused financial and personal ruin and damaged industrial production, had also made way for the emergence of smaller, local enterprises. The new government supported these while also trying to encourage trade and industry to get back on its feet. Internationally, the global market was starting to flourish again – but tensions were also building as Hitler's Germany was shaking up the fragile peace on the European continent.

World War II

In the weeks before World War II came to Norway, the government planned to follow the same line as 35 years before – staying neutral. They were also intent on not ending up on the wrong side, if things went wrong. Before dusk on April 9th, German ships were seen sailing into the Oslo Fjord. Norway was under attack, and it was taken by surprise. One of the German ships, Blücher, was hit by Norwegian fire and sank in the Oslo Fjord. This helped give King Haakon and the government enough time to escape from the city. Apart from the Blücher being hit, the Nazi forces were completely superior. The Norwegian government, which until now had clung to neutrality, decided to side with the Allies. It took the Germans

King Haakon VII and Crown Prince Olav photographed during an air raid outside Molde in 1940.

about three weeks to gain what they considered satisfactory control of the southern parts of Norway, but the battles were not over. In the areas surrounding the city of Narvik in Nordland county, Norwegian and allied soldiers drove the Germans out of the city and into the barren, mountainous areas close to the Swedish border. The Germans lost that battle – their first defeat, and the first victory on land for the Allied troops during the war. But the Germans were advancing in France, and so the Allied leaders needed more troops in Europe, which meant abandoning the fighting in Norway to transfer the troops back to the Continent. On June 7th 1940, the Norwegian government and the royal family fled from Norway to Britain, to continue the fight from there. In Norway, Vidkun Quisling's National Unity had become the only legal party, and only supporters of the Nazi occupants were given influential positions in occupied Norway.

The Nazi regime built defensive posts all along the coast of Norway. The German forces present in Norway numbered approximately 430 000 at the most; Hitler feared both the Soviet Union in the north and an Allied intervention from the sea. The Norwegian population numbered approximately

3 million people, so it is clear that the German presence made a severe impact on the everyday lives of the Norwegian people. Arbitrary imprisonments, torture and other sorts of suppression made lasting impressions on an entire generation.

A widespread civil resistance movement rose up, including people from all layers of society. During the war the resistance movement became more organized. The armed sections of the resistance movement carried out several sabotage attacks, representing a constant cause of irritation for the occupying forces – and perhaps most importantly, strengthening the Norwegian morale against the invaders.

As the war drew to an end, the Germans became more desperate. Northern Norway was left ravaged by the retreating occupants; as the Soviets forced the Germans further south, the Germans burnt everything and tried to imprison or chase away the local inhabitants. Housing and infrastructure in the north was severely damaged, leaving some settlements completely burned to the ground. Finally, on May 8th, 1945, the Germans surrendered. The King and the government could return, and the process for justice and rebuilding the country began. 93 000 people were investigated for collaboration with the Nazis, and eventually approximately 53 000 people were found guilty of treason and sentenced. 25 were executed. The collective trauma experienced by the Norwegian nation as a result of the war is still the subject of discussion and research.

Liberation, restoration and regulation

After the liberation, there was a general consensus amongst the Norwegian people to settle the war reparations quickly and get back to a normal life. The war tribunals were swiftly and efficiently set up, and the government and the Storting worked quickly to organize elections so that a legally elected government could get started on rebuilding the country. In June, a coalition government led by Labour party chairman Einar Gerhardsen, including representatives from all the political parties, went to work. On October 8th, elections were held, and the Norwegian people cast their votes – giving the Labour party a majority in the Storting. 110 of the 150 representatives in the Storting had never held parliamentary positions before. Democracy was restored, and a new era began.

Two of the greatest challenges facing the new government were restoring the material damage done to the country and getting the economy back on its feet while building a solid foundation for the future. The government's goals included a swift restoration, getting everyone back to work, stabilizing prices, and establishing and encouraging a fair system of income distribution. All over Norway, there was a great housing shortage. The transportation and communication networks had been severely damaged. The government faced huge challenges, and a very centralized way of governing would shape the following years in Norwegian politics. The Norwegian people had experienced a horrible war, but the war had also strengthened a sense of community among them. This experience of unification and shared responsibilities continued during the post-war years.

In 1947, Norway received about 3 NOK billion as part of the Marshall Aid from the United States, along with various goods and household necessities. Conditions for receiving Marshall Aid included liberalizing trade and economic activity. The Norwegian government regulated the economy strictly – keeping wages and price levels low and stable while encouraging a high level of economic activity and employment. The regulated, planned economy from the early post-war years had to change gradually into a mixed economy, or a controlled capitalist market economy. This has become known as the Scandinavian Model – combining economic efficiency and performance with minimal inequality and welfare state benefits.

The emergence of the welfare state

The Labour government led an active sociopolitical development of the Norwegian state, based on the idea that the state is responsible for the welfare of its people. The decades following World War II would bring about the founding of one of the world's most comprehensive welfare systems, which is possibly the main reason why Norway today ranks as the top country on the UN Human Development Index. Reforms and new services were introduced, based on equal rights and opportunities for all citizens. In order to maintain this system, Norway would be dependent on high employment and a solid economic growth. Pensions, health care, poverty assistance, unemployment benefit, free education, and free or subsidized cultural events were some of the services the government would prioritize in building the modern Norwegian state.

International cooperation and concerns

The world order had changed for ever following the war. Norway's cooperation with the other Allied countries led to a close relationship with Western Europe and the United States, and its hopes of a future, peaceful world order were established when Norway joined the United Nations in 1945. Its geopolitical position led to what might seem an inevitable involvement in the Cold War. Anti-communist movements and a great fear of the red neighbour in the east shaped Norwegian domestic and international policy. In 1949, Norway became a NATO member and the following decades were to bring about a substantial increase in funding for the Norwegian military. Throughout the 1960s, Norwegian military spending totalled about 4 % of the gross national product. Norway was also one of the first countries to start bilateral development aid programs. The first was in 1952 when the Storting decided to support a fishing project in Kerala in India. This type of help escalated during the sixties, and Norway reached the UN-recommended 1 % of GNP (in development aid) in 1980.

Changing political winds and an economic bonanza

As a whole, all industries in Norway flourished in the 1950s and 1960s. A rapid urbanization took place, housing standards improved, household consumption increased, and the welfare state grew stronger. There was also a great increase in new schools and universities. In 1965, Storting elections brought about a change in the long-standing political order – the conservative parties joined forces and formed the new coalition government. Economically, the new government based its policies on the existing developments and policies created by its predecessors. In 1971, the coalition government dissolved as a result of inner disagreements, conflicts and outside pressure. The Labour Party was once again asked to form a government, and the following years presented two hugely important events for the Norwegian people: The European Union question, and the forthcoming oil bonanza. In 1972, a majority of Norwegians voted against Norwegian membership of the EU (or the EEC as it was then). The opposition's main arguments for not joining the union were that it could be the end of small-scale farmers and fishermen living in the districts, and that it would take the power away from democratically elected Norwegian institutions to offices further away from the people in Brussels. Those who wanted to join the union thought that this was a chance to secure peace in Europe, and that Norway could now have a say in the forming of Europe. The 'no' vote in 1972 was repeated in another referendum in 1994, with the same result.

Norway's wealth today is largely due to its oil income. Full oil production began in the North Sea in 1975, and the production of crude oil and natural gas increased annually. In the 1960s, the Storting had decided that the state should exercise strict control over and secure a large income from the oil production. The goal was to build up a full-scale Norwegian oil industry, instead of just exporting the oil to other countries. By establishing an oil industry capable of handling all aspects of the oil process, Norwegian employment and income experienced a significant increase and long-term investment. The state-owned oil company Statoil, established in 1972, resulted in enormous economic growth - especially in the Stavanger region on the southwestern coast, where much of the oil industry was based. Not only did a new industry demand new knowledge, technology and labour, it also meant a whole new way of thinking in Norwegian politics. Oil would give Norway a financial surplus that has been compared to a real life fairytale. A large amount of the oil revenue has been spent building and securing the welfare state, and some has been invested in what is called The Oil Fund.

Towards the present

The debate about Norwegian membership in the European Union was not the only issue engaging people's interest. Additional protest movements rose up and brought different issues into focus, such as protecting the environment. In 1972, Norway became the first country in the world to have a Ministry of the Environment. Its job was to protect nature and endangered species. Feminist movements also grew stronger, promoting gender equality. Men dominated politics and working life, and the feminists wanted to change this. They also demanded the right to receive equal wages for equal work, public daycare for preschool children, and paid maternity leave. The feminist groups were successful in getting their views across on some issues, such as paid maternity leave. They also won another great symbolic victory when Gro Harlem Brundtland became Norway's first female prime minister in 1981.

The Sámi population also voiced their demands and grew into a powerful movement. Following the war, the state had given up its strict policy to

In two referendums in 1972 and 1994, Norwegians voted against joining the European Union (EU).

force the Sámi into mainstream Norwegian society. But the government had not done much to implement the new policy, partly because of the lack of a central Sámi organization to work with. The case that really put the Sámi struggle in the spotlight was the Alta affair, which started in the early seventies. To create a new power station the state wanted to regulate the watercourse of the River Alta, which had been a part of the Sámi territory for thousands of years. Even though the Sámi lost this case in 1981, it resulted in some sort of goodwill from the government, and in 1989 they were allowed to set up their own democratic government.

The 1980s were in many ways different from the preceding decades. People started to question the social democratic society and its values. Many people now wanted more individualism, both economically and personally. As a result of this, politics took a turn to the right. The Conservatives won the election in 1983. Many young people were able to get good jobs or important positions, due to an expanding economy and a higher level of education. The lifestyle of these people, known as the Yuppies, was characterized by a busy nightlife and flashy spending – and those who did not have the money themselves, borrowed it. Bank loans were much easier to get than before. The economy became overheated, and when the oil prices fell in 1986, many people went bankrupt and lost their homes, cars, and their social status. The interest rate on loans rose quickly, and those who had loans to fund their flashy spending were unable to manage.

The liberalism of the 1980s not only put people in financial positions they were unable to handle, in fact it also made society more tolerant and diverse. The 1990s continued the process towards gender equality. As of today, all the political parties have had a female leader. In higher education institutions, there is a majority of female students. The 1990s also saw an improvement in the rights of minorities. From 1993 homosexual couples were allowed to enter into civil partnerships, giving them most of the rights that married couples have, but not quite. A gender-neutral marriage law was passed in 2008. Immigrant cultures became a natural part of Norwegian society, although the immigration issue is still much debated.

Politically, the last three decades have brought several changes of government. Oil resources, employment rates, industry and production, international concerns, and domestic issues have in their turn dominated the political agenda. Governments have been forced to form coalitions and cooperate across party lines, which may have been a contributory factor in explaining the present stable political situation in Norway.

Chapter 3

Why is Norway a Wealthy Nation?

By Olav Arild Abrahamsen

Today Norwegians are extremely rich. They boast, together with the Swiss, the highest incomes per capita of all the European countries. The Norwegian standard of living ranks among the world's highest. In terms of gross domestic product per capita, Norway is one of the richest economies of the world.

Why then is Norway a wealthy nation? At first the answer may seem quite obvious: Norway's prosperity is due to the discovery in the late 1960s of vast reserves of oil and natural gas along the continental shelf of the North Sea. When the drilling rig Ocean Viking struck oil in the Ekofish field in December 1969, Norway stood on the threshold of the oil age. Today North Sea oil and gas fields account for between one-third and one-half of Norway's annual exports. Norway is the world's third- largest exporter of petroleum, after Saudi Arabia and Russia, and one of the world's top exporters of natural gas. The oil age, however, is if anything the epilogue of the story about how Norwegians became rich. The discovery of oil first of all brought a *new* source of prosperity to a relatively wealthy, industrialized country. The story begins in the nineteenth century when an industrial revolution took place in Norway, and the nation became integrated into the developed part of the world economy.

A backward country in the European periphery

An Englishman who visited Norway in 1800 told his friends after having returned to England: "There is no reason to help these people! These dirty, ignorant people produce far too many children. They do not want to work, and they are undisciplined. They misuse all the opportunities they are

In 1969, Norway struck oil in the North Sea. Today, Norway is the third largest exporter of petroleum in the world.

given. Every time they get any money, most of it is spent on alcohol and is just squandered. All the help we give them just encourages laziness and provides another opportunity for them to have even more children." This characterisation of the Norwegians in 1800 reflects attitudes and prejudices of a member of the "developed" world who has met people living in a backward country. Historians do not share this view on our forefathers, of course, but they do agree that at the beginning of the nineteenth century Norway was, in many ways, a poor country. Production and consumption per capita were low. A rather large proportion of the population lived close to subsistence level. Historians also agree that it was not at all clear that the Norwegians would become rich.

Norway had certain advantages in its resources. Forests covered more than one-quarter of Norway's surface, and softwoods were an important timber resource. For centuries Norwegians had harvested marine life from the surrounding seas. Norway also had some mineral resources which included modest amounts of iron ore. The prosperity of the urban population had for years depended on the export of timber, fish stocks and iron.

On the other hand, the obstacles to industrialization were numerous. Norway was a country with a low population density. In 1801 only about 10 per cent of the population was living in urban centres. Around 80 per cent of Norway's population obtained its livelihood from agriculture. Norway had an extreme shortage of arable land. Soils suitable for farming cover just 3 per cent of the country's total area, and furthermore, the climatic conditions are unfavourable. Norway had formidable inland communication barriers, and was, like Sweden and Denmark, a country with little coal. A further obstacle to industrialization was the presence of powerful competitor economies near at hand, primarily Britain, in a context of relatively open trading systems. Therefore, at the beginning of the nineteenth century, Norway can be characterized as a rather backward country on the European periphery, with a dual social structure consisting of a peasantry tied to subsistence agriculture and a small urban population whose prosperity depended on foreign trade.

Table 3.1   How rich was Norway in 1820?

Rich and poor states, 1820	
Country	Income per head in 1990 USD
United Kingdom	1 756
Netherlands	1 561
United States	1 287
Denmark	1 225
Germany	1 112
Norway	1 004
Japan	704
China	523

Source: Angus Maddison

The German historian Dieter Senghaas claims that the normal process for a "peripheral" country like Norway was to become "peripheralised", that is to become a supplier of raw materials to more highly developed countries. Against all the negative odds outlined above, however, Norway succeeded in industrializing and in sustaining its industrial growth. In the period between the 1840s, when the first modern textile factories were established, and the outbreak of World War I, modern Norway took shape. At the turn of the century the industrial sector represented 30 % of the national product. In 1920 the portion of the economically active population employed in the primary sector had been reduced to 37 per cent, while 28 per cent were employed in the secondary sector (industry) and 35 per cent in the service sector. As a result of the strong growth in the last two sectors – first of all in manufacturing industry, commercial activity and communications, together with the public sector – the section of the population living in towns and built-up areas rose from about 25 per cent in 1875 to 45 per cent in 1920.

The transition from a pre-industrial to a developed country was complex, with no single determining factor. Before we look into the historical process by which Norway became an industrialized country, it is important to bear in mind that if Norway was in its time "underdeveloped", the word must be understood quite differently from the way it is used today. The supply of capital and standard of living were substantially higher than in some developing countries of today. And culturally the outlook was even brighter: Norway was, after all, part of the same larger civilization as Britain.

Traditional Norwegian goods and services

In the eighteenth century exporting timber, mainly to Britain, had been a well-established Norwegian trade, but due to the Napoleonic Wars and British import duties, the European markets had more or less closed. Therefore, the economic growth in Western Europe from the 1840s and 1850s, and the British government's decision to reduce the duties on timber were of great importance. Norway was able to draw the full benefit from its favourable location with regard to the British market. Britain again became the main market for Norwegian timber.

Furthermore, the fisheries enjoyed a boom period after the Napoleonic Wars. A new influx of spring herring and a plentiful occurrence of cod in the fishing seasons led to an expansion of the Norwegian fisheries. These blessings from nature coincided with favourable developments in European markets. The growth of population in the rest of Europe meant an increasing demand for cheap food; salted herring, dried fish and *klippfisk* (split, dried and salted cod). Most of the catches were exported, and the prices on the European market tended to rise.

Finally, in shipping an uninterrupted period of growth began in the middle of the 1820s. By 1878 Norway was, in terms of tonnage, the third largest shipping nation in the world, behind the USA and Britain. Between

1860 and 1914 at least 40 per cent of the export income was usually earned by the Norwegian merchant fleet. Expansion was particularly marked from 1850 onwards, with the major stimulus from the international shipping market. The breakthrough came after the British repealed the Navigation Acts in 1849. Now Norwegian ships were in a position to compete for cargoes on the British market. Other countries followed the British example and reduced the protection provided for their own shipping, with the result that new markets were opened to free competition. At the same time, there was an explosion in international trade. This rapidly growing market for shipping services was exploited by the Norwegian shipowners.

Norway's domestic product appears to have grown considerably from the 1830s to the crisis years at the end of the 1870s. Forestry, fisheries and shipping were the growth engines or the forces that fuelled the growth, and a growing demand in Europe for these traditional Norwegian goods and services triggered developments. Due to its exceptional volume, the export of raw materials had spin-off effects on the economy as a whole. A large proportion of the population was directly engaged in activities connected with these industries. Production depended on seasonal work by farmers who caught fish or felled timber in the off-season. The young men went to sea for a time before they established themselves in local coastal communities as farmers and fishermen.

So far we have established that the Norwegian economy depended on exports in a few key sectors. The difficulty, however, lies in explaining why Norway was not marginalised, that is, simply turned into a supplier of raw materials to more highly developed countries. The next question is how opportunities were utilised and how Norway was industrialized.

The first wave of industrialization

The expansion of the export trades led to growth in the traditional industries, for example ship building and the sawmilling industries. However, more interesting was the emergence of the modern Norwegian textile industry and the engineering workshops, because both were important features of the modernization process. The first textile factories and the first workshops were established in the 1840s and mark the first wave of industrialization in Norway.

Historians emphasise initiatives from Britain when they explain this early industrialization. In 1843 Britain lifted the ban on the export of machinery, and machinery manufacturers began to export not only machines but whole factory systems, including engineers and sometimes workers. They sought active partners in countries where the conditions were right, and thus played an important role in the industrialization of the European periphery. The founders of the textile industry in Norway had a background in trade and were internationally oriented, but lacked technical knowledge. In the 1840s and 1850s they exploited the opportunities, so to speak, and imported "the industrial revolution" from England.

The second modern industry to be introduced in the 1840s was mechanical engineering. This industry too is an example of the importance of international diffusion of technology. The engineering workshops needed mechanics and technical know-how as much as machines. Norwegians travelled abroad, first of all to Britain, to learn the production process. Production under licence was widespread and many workshops employed British artisans and engineers.

The workshops were important for the future of industrial development in Norway. They played a crucial role not only for repairs and maintenance of steam ships and railways, but also for adapting production equipment to meet specifically Norwegian requirements in, for instance, pulp production.

The role of the central government

So far, in explaining the modernization process, we have stressed foreign factors like a growing demand in Europe for traditional Norwegian goods and international diffusion of technology. Now it is time to look at the process in the light of domestic factors or circumstances at home. As one historian has pointed out: Machines imported from Britain would have remained curiosities, had there not been a growing demand for them.

For more than 400 years, from 1397 to 1814, Norway was under Danish "colonial" rule. In 1814, Norwegians resisted the cession of their country to Sweden, and adopted a new liberal constitution. Sweden then invaded Norway, but agreed to let Norway keep its constitution in return for accepting a union under a Swedish king. The new liberal regime that came to power in Norway after 1814 was, as one of our most distinguished historians Francis Sejersted has shown, "founded on the idea of economic expansion" and had "a long term strategy" to modernize the country. Through extensive use of public measures, the central government aimed at the economic development of the nation.

In times of crisis, for instance, the state raised loans which it passed on to industry and commerce. The state was also active in the creation of an institutional apparatus for the provision of credit. Local authorities played an important role in the establishment of local savings banks, which became instruments of industrial development on a small scale.

The state played the main role in the development of the communications network which promoted growth and market integration. The purchase of the country's first steamship in 1826, *The Constitution*, was a state initiative. By 1855 the state owned 11 steamships. From the middle of the century both national and local authorities directed their efforts towards extending and improving the road networks. The state took sole responsibility for the telegraph service. A national network of lines was built in the years between 1855 and 1870. The government took a hand in railway construction. The state was responsible for both the building of the railway network and its operation. The only exception was the first Norwegian railway which was opened in 1854 and ran from Christiania (Oslo) to Eidsvoll. This line was built and partly financed by a British company.

The Storting (the parliament) passed laws that dismantled privileges and allowed enterprise and capital greater freedom of movement. Industry and commerce benefited from low taxation. Both customs policy and treaty negotiations strengthened the competitiveness of the Norwegian export industries.

The central government obviously played a key role in the modernization process, but state intervention alone is not enough to bring about economic development in a backward country. There must be driving forces in the private sphere, with which the public sphere can collaborate.

Francis Sejersted, who places great emphasis on the role of the state, points to the importance of the emergence of a new, small industrial and trading bourgeoisie who invested money in shipbuilding, wool spinning, engineering workshops, timber and later pulp production. The period following the post-Napleonic war crisis generated countless entrepreneurs.

Wood products industry

Towards the end of the 1870s, the forces that had fuelled the growth in the Norwegian economy appeared to be exhausted. The fisheries experienced hard times as the spring herring disappeared from the coast in the 1870s. The forests had been felled to such an extent that the traditional saw-mills along the Drammen and Skien rivers ran into difficulties. The large-dimension timber, suitable for turning into battens and deals, had been reduced, and as a consequence the saw-mill industry moved eastward, to Sweden, Finland and Russia. The expansion in shipping since the 1850s had been based on technology that Norwegian shipowners were familiar with – wooden ships under sail. However, in the 1880s and 1890s shipping was in the process of being left behind in the competition with steamships.

How did Norway meet this challenge? The answer is, to put it briefly, a switch to new products and the modernization of the means of production. While the 1840s and 1850s were the early childhood of Norwegian industry, the period from the 1870s to 1920 was its coming-of-age. Industry now became the dynamic force in the process of growth and the transformation of society.

Very few of the technologies in use in Norwegian industry have been developed within its boundaries. Norway was not an innovator, as many historians have emphasized, but rather a good imitator. Norway did not create new products. As outlined above, entrepreneurs imported machines, processes and skilled labour. After a time, however, Norwegian industry was able to carry the development further. The historians' favourite example is the establishment and the growth of the wood pulp industry, our first modern export industry. During the nineteenth century the demand for paper grew rapidly, and in Europe there was an intense search for an alternative raw material to textile fibres. Wood fibre was to be the solution, and the first production of mechanical pulp took place in Germany in the 1840s. The technology was comparatively simple and turned out to be the basis for a new growth industry. The pulp industry could manage with smaller-dimension timber, and so solved the raw material problem in the catchment areas of the Drammen and Skien river systems. With their surplus of water power these areas became the centre of the new industry.

The pulp industry was established in the 1860s, and developed in close cooperation with the mechanical engineering industry that had been established in the first wave of industrialization. The technological breakthrough had occurred in Germany, but Norwegian industry had been sufficiently developed to service the wood-pulp mills and to make its own independent contribution to further development. In the 1880s Norwegian wood pulp had a dominant position on the international market. The 1890s saw a developing production of chemical pulp or cellulose, and a number of factories were built in Norway. This industry, however, was developed by foreign capital, which leads us to the "second industrial revolution".

A hydro-power-rich country

At the end of the nineteenth century important scientific discoveries fuelled industrial improvements called the "second industrial revolution". The leading nations were Germany and the USA. Electricity began to be more widely used, replacing coal as a source of energy. Norway was a hydro-power-rich country and therefore had advantages on the energy side, but had disadvantages when it came to capital and technology. The accumulation of capital in the golden years of the traditional export industries and the credit supply systems which had emerged in the same period were well suited to the type of production found in the first phase of industrialization. Power stations and industrial plants, however, were bigger than Norwegian capital alone could cope with. The mechanical engineering industry, which had emerged in the 1840s and 1850s, proved well able to service and develop wood-pulp mills. However, the new technology, which was both scientifically-based and capital-intensive, had to be imported from abroad.

Hydro-electricity came to be the foundation for new industries which depended on cheap energy. Foreign companies invested massively in the acquisition of waterfalls and hydroelectric power stations as well as in the newer industries. By using abundantly available hydraulic power for the generation of electricity, the new heavy industry turned Norway into a major exporter of electro-chemical and electro-metallurgical products. Output included saltpetre, calcium carbide, cyanamide and aluminium, as well as different kinds of ferro-alloys and electro-steel based on scrap iron. A number of the factories began production just before and during the First World War. The construction phase of others was at its most hectic in the war years.

These new export industries were to leave their mark on the Norwegian economy for many years to come, and they represented a decisive step in

Norway's transformation into an industrial nation. They also left their mark on the Norwegian topography. Because so much energy was lost in the process of transferring electricity from one place to another, the plants had to be located near the sources of energy. The result was that industrial communities appeared in previously almost uninhabited areas, and furthermore, this energy-based industry created many communities that were dependent on the success of one or two companies.

Due to the massive foreign investments the Norwegian parliament found itself compelled to pass, between 1905 and 1910, restrictive investment laws, mainly with regard to the further construction of hydroelectric power stations using foreign capital. These laws or regulations in fact stimulated the Norwegian economy because they required the use of Norwegian workers and materials. Moreover Norwegian industries benefited from foreign investment through collaborative agreements, which brought in new technology, know-how and capital.

A more developed country

At the start of the twentieth century Norway was definitely on its way from a supplier of raw materials to a more developed country. The reasons for the successful development are varied and complex. The traditional export activities provided the dynamic growth. Relatively early, however, Norway switched from the production of unprocessed staple goods to the first stage of processing, which resulted in semi-finished and finished manufactures. Our finest example was the progression of the wood-based industry from the export of timber to the export of battens and deals to the export of wood pulp, and later on to the export of paper and paper pulp.

Broadly speaking the emergence of Norway as an industrial nation took place in two phases. From the 1840s local elites invested money in sawmills, shipbuilding, woolspinning and pulp production. In the years 1890-1920 foreign companies built up an electrochemical industry based upon cheap hydro-electric power. After the turn of the century, however, also industries producing consumer goods experienced increasing growth rates, notably those producing ready-made clothing, shoes and foodstuffs. The fish-processing industry began to modernize. The canning industry, with brisling sardines as its most important product, was founded in Stavanger in the 1890s, and grew ever more significant.

Industry was, of course, not the only factor behind growth and change. Urbanization and the development of communications contributed to the creation of markets which accelerated changes in agriculture. In the first decades after the turn of the century the fishing fleet was motorized. Fishermen could now follow the fish more easily and productivity increased. In the same years the belated transition of the Norwegian merchant fleet from sailing-ships to steamships accelerated. Shipping, therefore, continued to be of vital importance for the Norwegian economy.

But it was the transition to the industrial processing of raw materials on a large scale that provided the most important stimulus for social changes. Industrial environments laid the technological foundation for the lasting increase in prosperity that Norway was to experience right up to the present.

Between the wars

By 1920 the modernization of the Norwegian economy had taken a major step forward. Historians seem to agree that the years after the turn of the century mark the breakthrough for the Norwegian industrial society. Economic and social crises, however, left their mark on the inter-war period: Businesses went bankrupt and flourishing industrial centres saw all activity cease. Long-term unemployment compounded the difficulties. Poor relief was the only means of survival for large groups of the population.

Taken as a whole, however, the inter-war years witnessed considerable economic growth. While the export industries' contribution to growth diminished, due to restrictions on international trade and customs barriers, the home industries benefited from increased tariff protection. Many new firms were established in the rural districts, for instance the furniture industry in Sunnmøre in the county of Møre and Romsdal. The new location pattern was a product of several factors: the development of small electric motors, lower wages in the countryside than in the towns, no troublesome labour movement and modest capital requirements.

Against all odds, Norwegian shipping became a growth area in a period when world trade was shrinking. The fleet was expanded and modernized in the 1920s and 1930s because Norwegian shipowners took the lead in two important transformations. By 1930 Norway had the world's most efficient fleet because so many of its ships were oil-fired, and Norwegian shipown-

During the 1930s, Norway was a leading producer of whale oil.

ers had also become leaders in the tanker market. The financial surplus created by shipping made it possible to compensate for the deficit of trade with other countries, and hence is an important economic and political factor in Norwegian history.

Whaling increased even faster than shipping. By 1930 Norway produced almost two-thirds of the world's whale oil. This expansion, however, had tragic consequences, as it led to the first catastrophic over- exploitation of a marine resource.

In the 1930s Norway ranked fourth among the shipping nations. Moreover, its ships were modern and fast, and the fleet had a large proportion of tankers – every fifth one of the world's tankers was Norwegian. The merchant fleet was to become Norway's most valuable contribution to the Allied war effort in the Second World War.

The golden years

In the period 1945 to 1973 Norway experienced the longest continuous period of strong and stable growth in its modern history. The gross domestic product rose annually by an average of 5 per cent. In these golden years, when Norway definitely entered "the rich man's world", Norwegians were spared unemployment of any significance. Unprecedented economic growth and low

There was an urgent need for hydro-power in the new export industries in the decades after World War II. Consequently, the factories were located near water-falls. Here is the site of the aluminium works in Øvre Årdal surrounded by high mountains and the longest fjord in Norway, Sognefjorden.

unemployment meant unprecedented improvements in income. In Norway average pay more than doubled. Norwegians experienced a marked increase in material well-being, and new spending money was translated into the purchase of durable consumer goods. In the 1940s there were more than 50 people per car, by 1974 more than two of every ten people owned a car. The Norwegians were given more holidays and more free time, and they spent more money on visits to restaurants, hotel accommodation and package holidays.

The economic growth in this period was closely tied to the development of the Norwegian industrial society and later to the service society or the post-industrial society. Immediately after the Second World War it was the industries that produced consumer goods for the home market that grew the fastest: the food and drink industries, leather and rubber, and the textile and clothing industries. From the end of the 1940s, however, the fastest-growing industries were those serving the export markets, the chemical industry and the smelting works.

The industrial development in the 1950s and the beginning of the 1960s was reminiscent of the industrial expansion in the first decades after the turn of the century. New large-scale industrial concerns and new towns were established almost from scratch, producing semi-finished products for the world market using cheap water power. Roughly speaking: until the 1970s the industrial expansion was based mainly on the availability of inexpensive water-power resources and raw materials harvested from Norway's farms, forests, and seas.

During the 1950s the industrial workforce grew as a part of factory expansion, but by the 1960s, the relative proportion of factory workers began to drop, despite rising production. Workers in the service sector, filling functions as teachers, clerks, medical personnel, insurance and bank workers, rose rapidly in contrast. Half of all paid workers were in the service sector by the beginning of the 1970s, and the proportion rose steadily thereafter. Of the economically active population in 1977, only 8 per cent were employed in the primary sector, 37 per cent in the secondary sector and 55 per cent in the service sector.

The post-war years saw an increased governmental role in economic policy. Most European countries, including Norway, set up new planning offices, responsible for developing multi-year economic projections and for setting goals and the means to meet them. Most European post-war governments nationalized some sectors of industry. In Norway industry had the highest priority in the post-war years, and the central government made great efforts to channel investment to this sector. This occurred most directly through the state's own activities. State-owned enterprises – aluminium, iron, steel and mining industries – belonged to the expanding industry of the 1950s and 1960s.

Norway's economy was a mixed one of public and private enterprises, and the state also stimulated industrial growth in the private sector. Of greatest importance were large-scale investments in the construction of power stations. The power was delivered to industry at favourable prices. Energy resources were Norway's greatest competitive advantage on world markets.

A "flight" from the countryside to the towns took place in the post-war years. On the one hand this flight, or migration, of labour was a natural feature of a growing economy. There was an excess of labour on the farms and expanding industry and services offered secure work and higher wages. On the other hand the central government stimulated centralization and the transfer of labour by encouraging the growth of larger farms with increased mechanization and specialization. In fishing too, larger units were stimulated. As a result, rising food production and higher output in the fisheries were achieved with a steadily shrinking labour force.

Figure 3.1   Structural change and economic development.
Employment expressed in percentages, Norway, 1875–1990

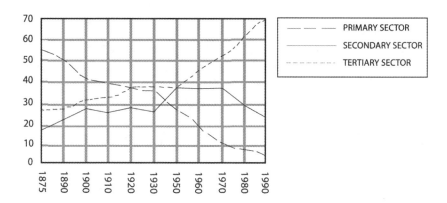

Economic structure deals with the relationships among the various sectors of the economy: the primary, secondary and tertiary sectors. In a modernizing economy with increasing productivity there tends to be a shift from people working in the primary sector to the secondary sector, and then to the tertiary sector. The figure above shows that the proportion of the labour force engaged in agriculture and fishing had fallen from 54% in 1875 (it was much higher earlier) to 6% by 1990, while during the same period the percentage of the labour force employed in industry rose from less than 20% to almost 40%. This is the first major structural change that took place in Norway. The second change involves a shift from commodity production (industry) to services. 70% of the population in 1990 were employed in the tertiary sector.

Which economic activities belong to the primary, secondary and tertiary sectors?		
Primary sector	**Secondary sector**	**Tertiary sector**
Products are obtained directly from nature	Products of nature are transformed or processed	Deals not with products or material goods, but with services
Agriculture, forestry, fishing	Manufacturing, construction	Domestic and personal services (e.g. cooks, barbers), commercial and financial (e.g. merchants, bankers), professional (e.g. doctors, lawyers), governmental (e.g. postal workers, bureaucrats, military employees)

So far we have mentioned the role of the state and its industry-friendly policy, productivity increase and transfer of labour as reasons for growth. Another important factor was the growing internationalization of the Norwegian economy. While the great depression and a protectionist climate left their mark on the 1930s, a growth in and a liberalization of the world economy characterized the post-war years. Both historians and economists have emphasized the increase in international trade when explaining the post-war growth in Norway. Important turning points were 1948, when the government decided to participate in the Marshall Plan, and 1960, when Norway became one of the founding members of the European Free Trade Association (EFTA).

In the 1950s and 1960s Norway, above all, became integrated into the western industrialized world. As the historian Tore Grønlie has pointed out, by the middle of the 1960s, Norway as a state was involved in more than 60 international organisations. Most of them had been established after 1945, and most of them were economic in nature and tied to international trade. Norwegian shipping expanded with the increase in international trade, and as outlined above, it was the export industries that expanded the most in the 1950s and 1960s.

The years 1972-1973 mark the end of the golden years and a turning point in the story about how Norway became a wealthy nation. In 1973 an international crisis was set off by a dramatic increase in the price of oil, engineered by the Organization of Petroleum Exporting Countries. The economic downturn was reinforced by a basic structural crisis in western industry. The crisis led to long-lasting problems in Norwegian industry and shipping. However, the discovery of oil and gas offshore in the late 1960s boosted Norway's economic fortunes.

The oil age

Oil from the North Sea became a new element of growth in the Norwegian economy. Large petroleum and natural gas reserves were first discovered in Norwegian areas of the North Sea in 1969, and petroleum production began on a trial basis in 1971. Foreign companies dominated exploration off Norway in the initial phase, and were responsible for developing the country's first oil and gas fields. The multinational firms were intended to play an important long-term role. At an early stage, however, the goal was to build up a Norwegian oil community. The strategy was to invite foreign oil-companies to the Norwegian continental shelf and receive certain services in return. The model was the investment laws passed between 1905 and 1910, which had reduced foreign dominance, and at the same time secured Norwegian enterprises know-how and technology.

The goals for Norwegian oil and gas policies since the early 1970s have been national management and control, building a Norwegian oil community and state participation. In 1972 Statoil was founded as a state-owned oil company. At the same time the Storting established the principle of 50 per cent state participation in each production licence. Later on the Storting decided that the level of state participation could be higher or lower than 50 per cent, depending on circumstances. In 2001 Statoil was partially privatised.

In 1974 construction of a pipeline to carry crude oil to Teesside in England was completed. By 1975 Norway was producing enough petroleum to satisfy all its domestic needs and also to export large quantities to Europe. Before offshore drilling for petroleum and natural gas began in the 1970s, mining was relatively unimportant in Norway, and the country had to import most of its fossil fuels. Today Norway is highly dependent on its oil production and international oil prices, with oil and gas accounting for one-third of its exports. The petroleum sector now accounts for about one-eighth of Norway's gross domestic product, and as mentioned above, today Norway is one of the biggest oil and gas producers in the world.

Table 3.2   Export of primary commodities

Export of principal commodities (2003)	
Commodity	NOK Million
Total	482 896
Petroleum (incl. products)	222 927
Gas (natural and manufactured)	70 874
Metals	29 407
Fish	25 161
Transport equipment (excl. road vehicles, incl. ships and oil platforms)	17 514

Source: www.ssb.no/english

In spite of Norway's strong image in the field of international co-operation, the Norwegians together with the Swiss are the only two decent-sized western European nations who have resisted the temptation to join the 25-member European Union. Norway opted to stay out of the EU as a result of referendum first in 1972, and then again in 1994. Both Norway and Switzerland have demonstrated that it is possible to stay out of the EU and still prosper. Euro-enthusiasts would probably say that the wealth of these two countries is more a cause than a consequence of their decisions not to join the EU.

With arguably the highest quality of life worldwide, however, Norwegians worry about the time to come in the next two or three decades when the oil and gas begin to run out. Instead of splurging out, they dutifully put much of their oil cash into a special savings fund for a rainy day. Norway has been saving its oil-boosted budget surpluses in a Government Petroleum Fund, which is invested abroad and now is valued at more than $388 billion (December 2007).

Chapter 4

Religion in Norway: A Bird's-Eye View

By Helje Kringlebotn Sødal and Levi Geir Eidhamar

Traditionally religion has permeated Norwegian society. During the last few decades, however, religion in Norway – as in most Western countries apart from the US – seems less socially important than previously. This chapter explores the significance of religion in Norway, historically and today.

There are historical, cultural, and legal reasons why Norway can be regarded as a Christian nation. Christianity came to the country more than a thousand years ago, and Norwegian culture, from language to art, is greatly influenced by this religion. The Constitution is based on the principle of religious freedom, but it also ascertains that "the evangelical-Lutheran religion remains the official religion of the state" (§ 2). Hence the king or queen must profess the evangelical-Lutheran religion and "maintain and protect" the state church called The Norwegian Church (§ 4), where about 86 % of the population are members. Four to five per cent belong to other Christian communities. The Christian religion has also left its mark on Norwegian education to some extent. Pre-schools and schools have a Christian objects clause, stating that the values of the education are rooted in the Christian tradition. The tension between religious freedom on the one hand and certain "privileges" for the Christian religion and Lutheranism on the other is strongly felt in Norway today. The state church as well as the Christian foundation of the education system give Norway a special position compared to other Western countries. Both are rooted in tradition and are in accordance with the preferences of the majority of the population. Even so, they are not directly compatible with pluralistic, partly also secular, post-modern trends.

Three main periods can be outlined in the history of religion in Norway: the pre-Christian period with the Norse religion up to about 1000 AD, the

Christian period up to the last decades of the twentieth century, and the pluralistic Christian period of today – where different religions and secular world views exist side by side with the still dominant Christian religion.

Christianity conquers the Norse religion

From about 800 AD Christianity gradually penetrated the areas that were about to be included in the nation of Norway. In this period of dramatic changes, Norwegian political and religious history are deeply intertwined. Ideologically Christianity stimulated the process of building a nation ruled by one king from several small, tribal kingdoms. Hence many of the pretenders to the throne fought for the new religion. Traditionally Olav Haraldsson, later St Olav, is known as the king who completed the Christianizing process, paradoxically when he died in battle at Stiklestad in Trøndelag in 1030.

The Vikings worshipped several supernatural powers, from named male and female gods, to unnamed powers of lower ranks, to ancestors. Norse mythology did not comprise an organized system of dogmas. Religious performance, especially the ritual of sacrifice (*blot*), took precedence over religious thinking. The Norse religion was concentrated on creating and maintaining fertility on earth, not on salvation in a life to come. The rituals were carried out collectively with the tribal leader as sacrificial priest. In *Heimskringla*, the Islandic writer Snorre Sturlason (1178/79-1241) tells the story of the Norwegian kings. In a paragraph on the 9th century petty king Halvdan Svarte, Snorre Sturlason writes about the death of King Halvdan. He drowned trying to cross a lake on porous ice. Here is what Snorre Sturlason writes about the relationship between a popular king and the fertility of the soil: "He had been considered such a popular king. People mourned over his death, so when it became known that he was dead, and his body had been brought to Ringerike in order to be buried, chiefs from the counties of Romerike, Vestfold and Hedemark showed up, and everyone demanded that they should have the body of Halvdan. They wanted to bury the corpse in their county, because everyone thought that this would bring fertility to the soil." In Norse religion, it was the king's responsibility to provide rain, sunshine and good crops.

Contrary to the Norse religion Christianity was universal, exclusive and proselytizing. It focused more on the community of the believers than on

King Olav Haraldsson, later named St Olav, is known as the person who completed the Christianising process in Norway. This sculpture is found in Nidarosdomen in Trondheim, the most famous church in Norway

the collective worship of the tribe or clan. It was monotheistic and proclaimed an almighty, holy and loving God. The many gods and powers of the Norse religion were believed to be strong and powerful, but they also had certain limitations and weaknesses. Whereas the Vikings valued strength, honour, power and self-assertion, Christianity preached about sin, mercy, obedience, humility and forgiveness. Such differences indicate that there was a great clash of beliefs and values between the two religions. Thus it is hardly correct to describe the transition from the Norse religion to Christianity as a smooth, syncretistic process. The Norse religion was not weak or dying at the end of the first millennium AD. It was a vital tradition superseded by Christianity, partly because the latter was more in accordance with ideological forces at that time. The kings with their politically centralizing ambitions profited from an allegiance with the centralizing and unifying Christian tradition.

A thousand years of Christian culture

Despite the fact that Christianity to some extent was thrust on the Norwegian population, the culture developed within a Christian framework for the following thousand years. The Roman-Catholic church with its clergy and its monasteries became an increasingly important factor during the middle ages. Churches were built all over the country. In the second half of the 13th century there were approximately 1200 churches and 2000 clergy, which probably meant that one priest served about 150 people on average. Nidarosdomen in present-day Trondheim became the most famous church and pilgrimage destination and housed the shrine of St Olav. The construction started in the 1150s, and the cathedral became the biggest medieval building in the Nordic countries. The stave churches – once about 750 in number but now 25 – represent a distinctively Norwegian contribution to the history of European architecture. The cult connected to the Norwegian saints – particularly St Sunniva, St Hallvard and St Olav, patron saints of Bergen, Oslo and Nidaros (Trondheim) respectively – helped "domesticate" Christianity. There is hardly evidence to support the idea that Norwegians in the medieval period were less influenced by Christianity than their contemporaries in other countries.

The laws were changed due to Christian influence (Kristenrettene). They prohibited Norse religion and the old tradition of killing unwanted children by leaving them to die in the forest, whilst making fasting at certain periods, abstaining from work on Sundays and baptizing children compulsory – to mention some examples.

In 1152 Nidaros was made the residence of a new, Norwegian archbishop. This further increased the spiritual and political power of the church. Priests were appointed exclusively by the bishops. The king and the rich landowners could no longer install priests in the churches they had built and lost the right of ownership of them. The bishops were to be elected by the church, without interference from the king. The king was crowned by the archbishop and had to declare his loyalty to the pope in Rome.

Since both the bishops and the kings sought political power, they could be bitter rivals. One of the most famous medieval kings, Sverre (ca 1150-1202), was excommunicated by the pope because of a complicated political conflict with the church. The Black Death hit Norway in 1349-50, and the plague may have killed half the population. Priests, monks and nuns deliberately risked contagion by attending to the ill and dying, and conse-

Stave churches represent a distinctly Norwegian contribution to the history of European architecture. This is one of the most famous ones: Heddal Stave Church in Telemark. The oldest parts date back to 1250.

quently died in even greater numbers. The whole church structure suffered badly, but even so the power of the church was strengthened. The spirit of self-sacrifice among the priests, monks and nuns had impressed people and led to a flow of gifts to the churches and the monasteries. Towards the end of the middle ages, the church had become the biggest landowner in the country.

Norway lost its national sovereignty in the 14th century and joined a union with Sweden and later Denmark, both countries richer and more powerful than Norway. Eventually this meant that the Danish-Norwegian kings in Copenhagen took major decisions pertaining to religious questions in Norway. Two German "imports" were particularly important, the Reformation and pietism.

The Lutheran Reformation

Geographically close to North Germany, Denmark was influenced early on by Martin Luther's theology. The kings could profit politically from the new religious movement since the Reformation favoured national churches rather than a universal church led by the pope. Taxation to Rome would cease, the king could appoint the bishops, and he could confiscate the huge, church-owned properties if Lutheranism became the official religion of the monarchy.

Kristian III (1503-1559) made the Lutheran church the only legal one in Denmark-Norway in 1536-37. He removed all the Catholic bishops, closed the monasteries, confiscated church property and proclaimed himself head of the new national church. In Norway Olav Engelbrektsson (1480-1538), the last archbishop and one of the most influential advocates of Norwegian independence, had to flee the country in 1537. Likewise, the Norwegian consultative body to the king (*Riksrådet*) was dissolved. In this way Kristian III used the Reformation to abolish the remaining elements of Norwegian political independence and make the country a Danish province. In Norway Lutheranism was introduced without much preparation or public support.

Roman-Catholic worship was declared illegal and the monasteries were emptied. The Catholic bishops were replaced by Lutherans who were loyal to the king. Most of the priests continued in their parishes, but had to adjust the services to the Lutheran decree. This meant that they had to get hold of the Bible in Danish (the first complete translation was available in 1550), Luther's two books of catechism and *Confessio Augustana*, which proclaims the main elements of the Lutheran faith. It is, however, hard to say how much ordinary people's belief was changed by the enforced Reformation. Probably the Lutheran doctrines needed generations before they were internalized by the population. Some historians claim that the main theological ideas behind the Reformation did not effectively make their mark on the Norwegian population until the end of the 18th century.

During the middle ages people generally interpreted their lives, religious life included, within a collective framework – the (extended) family, the local area, the church and the country. Collective worship rather than individual belief and practice characterized the period. The Reformation paved the way for a more individually based religion since Luther drew attention to the personal relationship between the individual and God, and focused less on the church as an institution and mediator between the divine and the human. One very important effect of this "individual shift" was the growing need for the church to educate the whole population so that everyone could read the Bible on their own.

In the 17th century – the orthodox epoch – theologians sought to consolidate and purify the teaching and preaching in an exclusively Lutheran way. Catholic supporters and reformed dissidents were persecuted. Church discipline was tightened up. The moral obligations for ordinary people were strict, and immorality was severely punished. The intimate unity between the Danish-Norwegian state and the Lutheran church reached a climax when King Fredrik III proclaimed himself absolute monarch in 1660. He became the ultimate leader and legislator of the state and its state church, and the distinction between church jurisdiction and secular jurisdiction was blurred. One example is the processes against the witches and wizards. They were convicted by secular courts of justice, but orthodox theology legitimated the trials to some extent. About 300 Norwegians were burnt as witches or wizards. More than 80 % were women. Some priests played an active part in the processes by refusing to give the accused absolution and communion unless she or he confessed guilt. Others fought for acquittal for the accused.

Pietism

Two rather different movements – Pietism and the Enlightenment – dominated religious life in Norway during the following period (18th and 19th centuries). The theological enlightenment originated from a broader philosophical current of enlightenment and reason in Europe and America. Pietism was a Christian movement from the onset. Despite obvious differences, pietism and enlightenment were to some extent related. Both were critical of orthodox theology and its preoccupation with dogmas. They focused more on subjectivity and individualism than orthodox theology did, and they wanted to educate people, admittedly for different reasons. The pietistic movement stressed the sinfulness of man and preached the need for personal conversion, redemption and moral piety. Experiences and feelings were regarded as vital elements of Christian life. Christians were warned against taking part in secular, cultural life – which allegedly could lead to moral corruption and apostasy. Instead they were encouraged to seek the community of true believers. Contrary to this, theologians influenced by the enlightenment focused on reason and the inherent goodness of man, and praised secular, cultural developments. Ideas from the enlightenment had a rather limited impact on ordinary people in Norway. These ideas were most influential among the intellectual elite, the clergy included. Pietistic thoughts, on the other hand, were widespread and created a strong, pietistic movement among lay people, which left its mark on Christianity in Norway for centuries to come.

Pietism was partly introduced from "above", i.e. by the central administration in Copenhagen because the kings favoured it, and partly from "below", i.e. through preaching in the churches and in small groups in private homes (*konventikler*). Pietism as the monarch's policy of religion (*statspietisme*) brought about some very important changes in Norway. Since its major aim was to educate the population in pietistic Christianity, confirmation was introduced in 1736. This conditioned systematic Christian education, and part of the confirmation service was an extensive oral examination of the dogmatic knowledge of the candidates. Being confirmed was practically speaking compulsory for all young people, since nobody could marry or be employed in certain jobs before they were confirmed. Because everybody had to be able to read in order to prepare for the confirmation, compulsory education was introduced in 1739. The main subjects were Christianity, writing and reading, the latter two being mainly regarded as tools in the religious education. Gradually more subjects were introduced.

Pietism started a strong missionary movement in Norway. The state supported missionary work, partly for political reasons. At the beginning of the 18th century the king wanted to convert the native Lapp population from shamanism to Christianity and to tie them to Denmark-Norway politically. The mission to Finmark was mainly carried out by the Norwegian priest Thomas von Westen (1682-1727). Schools and churches were built, and von Westen worked to raise the poor living conditions of the Lapps. The king also supported the mission to Greenland. The Norwegian priest Hans Egede (1686-1758) and his wife dedicated their lives to this cold and desolate mission field. Both von Westen and Egede soon learnt the native tongues and were greatly respected by the population. At that time as later, there was a certain ambiguity connected to the missionary work. On the one hand the missionaries helped the natives to preserve parts of their cultural identity, above all their language. On the other hand they stimulated integration and even assimilation to Western culture. The second wave of Norwegian missionary work started about 1840. At that time missionaries were sent to Africa and Asia. They were financed by the numerous lay missionary groups and by church collections. Until a few years ago Norway was the world's largest sending country of missionaries per capita.

Pietism continued the process of individualisation of religion started by the Reformation. The pietists encouraged individual study of the Bible and Christian literature. Devotions, prayers and other meetings were held privately, with or without the consent of the clergy, despite the fact that the law demanded that the local priest should supervise such arrangements in his parish. Women took active part in these activities that traditionally had been dominated by males.

Hans Nielsen Hauge – a lay pioneer

Hans Nielsen Hauge (1771-1824) is the most outstanding lay person in Norwegian religious history. He started a pietistically inspired lay movement within The Norwegian Church that has influenced Christianity in Norway to present time. Twenty-five years old, Hauge had a religious experience, which he interpreted as supernatural intervention, as he was working in the fields as a farmer. Soon he started travelling and preaching in large parts of the country, even though this was contrary to the law. He also established several factories and printing offices that published religious literature. Hauge actually became the most widely read author in Norway in the 19th century, having written more than 30 books. He organized his adherents in small "friendship groups". The "friends" throughout the country supported each other spiritually and financially, as Hauge preached about personal, Christian life *and* about being an honest, industrious worker. He was a pioneer both as a pietistic preacher and organizer, and as a successful businessman. Hauge and his movement can be interpreted as an example of the later Max Weber's thesis of "the protestant ethic of hard work". Hauge's activities were in conflict with several laws regulating religious activities, trade, freedom of the press and vagrancy. Thus he was put in jail in 1804. His health was broken by nearly ten years of imprisonment. But he continued to supervise and lead his "friends" when he was released, until he died ten years later.

Hauge made a lasting impact on Norwegian religion in several ways. He created and led the first major revival movement in the country. Secondly, this movement – consisting mainly of people from the lower social strata – worked partly as a protest movement against the dominance of the official class and seriously challenged the authority of the clergy. The lay movement within the state church has been remarkably strong in Norway ever since. Thirdly, Hauge contributed to creating religious equality between the sexes.

Hans Nielsen Hauge organized his adherents in small "friendship groups" emphasizing the need to take a personal stand as a Christian. He encouraged lay people to preach. Adolf Tideman's painting depicts a meeting of the "friends".

Contrary to tradition he allowed women to preach publicly and to be in charge of the "friendship groups". Many of his successors disagreed with Hauge on this point. Thus female priests were not ordained in The Norwegian Church until 1961, with the first female bishop in 1993. Today more than 50 % of the students of theology are women, and the dominating position of men in church leadership is on the wane.

Christianity in the 19th and 20th centuries

The 19th and 20th centuries brought about major changes in Norwegian society – politically, socially and religiously. At the beginning of the period Norway was a poor, underdeveloped country politically dependent on Denmark. During the period, however, this changed radically. The unions with Denmark and finally with Sweden were dissolved, and Norwegian society experienced urbanization, industrialization, egalitarianism and economic growth. These great changes naturally affected the church and the Christians.

The lay movement continued to grow in the 19th century and in most of the 20th. One important characteristic of Christianity in Norway is the many different lay organizations established within the state church. Most of them are either working to support missionary activities in foreign countries, or working for Christian nurture and spreading of the Gospel to different social groups within the country (*indremisjon*). The many "prayer houses" are a typically Norwegian phenomenon linked to the lay movement. They were built from the 1850s onwards. As the name indicates, they were used for prayer meetings, but they also housed a wide range of other arrangements including lotteries for the benefit of Christian work. The number of prayer houses throughout the country, now about 2600, exceeds the number of churches and chapels. Lately, however, the prayer house movement seems to have lost some of its vitality in many local communities. It is more difficult to recruit the younger generations, especially in some urban areas.

At the turn of the 19th century great cultural changes took place in the country. Institutionalized Christianity, Christian dogmas and values were criticised by modern literature, new theological movements and science. Faced by these cultural and theological challenges, most Christians chose conservative positions. But there was also a more liberal Christian faction. Theological controversy led to the division of the rather small Norwegian theological milieu. A private, theologically conservative seminary was established in 1908 and soon became the largest institution for educating clergy (*Det Teologiske Menighetsfakultet*). Conservative theologians in alliance with the strong lay movement agreed not to cooperate with liberal Christians at a conference in 1920. The split between conservative and liberal Christians characterized The Norwegian Church for decades, but is now less visible.

The Norwegian Church played an important political role during the years of German occupation (1940-45) by encouraging resistance against the Nazi regime. All the bishops broke with the state in 1942 and declined to carry out the official part of their work. Shortly afterwards nearly all the clergy followed suit. The Norwegian Church functioned as a free church, not a state church, during the remaining years of the occupation.

A debate on the relationship between the state and the state church began in the 1850s and was reinforced in the 20th century. The self-government of the church has been increased during recent decades. Many active Christians still find the dependence on the state unfortunate. Some of the political parties also want to abolish the state church. Even so, a larger proportion of the population want to keep the state church system (about 39 %) than those wanting to abolish it (about 20 %).

Towards privatized and individualized religion

There have been major changes in religious life in Norway during the last few decades. One is linked to the withdrawal of religion from the official to the private sphere. A remarkably high percentage of the population, more than 90 %, are members of a religious community. Still, Norwegians' church attendance is among the lowest in Europe. About 2-3 % attend church on Sundays, and 10 % say that they take part in organized Christian activities at least once a month. This does not mean that people no longer regard themselves as Christians. Only about 10 % claim not to believe in God or a religious power. The vast majority believe in God with more or less certainty. The dwindling church attendance indicates a shift of focus from collective religion to a privatized and individualized belief rather than religious indifference. Privatization of religion is more characteristic of Christians than of people belonging to non-Christian religions, and is more widespread among members of The Norwegian Church than among members of other Christian communities.

Privatized religion can be characterised in many ways. One important feature is that religious institutions and traditions have lost their strong hold over many people's lives. It is no longer regarded as necessary to practise religion together with other believers or to proclaim one's belief. Many feel relatively free to interpret, or even disregard, dogmas and the official teachings of the religious communities, and many refuse to submit to religious authorities. Loyalty towards one's own feelings and experiences seems to take precedence over acceptance of more or less "established truth" and reason-based religion. Freedom to choose what to believe and how to practise (or withdraw from it) is highly valued.

To sum up: The majority of the Norwegian population still believe in God, but they believe in their own, personal way. Their world view consists of Christian elements, and most people feel somehow linked to parts of the Christian tradition, like celebrating Christmas, baptizing their children, marrying in a church and being buried in a Christian way.

The active Christians

The active Christians, about 10 % of the population, take part regularly in Christian activities. Geographically there are more active Christians in the southern part of the country than elsewhere, and Kristiansand is probably the "Christian capital" as far as religious activities are concerned. Women are slightly more religiously active than men. Children, middle-aged and elderly people are more active than other age groups. There is no strong connection between religious activity and social deprivation in Norwegian society today. The majority of the religiously active are relatively well off economically and socially and could be labelled as "middle-class".

Generally speaking, members of Christian communities other than the state church as well as members of non-Christian religions like Islam and Buddhism are more active than members of The Norwegian Church. Estimates indicate that about 60 % of Christian activity in the country is carried out by members of The Norwegian Church. The members of the free churches, 4-5 % of the total population, take care of the remaining 40 %. One of the most alarming developments within The Norwegian Church is that relatively few from the younger generations go regularly to the service on Sunday morning, which traditionally has been regarded as the most important collective Christian gathering of the week. The Norwegian Church is probably experiencing the same declining tendency as many of the traditional churches, for instance the Anglican and the Methodist Church, experience in the West. But so far The Norwegian Church has maintained approximately the same membership rate despite the fact that the active part of the church members are getting older.

Today charismatic, ecumenical and ritual currents seem particularly important within Christianity worldwide, as in Christian communities in Norway. The charismatic movement came to Norway from countries like the USA, England and South Korea in the 1970s. The charismatic current developed in two different directions in Norway. On the one hand it became a broad movement within the state church. On the other hand it resulted in the establishment of several independent congregations theologically related to traditional Pentecostalism. Some of these new congregations are recruiting lots of young people and aiming at re-Christianizing Norwegian society.

Norwegian Christians, like many of their fellow believers in other countries, now seem less preoccupied with theological differences than before. Ecumenical work on many levels – from arranging common out-reaches, aid programs and revival meetings to theologically based dialogs between different denominations – has become increasingly important.

There is also a rather strong movement of re-traditionalisation, particularly within The Norwegian Church. This movement focuses on liturgy, meditation, spiritual retreat and aesthetics as important parts of Christian life.

Towards religious plurality

The process of plurality started within the Christian tradition in the 19th century. The draft of Norway's first Constitution from 1814 originally contained an article stating religious liberty for all citizens. For unknown reasons it was dropped in the final version of the law. The breakthrough of religious freedom came with the so called "Law of Dissidents" in 1845. This law allowed different Christian communities to organize and hold public meetings. The Roman Catholics, the Methodists and the Baptists were among the first to establish churches in Norway and were soon followed by a large number of others. The law did not protect religious groups that were not defined as Christian. This applied for instance to The Church of Jesus Christ of Latter-Day Saints, which came to Norway about 1850. Some of the early Mormon missionaries were brought to court, fined and imprisoned. The Constitution also prohibited Jews from entering the kingdom. "The Jew paragraph" – which mainly was motivated by commercial reasons – was abolished in 1851. In principle full religious freedom was not granted until 1969 when a new law permitted any religious community or groups with secular world views to establish and register as "faith communities". Registered groups are given financial support annually based on membership. The state, however, cannot interfere with internal questions in a registered, religious group.

Modern pluralism

About 3.5 % of the Norwegian population belongs to non-Christian religions. A statistical survey from 2004 reveals that the Muslims constitute the largest group by far:

Table 4.1

	Organized members	Stipulated number of adherents
Muslims	80 838	120 000
Buddhists	9 968	20 000
Hindus	3 021	10 000
Sikhs	3 110	5 000
Jews	961	1 100
Bahá'is	1 000	1 000

Source: www.ssb.no

The vast majority of Muslims, Buddhists, Hindus and Sikhs are immigrants having settled in Norway after 1970. Religions like Judaism and Bahá'i have longer historical roots in the country. Most of their adherents are ethnic Norwegians.

The first Jewish congregation was established in Oslo in 1892, and the synagogues in Oslo and Trondheim were consecrated in 1920 and 1925 respectively. These buildings are still the only synagogues in Norway, and the synagogue in Trondheim is the northernmost in the world. When Norway was occupied by Germany in 1940, the Jewish population numbered about 1800. Some escaped to Sweden, but 760 were deported to German concentration camps. Only 25 of the deported Jews survived. The Holocaust had a lasting effect on Judaism in Norway, and today there are only 1100 Jews in the country. But the congregation in Oslo is active and has its own rabbi, Sabbath services, cheider (religious school for children) and a kindergarten. As in many European countries, Norwegian Jews now experience growing anti-Semitic currents.

The first local spiritual assembly of Bahá'i in Norway was established in 1948. The majority of the roughly thousand Bahá'is are ethnic Norwegians, but there is also a large group with an Iranian background.

The presence of the four largest non-Christian religions in Norway – Islam, Buddhism, Hinduism and Sikhism – is almost entirely a result of immigration. A few hundred Muslim and Buddhist Norwegian converts do not change this fact. Thus the history of these religions in Norway is closely linked to the history of immigration. There are mainly two types of Norwegian immigrants – labour immigrants and refugees.

Labour immigrants, who mainly came to the country before 1975, could settle down wherever they wanted. Most of them chose the Oslo area, and most of them were Muslims. The refugees, on the other hand, were placed in different parts of the country by the government. Certain areas were selected for certain nationalities. Thus fishery communities in Finmark, the most northern county of Norway, received Tamils from Sri Lanka, while Agder, the southern region, was chosen for the Vietnamese. Due to this, Hinduism is relatively strong in Finmark, while Buddhism has more adherents in Agder.

The Diaspora situation adds new functions to religious life. They have become vital in preserving ethnic, cultural and linguistic identity for the immigrants and their descendants. Mosques, temples and gurudwaras not only house religious ceremonies but are places to meet fellow countrymen, speak your mother tongue and eat traditional food from the home country. None of the world religions appears as monolithic and homogeneous. They are divided into different factions and ethnic groups.

The estimated 120 000 Muslims in Norway constitute a diverse mosaic of nationalities, traditions and beliefs. The largest groups originally come from Pakistan, Turkey, Iraq, Iran, Somalia, the Balkans and North Africa. Several mosques were established in flats and factory buildings from the 1970s. Mosques cannot be financed by loans, because Muslim law prohibits interest. Therefore only two buildings have been constructed as mosques in Norway. The newly raised mosque in Urtegata in Oslo houses the largest Muslim congregation in Scandinavia.

The variety of different Sunni groups has organized The Islamic Counsel of Norway (*Islamsk Råd Norge*). This body communicates Muslim views to Norwegian society, the media in particular. The majority of Shias are refugees escaping the strict Islamic regime in Iran. They are generally quite secular and have not established their own mosques. The few Shia mosques are run by Shias from Sunni-dominated countries.

The new generation of Muslims growing up in Norway usually tend to distinguish between the traditional culture of their parents' home countries and what they regard as "pure Islam". Some try to unify secular Norwegian values and individual interpretations of Islam. Others study the *Quran* and *Hadith* in search of true Islamic values. Muslim student organisations and homepages help promote the latter, conservative trend.

In the Oslo area different ethnic groups are large enough to keep their own congregations. For instance, there are separate Pakistani, Somali and

Girl studying a modern Muslim textbook. Photo from the mosque in Urtegata in Oslo.

Bosnian mosques – which help preserve an ethnically based religion. In areas outside Oslo different nationalities may establish one mosque together, where Norwegian is used as the common language. Young Muslims outside Oslo seem to be more liberal and influenced by Norwegian values than Muslims of the same age in the Oslo area.

As in most European countries, there tend to be some clashes of values between Muslims and Norwegian society. Topics like Muslim terrorism, arranged marriages and female circumcision are regularly debated in the mass media. These debates have revealed diversities between liberal and conservative Norwegian Muslims. The debate is now increasingly dominated by the Muslims who have grown up in Norway. They speak Norwegian and are familiar with Norwegian culture and values.

The Hindus in Norway constitute two distinctly different groups, Indian and Tamil Hindus. During the seventies Hindi-speaking Vishnuits from North India came to Norway as labour immigrants. By 2005 they formed a group of about 2 500. After the Sri Lankan civil war started in 1983, many Tamils fled to Norway. In this way Norway became one of the countries that received most Tamils. Today there are about 10 000 Tamils in the country. About 7 000 are Shivaite Hindus, while 3 000 are Catholics. The two groups of Hindus have different ethnic, linguistic, national and theological backgrounds. Usually the two groups have separate temples, where puja ceremonies of quite different styles are performed.

There are approximately 20 000 Buddhists in Norway, but only 8 500 belong to a registered Buddhist organization. About 700 ethnic Norwegians have converted to Buddhism. The Vietnamese, who escaped the communist regime in the seventies, constitute the largest group of about 10 000. They belong to the pluralistic Mahayana tradition. The Vietnamese have built Khoung Viet Temple on the outskirts of Oslo. This is the largest Buddhist temple in Scandinavia and contains the only relic of the historical Buddha in the Nordic countries. About 5 000 Thais belong to the more conservative Theravada tradition. The majority of the Thais are women who have married Norwegian men. Buddhists immigrants are generally well integrated in Norwegian society, and most Norwegians value Buddhism as a religion of peace and high moral standards.

Most of the estimated 5 000 Sikhs live in the Oslo area where they have two gurdwaras.

In addition to the many different religious groups, Norway has the largest number of organized secular humanists in the world, not only in percentage, but also numerically, with almost 70 000 members. The Humanist and Ethical Society (*Human-Etisk Forbund*), which organizes the secular humanists, was founded in 1956. The Humanist and Ethical Society arrange ceremonies connected to rites of passage, like celebrations when babies are named, secular confirmations, wedding ceremonies and funerals.

Future religion

Norwegian institutions have become increasingly secularized during the last two centuries. On the individual level, Norway, like most European countries, experienced a marked decline in Christian activity about 1970. After this the decline has not been dramatic. Some Christian communities are growing, while others are facing stagnation. Non-Christian religions are increasing in numbers and importance. Plurality within the Christian tradition and among the many other religious traditions is characteristic of the present situation, but sociologists of religion find it hard to predict whether Norwegian society is facing even further secularization.

Should religious leaders have more power in society?	
An international survey asked people if they wanted religious leaders to have more power in their home country. How many percent answered "yes":	
Nigeria	72 %
Indonesia	56 %
Philippines	50 %
Pakistan	39 %
Italy	24 %
USA	15 %
Canada	7 %
Norway	4 %
Denmark	3 %
Sweden	1 %

Source: Gallup International "Voice of the people"

Chapter 5

The 17th of May.
A Historical Date and a Day
of National Celebrations

By Knut Mykland

The United States has the 4th of July as its National Day commemorating the American Declaration of Independence. The French celebrate the 14th of July in memory of the storming of the Bastille and the downfall of l'ancien regime. The 17th of May is Norway's National Day. In the history of Norway, 17 May 1814 marks both the country's declaration of independence and the triumph of constitutional government. In order to understand the dominant place occupied by the celebration of the 17th of May in the national consciousness it is necessary to view it against its historical background.

In 1319 Norway was linked with Sweden in a union after over 400 years as a self-governing and independent realm. In 1380 Norway and Denmark were united under the same king, a union which eventually led to Norway's being integrated in a Danish-Norwegian single unified state with Denmark as the realm's dominant partner and Copenhagen as the unchallenged capital of the kingdom. It was not until 14 January 1814, the date of the Treaty of Kiel, that the Danish-Norwegian dual monarchy was dissolved and King Fredrik IV of Denmark was forced to cede Norway to the King of Sweden.

It is true that from the middle of the 18th century there had been a certain amount of discontent in Norway over the fact that the country's interests were disregarded to Denmark's advantage and, above all, to the advantage of the dual monarchy's capital, Copenhagen. There were repeated Norwegian requests that the country should have its own university and its own national bank, but it was not until 1811 that the demand for a university was finally met. The demand for a bank continued to be rejected out of fear that the dual monarchy could break up if Norway were to acquire a separate and independent monetary system.

When Denmark-Norway was drawn into the whirlpool of the Napoleonic wars in 1807, Fredrik VI opted for alliance with France and war with England. His choice was determined exclusively out of consideration to the Realm's continental portion, Denmark and the two duchies of Schleswig and Holstein. As far as Norway was concerned the war with England meant blockade, crisis and hunger. In this situation there were clear signs of a growing separatist movement in Norway and increasing disenchantment with the existing regime and the union with Denmark. Some Norwegians, among them Count Wedel Jarlsberg, went so far as to advocate Norway's separation from Denmark and the establishment of a union with Sweden. However, this discontent never reached such proportions as to threaten the existence of the dual monarchy. When Norway was separated from Denmark by the Treaty of Kiel on 14 January 1814, this came not as a result of dissatisfaction in Norway, but rather as a consequence of the policies Napoleon's former marshal, Jean Baptiste Bernadotte, had pursued after he was elected Crown Prince of Sweden in 1810 and as heir-presumptive to the Swedish throne adopted the name Carl Johan. Norway was the reward of the victorious commander in the field, in return for his and Sweden's support to the allies in the final reckoning with Napoleon.

From the spring of 1813 the young heir-presumptive to the Danish-Norwegian crown, Prince Christian Fredrik, resided in Norway as "Stattholder". At the end of January, when he received news of the Peace signed at Kiel and the cession of Norway to Sweden, he decided to prevent the realization of the cession of the Kingdom by placing himself at the head of a Norwegian independence movement, with reunion with Denmark as his unexpressed secret hope. King Fredrik VI of Denmark was well aware of the Prince's plan, was in sympathy with it, and himself supported the independence movement in Norway by supplying large quantities of grain.

When Christian Fredrik incited the Norwegians to fight for their independence, he was in no doubt that he enjoyed the support of large sectors of the population. The Norwegian independence movement received encouragement from many different traditional sources: the attachment to the old royal house, hopes for reunion with Denmark, anti-Danish feeling, recollections of bygone days and fear of a union with Sweden. From these vague and confused dreams, there developed in Norway, during the winter and spring of 1814, a powerful and heady desire for independence: Norway was once again to join the ranks of independent states as a free, self-governing realm, as she had been many centuries earlier.

There was one point on which Christian Fredrik's political plans after the Treaty of Kiel were frustrated by the desires and hopes of the upper stratum of society. After the news of the Treaty of Kiel and the cession of the Kingdom reached Norway, Christian Fredrik had the intention of ascending the Norwegian throne by virtue of his alleged right of inheritance and of governing the Kingdom as the only rightful absolute monarch. However, many prominent office-holders and other citizens nourished a strong desire for a free constitution, a desire to which the Prince would have to give way if he were to bring his policy of independence to a successful conclusion. On 10 April 1814 the popularly elected National Assembly met at Eidsvold Iron Works outside Christiania (Oslo) for the purpose of giving the country a constitution. As one of the representatives described this Assembly: "Here was to be seen a selection of men from all parts of the realm, of all ranks and dialects, men from court circles as well as landowners come together in no set order for the sacred purpose of laying the foundations for the rebirth of the nation." Six weeks later, on 17 May 1814, the National Assembly had completed its work on the Constitution, and on the same day closed its proceedings by electing Prince Christian Fredrik King of Norway. The solemn proceedings ended with a short and powerful speech by the President, Georg Sverdrup, linking the old free Norway to the Norway which was now emerging: "Thus within Norway's boundaries is resurrected Norway's ancient seat of Kings, which was graced by Athelstans and Sverres and from which, with wisdom and might, they ruled over Norway of old."

The fact that Christian Fredrik was able to unite the Norwegians in the struggle for independence and, in cooperation with the National Assembly, to organize the government of the new state in the course of a few hectic weeks prior to the 17th of May was due to Carl Johan's continued involvement on the Continent with the main Swedish army. But after Napoleon was forced to abdicate at the beginning of April, the Crown Prince of Sweden had fulfilled his obligations to his allies and, towards the end of May 1814, he was able to return to Sweden with the Swedish army. Despite bombastic statements from Norway, and despite the declaration "Death before slavery", after a short war Norway was forced into a union with Sweden, the union became effective when the Storting (the Norwegian Parliament) elected Carl XIII of Sweden as King of Norway on 4 November 1814. But the constitutional form of the Kingdom was in all main respects such as was laid down in the Constitution of 17 May, and the union with Sweden was so loose that it could be dissolved in 1905 without either kingdom being seriously affected as a result.

There are therefore good grounds for regarding 17 May 1814 as the pre-eminent date in Norway's history. After centuries as a dependency Norway once again joined the ranks of free states as an independent realm, and the new union with Sweden proved only to be an intermezzo, with no influence on the inner development of the country. From being subjected – at least in theory – to a most extreme form of despotism, the country emerged with a more liberal Constitution than any othercontemporary state. While other free constitutions in Europe, drawn up during the Revolutionary and Napoleonic eras, were rescinded and substituted by more authoritarian regimes, the Norwegian Constitution remained standing.

As early as the 1820s people started to celebrate the 17th of May, and since then this day has been established as Norway's National Day, Norway's Liberation Day, even though the celebrations have in the course of time changed their character and form. The history of the 17th of May celebrations in Norway reflects in many ways the main features of the country's history from 1814 until today.

When Carl Johan, as the victor of 1814, accepted the 17th of May Constitution as the basis for government in Norway, within the framework of a union with Sweden, there were many reasons for this policy: hope of once again being able to play a role in French politics, fear of a Gustavian restoration in Sweden, fear of a winter war in Norway, the desire to win the Norwegians over to the idea of a union with Sweden through concessions and a policy of appeasement. Among these motives, there was one which had the future in mind: the hope of later winning back what he had been obliged to give up in 1814. It was this last motive which formed the basis for Carl Johan's policy vis a vis Norway after becoming King in 1818. Deliberately and systematically he pursued a policy aimed at restricting the powers of the Storting such as they were prescribed in the Constitution, extending the powers of the Crown and creating a closer union between Norway and Sweden. Norwegian policy in the 1820s was characterized by a struggle to defend that which had been gained in 1814, the defence of the Constitution which formed a bulwark for national independence. These events also formed the background for the 17th of May celebrations in the 1820s. They took the form of an outer manifestation in support of the national liberation efforts of 1814 and for the will to defend the Constitution and national independence. It is significant that the slogan "Guard the Constitution" was the running theme of the banners used in the first 17th of May processions.

Around 1830 Carl Johan changed his policy on Norway. In reality he gave up the idea of a thoroughgoing revision of the Constitution, and his successors to the throne were to follow the same line of policy. Thus the 17th of May celebrations took more and more the form of a national day of celebration. The defensive watch-dog attitude which characterized the first 17th of May celebrations was superseded by a form of celebration characterized by a feeling of springlike optimism, by the joy of having a free constitutional government, by a people seeking to stress their own identity. It is a characteristic feature of the change that, in addition to the solemn procession of the citizenry, the children's procession was introduced, which, in time would come to be the most striking and colourful feature of the Norwegian 17th of May celebrations.

It was above all the holders of "embete", or higher office, who were responsible for creating the Constitution of Eidsvold. It was this group which stood guard over it against Carl Johan's encroachments in the 1820s. It was also this group which in fact ruled the country during the first two generations after 1814. From the 1830s the farmers began to awaken and became conscious of the power given them under the Constitution, and the 1870s and '80s were characterized by the fierce political struggle between the old ruling class – the senior office holders and bourgeoisie – on the one side, and the farmers and the liberal urban citizenry on the other. The conflict erupted into a bitter and uncompromising struggle in the Storting, which led to impeachment, the victory of parliamentary government and the establishment of the two political parties, the Conservatives (Høyre) and the Liberals (Venstre). In this situation the 17th of May celebrations again changedcharacter. The day was no longer regarded as a day of national unity, but a day of strife, when conservatives and liberals voiced their political standpoints in town after town, each with their own 17th of May speakers and their own 17th of May processions.

On 7 June 1905 the union with Sweden was dissolved by a decision passed in the Storting. The dissolution was supported by a united population, more united perhaps than at any time before or since. This attitude was also to be reflected in the 17th of May celebrations. The differences between the parties were to give way to the feeling of unity. The 17th of May processions were now characterized by a feeling of fellowship and of rejoicing that the country had at last gained full independence.

But time brought changes. In the 1880s and the 1890s, the Norwegian political scene had been marked by the struggle between the Conservatives and the Liberals, between the old regime of officialdom on the one hand and on the other the alliance of farmers and urban liberals. In the 1920s and '30s the clash of interests between the middle class and the working class formed the main area of conflict in Norwegian political life and this state of affairs was intensified by unemployment, strikes and labour unrest. The bourgeois parties put full emphasis on the national element in politics. As far as the working class was concerned, politics centred on international fellowship in tune with the slogan: "Workers of the world, unite". This conflict-ridden situation was also to set its stamp on the 17th of May celebrations. While the middle class celebrated the day with massed processions in the towns, processions often featuring slogans directed against the workers' internationalism, the working classes largely avoided the 17th of May celebrations altogether. "It is not in cooperation between the classes, but in the class struggle to the bitter end that the answer is to be found – on 17 May as on the other days of the year", wrote Martin Tranmæl, editor of the Labour Party's main organ. The Labour party and the unions in Oslo supported the party line in a declaration in which they urged the workers not to take part in "the bourgeois celebrations of 17 May. Boycott the arrangements of the bourgeoisie."

During the German occupation of Norway from 9 April 1940 until 7 May 1945, the feeling of national fellowship predominated. The Nazi regime, with all its terror, imprisonment and torture, united the population. During the German occupation, the 17 of May celebrations were strictly forbidden, but there can scarcely have been any time when the day occupied a more important place in the national consciousness than just then in the occupation period, as the writer Nordahl Grieg phrased it in a poem which was soon the common property of all Norwegians:

"Now stands the flagpole bare
Behind Eidsvoll's budding trees,
But in such an hour as this,
We know what freedom is"

Children celebrating the 17th of May outside the royal castle in Oslo.

The bitter conflicts which had marked the 17th of May celebrations in the 1920s and '30s were replaced after the war by a feeling of fellowship resembling that of the years around 1905. But there was a difference. Then, it was on full national independence that the 17th of May celebrations and the public rejoicing were centred. In the post-1945 period, the main stress was laid more on democratic rights, constitutional government, freedom of the press, and law and order, in contrast to what had been experienced in the war years – violence, terror, concentration camps and dictatorship.

The discussion of Norwegian membership in the EC in 1971 and 1972 again led to a major split in public opinion. The Norwegian population found itself divided into two main factions: the supporters of membership and its opponents. The hostile feelings were just as intense as in the 1880s and the 1930s. This dissension was at the same time a struggle over the national symbols, a struggle where traces were visible in the 17th of May celebrations in 1972. But after the question of membership had been decided by a public referendum on 25 September 1972, antagonism gradually faded, and in the years that followed the feeling of fellowship was again to come to the fore.

If the 17th of May celebrations in Norway are viewed in the long-term perspective, one is struck by the manner in which the annual celebrations have changed in character and content over the years. The 17th of May has been a day of strife, as well as a day when the people rallied around the Constitution, national independence and democratic rights. Viewed against this background, the question inevitably arises: despite all this, how is it that the National Day has managed to retain its central position in the public consciousness and remain Norway's great ceremonial day? One reason is to be found in the physical features of the country.

The 17th of May has remained the great spring festival in Norway, in a country with a winter that is both long and cold. For this reason the 17th of May has more and more taken on the character of a children's festival. The children's procession has become the colourful focal point in the celebrations, from the most remote coastal settlements to the capital city where literally thousands of schoolchildren, marching along behind their school bands and banners, file past the Royal Palace in salute to the King.

Another reason for the central position the 17th of May celebrations have occupied and continue to occupy in Norway is to be found in the country's relationship with other countries. From 1814 to 1905 Norway was joined in a union with Sweden, and although the country held an independent position in this union, nevertheless in the Norwegian consciousness the union always represented a potential danger, able to arouse feelings of nationalism and lead to closing of ranks around the national symbols, as in the 1820s and the period around 1905.

Jumping from the time of the Union to our own globally-minded era, a similar tendency may be seen. The German occupation during World War II provided evidence of the fate which could befall a small country in a world ruled by the great powers. Experiences from that time were kept alive in people's minds in the post-1945 cold war, in which the small states were often treated as no more than pawns in the great powers' ruthless game. There are still many countries which have not yet attained national independence. There are still many peoples who continue to live under dictatorship and despotic forms of government. Viewed against such a background, the ideals from Eidsvoll still retain their relevance and significance, representing values which are able to give the 17th of May celebrations a deeper meaning.

Part 2

Society

Chapter 6

The Norwegian Welfare State

By Olav Helge Angell

Political system

Norway has been a constitutional monarchy since 1814, after the approval of the first democratic constitution. Almost one century later, in 1905, the country gained independence from Sweden. Contemporary Norway has a three-tiered parliamentary system, with each tier governed by a popularly elected body: the national parliament (the Storting), the county councils and the municipal councils.

The Storting has 165 members, and is elected by proportional representation for a four year period. Although formally a one chamber parliament, it splits up into two chambers after elections, and both of them have to approve legislation. The King is formally the highest executive authority, although in practice the government (*regjering*) – comprising the prime minister (formally chosen by the King) and his/her cabinet (selected by the Prime Minister) – is the head of executive power. Parliament members must leave the parliament if they are chosen to serve in the government. In 2007, there are 19 counties and 431 municipalities. County populations range from 73,000 to approximately 550,000 inhabitants in the case of Oslo. Municipal populations vary widely in Norway, ranging from 214 to 550,000 inhabitants per municipality. There are about 30 municipalities with fewer than 1,000 inhabitants, and one third have between 2,000 and 5,000 inhabitants.

Politically, the country has been stable, with a dominant Labour Party in office between 1945 and 1965. From 1965 to the present, Norway has had 24 additional years of Labour government – alone or in coalition government, intertwined with periods of various Conservative-centre coalition governments. The shifts in government in the period after the Second

Norway was in acute need of housing in the decades after World War II. Not everything was left to private initiatives. The building of apartments and small houses was also looked upon as a public concern and an important factor in the development of a welfare society. The Norwegian National Housing Bank (Husbanken) was established in 1946, providing long-term loans with low interest rates. Two-thirds of all houses in Norway were built with the support of the National Housing Bank between 1946 and 1985. In the suburb of Lambertseter in Oslo (above), housing for 18 000 people was provided in the years between 1950 and 1958.

World War have not implied significant variations in welfare policy. Overall, one may say that there has been a consensus on the general principles.

The organisation of the welfare state

Broadly speaking, the division of responsibilities and duties among the three tiers mentioned in the preceding section is as follows:

1   At the *national level*, the parliament serves as the political decision-making body. The ministries are the executive bodies with special responsibility for legislation, capacity expansion, budgeting and planning, information management, and policy design. Since 2002 the state has become responsible for the delivery of specialised health care services, through regional health care enterprises (see below).

2   At the upper *middle level*, in matters of health care regional units have, since 2002, become responsible for the planning and provision of specialised health care. This used to be the responsibility of the counties. Norway is divided into five regional units in matters of health care, each of which comprises three to five counties. Each region is organised as a health care enterprise, directly subordinate to the Minister of Health and Care Services (see above).

3   At the lower *middle level* the counties are responsible for e.g. dental services, cultural matters, and upper secondary education.

4   At the *local level* the municipalities cover e.g. the domains of health promotion, primary health care, care of the elderly, care of the handicapped and mentally handicapped, kindergarten and primary and lower secondary education, social work (child protection and social protection), and local culture.

The years following the Second World War can be described as a continual process of reform in the relationship between state and local government, in health and social care, as well as in other sectors. The goal has been to find an acceptable balance of power between these two levels of government. There has been an ongoing process of devolution of central power to local authorities, with the aim of focusing as much as possible on the municipal level. For instance, responsibility for institution-based care for the frail elderly has been moved from county to municipal level (1988) and so has the care for mentally disabled persons (1991). In the former case the change helped the municipalities co-ordinate institution-based and home-based services. In the latter case the decentralisation of responsibility at the same time implied that big institutions were closed down, with instead the building up of small local residential centres where the users were provided the necessary welfare services, facilitating their social integration in the local community.

The philosophy behind this is that decentralisation is an expression of applied democracy. It brings decision-making closer to those who are affected and promotes popular participation in local political affairs. Moreover, it is believed that delegation of authority usually leads to simplification of administrative procedures. The central authorities are responsible for national policy, for drawing up general guidelines, for advising, and for ensuring that services offered comply with national goals. Maintaining the principle of equal access to public service is a critical role of the central authorities in a decentralised system.

The scope of the welfare state

Norway, along with the other Scandinavian countries, may be characterised as a state-friendly society. What distinguishes the Norwegian welfare state is the relationship between the public sector and the labour market:

- A large public sector,
- A system of "full employment" and a high labour market rate for women,
- A wide-embracing system of more or less universal rights,
- A residual system of social assistance, and
- A comparatively strong element of vertical re-distribution

What should be added is that retirement age is high (67 years of age), and that the public welfare system does not include public or insurance coverage for dental treatment for persons above 18, with minor exceptions. Compared to the other Scandinavian countries, Norway's public system of kindergartens is not very well developed. The public system is complemented with privately owned and run kindergartens.

Childcare

In 2006, a total of 234 000 children ages 0-5, 67 % of the children in this age group, were enrolled in kindergarten. 54 % of these children were enrolled in public childcare, 46 % in private institutions.

One of the ideas behind the Norwegian and Scandinavian welfare model with its system of universalistic orientation is that it protects its members against social risks connected with a normal work and family life. As long as the members are active in the labour market, the national insurance system will protect the individual and the family against poverty. Therefore, active interventions in the labour market and active employment policies, are a central element in the welfare policy system as a whole. The goal of employment policy has been to stimulate the economy in such a way that the demand for labour from economic enterprises will provide job opportunities for everybody, i.e. full employment.

The problem with this system is that it does not provide very well for those who are not integrated into the labour market, either because they are not able to enter or because they are otherwise excluded. The Scandinavian welfare model, including Norway, does not bestow such rights on people by virtue of their citizenship. Since the basic arrangements (the National Insurance Scheme) are so closely connected to labour market participation, the source of income provided by the welfare state for those who are not directly or indirectly integrated in the labour market is the needs – based (residual system of) social assistance.

In 1999 the Conservative-centre government presented a white paper on poverty in which its commitment to the welfare state was expressed through the following statements on some basic goals:

- Security for all
- Improved distribution of incomes and living standards
- Equal rights and obligations for all
- An equal range of high-quality services
- Better opportunities for work for the most financially disadvantaged
- A more finely-meshed social safety net

In another connection the main objective in welfare policies is described as to improve the quality of life, social independence and self-reliance for the disabled and the chronically ill. Irrespective of "political colour" the governments have ascertained their willingness to maintain strong public responsibility for the welfare system.

The work approach to welfare

A policy of full employment has been a fundamental element in the welfare state during the post-war period. The government has not hesitated in increasing deficits and internal demand during periods of recession in order to maintain a low unemployment level. Oil revenue has made it possible to pursue this policy for longer periods than in other European countries.

The most important measure introduced to integrate unemployed people in the Nordic countries in ordinary paid employment has been an active labour market policy, where unemployed workers have had to participate in education and training schemes of different kinds.

The labour market policy in Norway has involved an active commitment by the government in economic policy. Post-war governments have committed themselves to maintaining scattered settlements in the peripheries in Southern and Northern Norway, thus maintaining a settlement pattern which is unlike e.g. that of Sweden. The decentralised settlement pattern helps explain the expansion of public employment and the labour force from the 1970s and the substantial increase in job opportunities in the welfare sector, in personal social services, education, and health services in the same period.

In Norway the government's white paper on welfare policies from 1995 declares as a main principle that "social security policy must emphasise that work must be the preference". This emphasis has been confirmed by later governments. One particular challenge has been the high rate of people on disability pension. In an international perspective the Norwegian labour market sees a fairly low exit rate of elderly workers, both women and men. The high participation rate is partly due to the high retirement age of 67 years; possibly partly explained by the type of early retirement scheme on offer and the way it has worked so far.

The National Insurance Scheme

The National Insurance Scheme is the very core of the Norwegian welfare system. The primary aims of the scheme are:

- to provide financial security by ensuring income and compensating for certain costs during unemployment, pregnancy and childbirth, for one-parent childcare, care of the elderly and in the event of death

- to help equalise incomes and living standards, during the lifetime of individuals and groups of persons, e.g. connecting levels of unemployment and sickness benefits as well as old age pension to the level of employment income

- to promote self-support and the best possible daily self-care for each individual, e.g. through schemes of occupational rehabilitation.

The National Insurance Scheme provides short-term assistance for those of working age, assistance for a transitional period for those who are unemployed for a few years, and permanent assistance for those who have finished their working careers.

Membership of the National Insurance Scheme is mandatory and universal. All residents of Norway or people working as employees in the country are insured under the National Insurance Scheme (NIS). Persons insured under the NIS are entitled to the following benefits:

1	Old-age, surviving partner's and disability pensions
2	Basic benefit and attendance benefit in the case of disablement
3	Rehabilitation benefits, granted if the person concerned has a permanently reduced work capacity or substantially limited opportunities in the choice of occupation or place of work. Benefits are also granted for improvements in general functional capacity if this has been substantially reduced due to illness or injury
4	Occupational injury benefits
5	Benefits to single parents
6	Monetary reimbursement in the case of sickness, maternity, adoption and unemployment
7	Medical benefits in the case of sickness and maternity
8	Funeral grant

Scope and expenditure of the National Insurance Scheme

In 2005 about 1.26 million persons (about one quarter of the population) received financial assistance from the National Insurance. Just over 1,000,000 of these received pensions (old-age pension, invalid pension, or survivor pension). Total expenditure from the National Insurance amounted to approx. EUR 1,200 per employed person. The areas with the greatest costs were old-age pensions, invalid benefits and sickness and maternity benefits.

The NIS is financed mainly by contributions from employer tax (about 40 %), National Insurance contributions from employees, self-employed people and pensioners (about 30 %), and the state (about 30 %). Levels of contribution rates and state grants are determined by the parliament.

The Norwegian health care system

The organizational structure of the Norwegian health care system is built on the principle of equal access to services. All inhabitants of the country shall have the same access to services, independent of social status, location and income. To fulfil this aim, the organisational structure has three levels following the political tiers described in an earlier section: the central state, the regional health care enterprise/county and the municipality. The role of the state is to provide national health policy, to prepare and oversee legislation and to allocate funds. The Ministry of Health and Care Services has the responsibility of implementing the policy at a regional level through the health care enterprises. The main responsibility for the actual provision of health care services lies with the regional health care enterprises and the municipalities. The enterprises assume responsibility for planning and operating the hospital sector (including both general and psychiatric institutions) as well as other specialised medical services, such as special care for alcohol and drug addicts.

Norway's health care system provides a wide range of services not only in the major urban areas, which are concentrated in the southern part of the country, but also in the most sparsely populated parts. Apart from socio-cultural and political considerations, this is a reason why, in Norway, the provision of health services has traditionally been in the hands of the public sector. Except for a few specialised private hospitals in the main urban areas voluntary sector health agencies such as the Red Cross and the church-based agencies, or those with a regional focus, are fully embedded in the system. By contrast, a significant private provision of ambulatory health care (physicians, dentists and physiotherapists in private practice) has co-existed with the public system.

In addition to the public hospital sector mentioned above, there is only a small private hospital sector consisting of a few small private hospitals with outpatient clinics – representing about 2 per cent of the total number of hospital beds and 5 per cent of the outpatient services provided in Norway. These private clinics have, among other things, specialised in open heart surgery, hip surgery and other minor surgery, in response to long waiting lists for such care at public hospitals. Norwegian law imposes tight restrictions on establishing such private hospitals.

Since 1984 primary health care has been the responsibility of the municipalities. Although municipal populations vary widely in Norway, each municipality must (by law) offer services for disease prevention and health promotion, diagnosis and treatment of illness, rehabilitation, and long-term care. Dental care for children and adolescents up to the age of 18, as well as for disabled persons and patients in nursing homes or receiving home care, however, is provided free of charge by specialised services owned by the counties. The task of running nursing homes belongs to the municipalities and so is, since 1991, the care of mentally disabled persons.

Financial aspects

Hospital services are financed through block grants from the central government to the health care enterprises. The municipal health service is financed through a combination of grants from the local government, retrospective reimbursement by the National Insurance Scheme for services supplied and out-of-pocket payments by the patients. The municipalities, in turn, receive block grants from the central government based on certain criteria.

The National Insurance Scheme fully reimburses all individual expenses for childbirth, treatment of children under the age of seven years and treatment of industrial injury. It also administers the public pension system and other income transfer programmes, such as sickness, disability, unemployment and rehabilitation benefits.

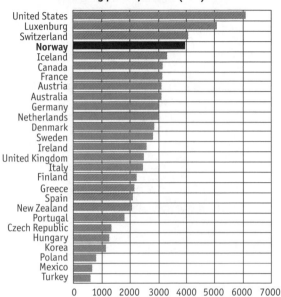

**Total health expenditure per capita. 2004.
Purchasing power parities (PPP). USD**

Source: Statistcs Norway

Social care

Social care in Norway includes social welfare services, care for the elderly, the disabled and psychiatric patients, and care for people with alcohol and drug problems. During the past ten years, municipalities have had increasing responsibility for providing health and social care services. This expansion, however, has not reduced the amount of care, in terms of time, provided by family members.

The state defines national goals and draws up the framework for social care services, and provides government guidelines and advice. There are no taxes or charges that are earmarked for special services in Norway. The allocation of resources to different public goods (like health and social services) is mainly a political matter in the parliament, in the counties and in the municipalities.

The basic principle of care for the elderly and the disabled is that services and individualised support should be arranged in ways that enable care in people's home communities. The elderly and persons with disabil-

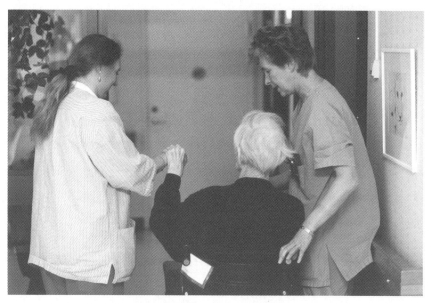

The basic principle is that old people are cared for in their own homes as long as possible. 77 % of those in institutions are 80 years and older.

ities should have the opportunity to live in their own home for as long as possible. Most of the municipalities (80 %) now provide home care services 24 hours a day.

It is the responsibility of the municipalities to provide residential care as needed, including nursing homes, service homes and group living for people with senile dementia. The vast majority of the population in institutions (77 % in 2005) are 80 years and older. The day care activities include day centres and rehabilitation. The users pay an out-of-pocket fee for some of these municipal services. For health care, there is an upper limit on the yearly out-of-pocket fees. For home care and inpatient care, the size of the fees varies among the municipalities. There is a national debate about whether there should be national guidelines as to the size of the fees. The fees, however, are supposed to be so low that services are available for everyone. The availability of the care services varies. It is good in the districts and not very good in the larger cities. The quality of care services also varies and is a recurring topic of concern in the mass media.

In general, the municipalities provide the social services, and the personnel working in the sector are directly employed by the municipality. Some nursing homes and day care centres belong to and are managed by voluntary organisations, including church parishes and other church-based organisations. However, they are staffed by professionals, and are funded by the municipalities. Up until the present time, very few enterprises involve commercial entrepreneurs.

The overall need for nursing and care services is expected to increase. This is due to the age structure of the population, and especially the expected increase in the number of elderly people over the age of 80 years.

The family in the welfare system

The degree of public intervention in the care of children and the elderly is decisive for the importance of the family in social policy. It has been claimed that Norwegian family policy has its distinctive feature in its combination of ideological individualism and public family policy. In a way the mutual family responsibility was removed with the introduction of the old age pension system in 1936. The system introduced a means-tested individual pension, based only on the individual income, irrespective of children's income. Until 1964 there was a mutual financial responsibility of children and parents, and until 1973 students' access to loans and grants from the State Educational Loan Fund was dependent on parents' income.

Family policy is most often understood as policy to support families with children. Female participation in the labour force has been accompanied by both private and public initiatives to improve professional child care. In 2006 the total number of children 1–5 years of age in kindergartens made up 80 per cent of the whole population in the age group.

Child benefit may be seen as an instrument to strengthen the financial situation of families with children. The Norwegian allowance level ranks in the middle of European countries when compared to the income level of the average net wage of a production worker. The parental benefit scheme enables parents to stay at home with their child during the first year of the child's life. The parental leave period in connection with childbirth has gradually been extended. Parents receive (2007) parental benefits for 54 weeks at 80 per cent pay or 44 weeks with full pay. Parents may choose to divide the period of paid leave between them. Six weeks of the total benefit period are reserved for the father (the paternity quota). As to the remainder of the allotted time, the parents themselves may decide whether one of them will stay at home with the child for the duration, or whether they wish to share the leave between them. The weeks reserved for paternity leave are non-transferable, and will be lost if they are not utilised by the father.

The family is still very important as a social support system, but the government and the municipalities have taken over the responsibility for the care of the elderly and children to a great extent. Family policy is closely related to gender policy and this section should be read in connection with the following section on the welfare state in a gender perspective.

The welfare state in a gender perspective

Gender distribution in education and the workforce

The participation of women in the Norwegian labour market is among the highest in Europe. According to recent figures (2007), 77 % of all women aged 25-66 are in the workforce, while the percentage for men is 84. Women have been in the majority in higher education since the 1980s. Close to 60 % of all students at Norwegian universities and university colleges are women, and more women than men have completed a four-year university or college education. In 2000, women comprised approximately one third of all doctoral degree graduates.

Women with small children are also highly represented in the workforce. In 1965, nine out of ten mothers with small children were housewives. Today the situation has been nearly reversed due to the emergence of a strong system of public welfare and an explicit policy aimed at helping women and men to reconcile the demands of family and working life. Particularly important in this context are systems for publicly financed daycare institutions and parental leave (including the paternity quota).

In 2006 44 % of all employed women worked part-time, as opposed to only 13 % of the men. Fewer women and more men work part-time today than ten years ago. The average number of hours of paid work per week is 30.7 hours for women compared to 37.5 hours for men. Norway continues to deal with the problems of an existing gender pay gap, and wages still tend to be lower in sectors dominated by women employees.

The labour market in Norway is one of the most segregated along gender lines in the Western world. More than half of all women employees work in the public sector, and women comprise more than two thirds of all employees in this sector. In the health and social sector, which primarily consists of public services, more than 80 % of the employees are women. In typical private sector professions such as construction and entrepreneurial activity, only 8 % of the employees are women (figures from 2006, Statistics Norway).

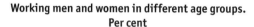

**Working men and women in different age groups.
Per cent**

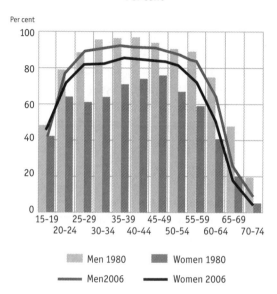

The general lack of women in decision-making positions in both the private and the public sectors continues to be a matter of national concern. The number of women serving on boards of directors has increased over the last five years, not least due to provisions concerning gender representation in boards of directors of public limited companies requiring at least 40 % representation of each gender by the end of 2007. The same provisions apply to the gender composition of boards in state owned companies. No gender representation rules have been proposed for private limited liability companies.

The number of women in top administrative positions in the private sector is small but increasing. Women comprise only 22 % of the top managerial staff in private companies and 27 % of the middle-level managers (2005). Women continue to be under-represented in the ICT industry, as teachers of technology subjects at all levels, and as editors-in-chief of newspapers and other media.

The proportion of women in leading positions in the public sector is not very different; they make up 22 % of the top managers in central government administration, while the corresponding figure for local government administration is 23 % (2005).

Measures and methods in gender equality efforts

The Norwegian Gender Equality Act was adopted in 1978. The Act prohibits all discrimination on the grounds of gender and is applicable to all areas of society, including education, employment and cultural matters. It also stipulates that public authorities, employers and the social partners are responsible for actively promoting gender equality within their spheres of responsibility.

One of the most important elements of the Act was the establishment of a Gender Equality Ombud as an independent body responsible for enforcing the Act. The Gender Equality Ombud's services are available to the public free of charge. In addition, the government-funded Gender Equality Centre has been established to monitor, promote and mainstream gender equality and equal opportunity measures in all areas of society.

Pursuant to the Gender Equality Act, it is the responsibility of the public authorities to promote gender equality in all areas of society. A gender mainstreaming strategy was introduced in 1986 and is still being actively applied. It is the responsibility of the relevant public authority to ensure gender equality, e.g. in working life, in education, in the health care system, in terms of social rights, income, etc.

The equality paradox: gender and work in welfare society

Norway is reputed to be one of the best countries in the world for women. The UNDP has developed two indices measuring gender equality, GDI (Gender-related development index) and GEM (Gender empowerment measure). On both indices Norway ranks on top of the list. At the same time the labour market in Norway is extremely segregated, as already noted. On the other hand, many women hold central positions in the political system, in the political parties, in the parliament, and in the government.

In Norway, as well as in other Scandinavian countries, the welfare state has been important for the labour market participation of women. Eco-

The feminist movement was an important feature of society in the 1970s and 1980s. Gro Harlem Brundtland's "government by women" in 1986 (8 out of 17 members were women) aroused international attention.

nomic growth and expansion of the public sector in the 1970s, especially at the municipal level, increased the demand for labour. Care for the elderly, education, social service offices, kindergartens, and public administration were organised and expanded everywhere. Many of the jobs created in this way were in care work, typically "women's jobs". The welfare state offered jobs where people lived; paid work was offered to women in the local community.

"State feminism", the peculiar form of the policy of gender equality in the Scandinavian countries, has "the women-friendly state" as a precondition. The policy implies that a women-friendly society would be the result of public policies, family and social policies, and an explicit gender equality policy. A women-friendly welfare policy based on the perspective of women in their role as mothers contributes to maintaining a high level of participation by women in the labour force. Through benefits at child birth and cash-for-care (*kontantstøtte*) it is possible for women with children to withdraw from the labour market for shorter or longer periods to care for children without losing their job or suffering a significant loss of income. On the other hand, this focus on women as mothers tends to maintain the traditional view of women (of fertile age) as unstable labour, with consequences for the return on their "investment" in the labour market; lower wages and fewer chances of promotion, other things being equal. On this basis the women-friendly welfare state has been criticised for being characterised by a "feminism of difference", emphasizing the differences between men and women, and not what they have in common. In this respect the welfare state is "gender conservative" as women are primarily defined by their family ties and not as individuals. On the other hand, this orientation may also be seen as contributing to a child-friendly state.

Gender equality in a multi-cultural society

Immigration and multi-culturality pose challenges to dominant under-standings of gender equality in Norwegian society. Norway has only recently become a multi-cultural society, having traditionally been a homogeneous society. A certain set of values related to e.g. norms of soli-darity and the idea of a national community has been a taken-for-granted basis for how the welfare state is perceived. Public policies based on such conceptions have become more problematic in the wake of the influx of immigrants whose cultural ideals may be at variance with dom-inant values in the Norwegian public discourse. Family violence, forced marriages, and more generally oppression of women among immigrants of non-western cultural origin, and how the Norwegian welfare state should deal with this, have been among the recurrent issues in the Nor-wegian public debate.

With regard to gender equality we may conclude that it becomes more complicated when we no longer relate to a Norwegian, all white society. We can assert that Norway is not necessarily the best of countries to live in for those women who are not ethnically Norwegian.

Critical views of the welfare state

The period since World War II has seen significant changes in people's way of life in our part of the world. A society in which experiences in life and work were fairly much the same, characterising whole social classes, has changed into a new form of society where life and work experiences are more differentiated than before. From the 1980s welfare state arrange-ments were criticised for rigidity, for not having adapted to the changed situation. The system was accused of being too standardised, not reflecting more differentiated life situations and more diverse local and individual needs. It was argued that a plurality of service providers and models for provision were needed to serve a plurality of needs. A major source of this criticism was the feminist movement. They argued that the welfare state system was better adapted to serve the needs of middle aged men in their life situation than the needs of women in their life situation. The state has – at least to some extent – complied with this criticism.

Another aspect of the welfare state criticism appearing from the early 1980s implied a critical view of the future of the Scandinavian welfare state: The welfare state was considered to be in a crisis in the face of globalisation and increased market orientation. It was predicted that the most developed welfare states would be forced to perform substantial cutbacks in order to accommodate the demands of private business to reduce taxes and increase the flexibility of the labour market in an ever tougher international competitive climate. Twenty-five years later we know that the Scandinavian welfare states have survived. Rather than crisis, social science research portrays the situation as one of consolidation and stability. The period has seen both increased international competition and expansion of the welfare state. Several arguments can be put forward to explain the development. One argument is that the welfare state was historically developed to protect the vulnerable against the risks of the market; thus, the welfare state came into being because of the market, not in spite of it. Public opinion in Norway has been stable in favour of a strong welfare state along these lines. Another argument is that it has turned out, empirically, that countries with a well developed welfare state have a very efficient and readjustment-oriented economic sector.

Current and future challenges to the Norwegian welfare system

Of the many challenges to the Norwegian welfare system which are publicly under debate four have been selected for further elaboration in this section. They have been selected because they rank high in the media and the public debate and represent recurrent concerns in the political and economic debates in the parliament and the government. In a way they also epitomise problems and challenges to the specific model on which the Norwegian (and Scandinavian in general) welfare system is based.

Rapid increase in the number of people receiving disability pension

The effective age of retirement in Norway has fallen over the past decade. This has been encouraged by the implementation of the early retirement scheme (*AFP*), but also by a considerable growth in the inflow into the disability pension scheme. This pension is granted to people who have lost at least half their "income potential", i.e. their ability to earn their living through wage labour. At the same time there has been a strong growth in the sickness absence scheme. Measures to reduce the strong growth of early retirement, disability pension and sickness leave are the most urgent political priorities in social protection in Norway today. Public authorities are concerned about the large number of and growth in new disability pensioners. The rising number of disability pensioners not only increases public expenditure, it also reduces the working population and thus the capacity to finance public welfare. It is a main political objective to reduce the high level of sickness absence and to limit the number of new entries into the disability pension scheme.

The problem for the Government in this case is that there exists a plethora of possible explanations which are difficult to test scientifically. In the public debate a mixture of structural, health and moral factors have been put forward to explain the increase. The political measures taken to prevent further increases have concentrated especially on making it more difficult to come within the scope of the scheme. The long-term development in the number of pensioners seems to indicate that such efforts are inefficient in the long run. The tightening up regards decisions in a field where discretion is important and where the criteria to be used in the decision-making have not been very precise. Recently a major government strategy has been to take steps to make it easier to combine work and pension and to take initiatives to make conditions more favourable for an "inclusive labour market", i.e. to help promote the chances for those who normally would have trouble succeeding in the labour market.

Poverty as an issue in Norwegian public debate

Poverty is one of the current issues in the Norwegian welfare debate. Eradication of poverty was among the main goals of the post-war government, against the background of the experiences of the consequences of the economic recession in the 1930s. In the wake of the mass poverty experienced in this decade both Norway and the other Scandinavian countries developed a welfare policy based primarily on three elements:

1   Poverty is primarily to be explained at a societal level, and should not be understood as a moral defect in the individual

2   It is the role of the state to take responsibility to secure the individual and the family against poverty

3   In the long run poverty will be eradicated through the transformation of the capitalistic class society into a welfare society based on a mixed (market) economy.

In 1979 the prime minister from the Labour Party stated that "it is the first time in the history of this country and the other Nordic countries that we can ascertain that poverty and social misery have been eradicated". Some 20 years later, this former prime minister, now retired, had to admit that "it is a shame that we have seventy thousand poor children in our country". It is interesting that poverty has become a public issue in Norway over the last decade despite the fact that it is of very limited extent, though depending on definition. In this respect Norway seems to be peculiar because of the role claims about poverty have come to play in the political debate. In contrast to earlier debates the current debate on poverty has moved the focus away from more or less "unworthy needy" social assistance receivers and their problems to broader groups of "worthy needy", retired people with only a low pension, i.e. people who have done their duty by society and receive little in return, and disadvantaged children.

The discourse on poverty has once more revived the idea of a general Guaranteed Minimum Income (GMI). The roads to poverty have gone from being simple and common to becoming more complex and individual. The current "welfare contract", which has the duty of work as the central element, provides less security than before since employment is less secure and the demand for flexibility greater than ever. Existing arrangements to protect against poverty are less accurate than they used to be, in a more changeable life situation. But the work approach (see p. 106) is still the strategy given the highest priority by the government in its effort to reduce poverty.

An ageing population

In Norway, like most western European countries, changes in demography will continue towards an increasing number and larger proportion of the elderly in the population, i.e. a significant ageing of its population. But the country starts from a favourable position: employment rates of older people are among the highest in the OECD, pension outlays are currently relatively low and substantial financial assets have been accumulated in the Government Pension Fund. However, without reforms, due to the maturing of the pension system, ageing will lead to one of the biggest increases in pension spending as a share of GDP in OECD countries over the next 50 years.

The dilemma Norway and the other Scandinavian countries now face is: as the standard of living improves and people's life expectancy increases, there are new challenges with an ageing population and a growing number of people with chronic illnesses. One of today's health dilemmas is that medical technology has advanced to a level where its ability to perform exceeds what society in general can afford to pay. This poses a new type of challenge in a society where the basic rule for generations has been that medical costs are a societal responsibility.

Medicine will be expensive, and an ageing population will require continuous care, rehabilitation and services for the chronically ill and disabled. The result will be an increase in need and demand for health services. New potential areas for treatment will emerge, which will increase the pressure on limited resources. This is a question of both technology and expectations of the general public and the medical staff as to what is possible to achieve.

Finally, expectations come from the general growth in wealth and social development. There has been an increased standard of living and an increase in the general expectations of the population. Also, many of the factors affecting the incidence of disease lie outside the traditional domain of health policy, but need to be addressed by the health care sector through illness prevention and health promotion practices.

The paradox connected to the wealth in Norway's oil resources in the North Sea is that it cannot be spent too fast without putting too much pressure on the economy and stimulating inflation. This is coupled with a lack of educated and well-trained health personnel like doctors and nurses. The other side of this challenge is probably an increased dependency ratio. It is likely that the increasing number of elderly people in the population will be accompanied by a decreasing labour force and a possible shortage of manpower. One way of overcoming this problem is through increased immigration, but so far this alternative seems to meet with a certain resistance in parts of the population and in at least one of the major political parties (the right-wing Progress Party). Another way is to reduce or remove incentives for early retirement. Even though retirement age in Norway is 67 years, only 26 per cent of those aged 65–66 are in the labour force. A paradox is that while government policy and the Confederation of Norwegian Enterprise (NHO), the largest association of employers in Norway, aim to encourage seniors to postpone retirement and employers to employ them, elderly people are to some extent excluded from the labour market through the recruitment behaviour of the employers, the members of the NHO.

At any rate, the demographic future of any population is uncertain. The three main determinants are mortality, fertility, and migration. Among those factors the first is the least uncertain.

The capacity of the hospital system

The most urgent problem facing the Norwegian health care system is the insufficient ability of both general and psychiatric hospitals to absorb patient inflows. Opinion polls show that long waiting lists and reduced freedom of choice of hospitals for patients are widely considered to be unacceptable. As a result, there seems to be a general impression that the hospital system is undergoing a crisis. As this problem is deemed to undermine the popular support for maintaining a fully public health care system, e.g. by inducing private insurers to create specialised centres for non-emergency treatment, it figures high on the political agenda. Recent opinion polls show that people's confidence in the public health system is less than desirable (2006 and 2007). Almost half the population said they were worried or to some extent worried that (public) health services would not be provided as required when they needed such services. Still, only about 1 % of the population is covered today by private insurance schemes. A representative of one of the world's largest pharmaceutical companies present in Norway gave as a possible explanation that an economic discourse has supplanted the type of discourse most people are familiar with as regards the health care system and its tasks, i.e. prevention, treatment and palliative care. When politicians' primary perspective on health care seems to be as a cost instead of an investment, people may fear that the politicians will not give consideration of people's health first priority.

There are also reasons to believe that the reported waiting times are used strategically by the health care suppliers to obtain more public resources, whereas there are no financial incentives that would motivate the hospitals to shorten the waiting lists or to meet the waiting-time guarantees.

Chapter 7

Education in Norway – Equality, Nature and Knowledge

By Arvid Hansen

You do not have to deconstruct the kitchen if the food doesn't taste you! This sigh came from the depths of an experienced teacher's heart in a recent debate about school reforms. International tests and the following comparisons of countries and schools have led to discussions about education all over the world. No politicians seem to be comfortable with a low ranking, but it seems difficult to find the right tools to change the situation. When countries with quite different methods end up with the same result, it is not easy to choose the right medicine.

15-year-old students in Norway have participated in the PISA tests since the first assessment in 2000, and find themselves in 2006 slightly *under* the average for the participating countries. Indeed, this has influenced the debate! But the reactions are not unanimous. Until now there has been consensus in Norway that the school should be a place for both social and democratic development *and* for teaching knowledge and skills. Consequently, a schism is evident in the Norwegian debate on education, between those who think that good, visible results are most important, and those who are willing to pay the price for working in a broader perspective. In one study that tested 14-year-olds in 28 countries, including 17 OECD countries, on their knowledge of civic-related issues (social and democratic skills), Norwegian pupils had high scores. But such tests are no comfort for the politicians. The Finns have been ranked highest on the internationally standardized assessments for 15-year-olds, and some think there is a Finnish "ghost" from PISA hanging over the country – implying that Norway should copy their educational strategies. The Finnish school is different from the Norwegian one, as are the two societies. It is interesting to note that Finnish educationalists come to Norway to learn about the well-being of the Norwegian students.

What will a foreign visitor experience in a Norwegian school?

Normally the size of the schools comes as a surprise. Around 600 000 pupils in primary and secondary school share 64 000 teachers and 3000 school buildings. That means an average of 200 pupils per school and about 10 pupils per teacher. There are, however, significant differences between urban and rural districts. There may be schools in some places housing fewer than 10 pupils. In scattered communities schools are permanently threatened by centralisation. For example, the number of schools in 1875 was more than 6000. Nevertheless, we can still claim that the country has a decentralised school system. An interesting reaction in the local communities, when the public schools are closed, is to establish so-called independent schools. These are also funded by the state, which is one the reasons why Montessori schools can be found in the rural areas of Norway.

The technical standard of schools is mainly good. Even though teachers and parents in Norway criticize school buildings and equipment, visitors from other countries will often find the situation positive, with colourful interiors adapted for children. There are many newly-built and renovated schools, because the last two school reforms have challenged the traditional classrooms when it comes to working methods. Project work has been emphasised and also individual work, with or without a computer.

A foreign visitor will not find a quiet, authoritarian school. According to PISA 2003, the students report that they are often disturbed by noise in the classroom. Some will experience that this is a reality, while others comment on the very active and happy children and the positive dialogue between teachers and students. Some will think of it as a lack of respect that pupils call their teachers by their first name, but for Norwegian teachers this is quite natural.

One will also observe that in "normal" classrooms, there can be children with special needs From 1976 the law concerning special schools and institutions for such students was replaced by new legislation that required these children to be educated in their local school. Furthermore, Norwegian students have little to fear from assessments. Since the reform in 1974, no marks have been given in primary schools. There are still marks given in lower secondary schools, but there is an ongoing discussion about this, since almost every student gets her/his first choice when applying for a place in the upper secondary school. "Is this school - or paradise?" a German colleague asked.

Nearness to nature – also during the school day

After first having stated that the Norwegian school buildings are nice and warm inside, the next thing to observe is that a lot of time is spent outside the buildings. "Never bad weather, only bad clothes!" is a familiar saying in Norway. Many municipalities have stipulated that teachers shall spend at least one day per week with the pupils in the nearest woods or on the nearest island, making bonfires, climbing trees and learning certain subjects in a practical way. The different classes often have one "home area" where they come back every week, all through the year. Visitors from other countries often comment on this. They find it strange that Norwegian teachers work outdoors in heavy rain or snow. What is the reason? One primary school in Oslo argues as follows on their home page: "The students experience an adapted learning situation; they learn through excitement, activity and joy in a holistic cross curricular perspective."

The development of schools in Norway in a historical perspective

Norway has child-centred schools that are based on equality. On the Ministry of Education's website, we find this expressed in the following manner: "No matter where they live in the country, all girls and boys must have an equal right to education, regardless of social and cultural background and any special needs. All public education in Norway is free up to and including the upper secondary level. The standard of instruction in schools and workplaces is of paramount importance for the quality of our society."

Let us have a short look at our education history. Presenting a country's school history in a few pages is a challenge similar to playing all Ibsen's masterpieces in 60 minutes. It involves making a lot of choices. The story told here is based on a teacher's perspective and divides history into sequences that describe the teacher's work and role.

Itinerary teachers (1739-1860)

The history of schooling in Norway starts more or less in 1739. That year a royal decree, "The 1739 School Ordinance", was issued, requiring all young people in the country to attend school. The purpose was to lay a foundation for the Christian faith. All children were expected to attend school from the age of seven, and remain at least until they were ten to twelve years old, or until they could read and undergo a Christian confirmation, about the age of fourteen.

This represents the introduction of a relatively early compulsory education program compared with the rest of Europe. Most European nations postponed such mandates until the end of the next century. In Britain, elementary education was not made universally compulsory until 1880. In France, compulsory primary education was not established until 1882. Even in Sweden, compulsory schooling was not introduced until 1842.

Unfortunately, the initial plan for Norwegian schooling had been worked out for the Danes by Germans, who knew next to nothing about the conditions in Norway. Consequently the royal decree dictated that permanent schools should be established wherever possible, and that the bell ringer in each parish was responsible for running the school. However, this was simply not possible in a country where more than 90% of the population lived in isolated farming households, and the decree encountered great resistance. Consequently, in 1741 adjustments were made, stipulating that each local parish was responsible for making their *own type* of common school.

"The 1739 School Ordinance" actually applied only to rural schooling, because the towns remained self-governing corporations. Common schooling had been easier to establish in most towns, and a general schooling process was well under way.

The early schools rarely taught the children to write. In Scandinavia the purpose of lower schooling was to teach children religion and reading. Writing had little connection with these needs, and so it was often neglected. Despite that, even prior to independence in 1814, Norwegians were generally proud of themselves for being literate.

We do not know very much about the early years of education, but schools were in the beginning considered a strange institution by people in the countryside. Working on the farms for survival had a much higher priority. Establishing schools for the farmers and other people living outside the cities made it possible to say that Norway had "a school for all" because

School bulidings like this one were built all around Norway in the latter part of the 19th century.

most of the population lived in rural areas at that time. The notion that "the teacher is the school" comes from this period, and tells us about the lack of both money and school-buildings, and also about the difficult conditions for the teachers. Because of long distances, a scattered population, and a weak economy, it was impossible for most of the local communities to build school buildings. Instead, the teachers walked from place to place, from farm to farm, and taught children under difficult conditions: in churches, in the living room of the farms, in barns and even in tents in areas populated by the Sámi people. It has been calculated that the number of itinerant teachers was 900 in 1750. Sixty years later, the number was more than doubled. Statistics from 1837 tell us that there were 2024 teachers walking around the countryside, compared with only 118 teachers working in primary education in cities.

In the same period, we also find teachers that were lucky enough to teach in schoolhouses. The size of the schoolhouse was however dependent on the number of people in the catchment area, and often the building consisted of one classroom only. In the beginning, teaching in schoolhouses was not the norm, but as time went by and more schoolhouses were built, "schoolhouse teachers" became the norm. In the middle of the 19th century, there were about 7000 itinerant teachers. At the same time there were only 420 schoolhouses. During the next fifty years almost 2800 schoolhouses were built. But even as late as 1930, there were still 9 itinerant teachers.

Teaching was usually a "combined occupation", meaning that teachers were doing more than one job. Often teachers combined teaching with, for example, bell ringing, farming, playing the organ in a church, or some kind of crafts. This combination of different jobs was possible because of a very short school year. Combining different kinds of work was also necessary because of the low wages teachers were paid. Despite the fact that teachers in schoolhouses were paid 3 to 6 times more than itinerant ones, they also had to do other work in addition to their teaching. Who were recruited as teachers in this period? Teaching was, up to the 1870s, an occupation for men only. It was illegal for the local? priest to hire "unknown vagabonds, dismissed military officers and women."

Teachers as nation builders (1850 – 1950)

This period, also the length of a century, is marked by Norway gaining independence and experiencing nationalization. In 1814 Norway became independent after 430 years as a Danish dependency. The new nation started out facing gigantic challenges. Its population of less than one million was scattered over a vast territory, averaging one person in every eight square miles. It was exhausted from a brief but debilitating conflict with Sweden, and its government, which had been located in Copenhagen, was now without resources and almost bankrupt.

Norway was without any national system of education. The first thirty years after independence from Denmark has been described as a period of *stagnation* with regard to education. The reason for this was that the country did not immediately move to adopt a school system that reflected its democratic constitution. It was not before the middle of the 19th century, when the folk school legislation for towns was introduced, that a hint of the educational reforms to come became evident. The home was, accordingly, still the primary agent of education, with schools providing a supplementary service.

In 1860 new legislation concerning rural schools was passed, introducing many changes. First of all, the government became responsible for the funding of schools. New secular subjects, such as mathematics, history and science, were introduced. The new legislation also accepted women as teachers. But, women did not become teachers, with some few exceptions, before the next round of education legislation in 1889. With this law the length of the school year and the number of lessons were expanded, and more subjects were introduced. Social studies became an integral part of the curriculum, and nature studies were no longer limited only to the people, the land and the natural surroundings of Norway.

In the latter part of the nineteenth century, the concept of a common school that would form the foundation of all subsequent schooling, finally became a reality. Norway was among the first countries to pass legislation that provided for schooling intended to be free and available for all children, regardless of social background.

The period from 1900 up to 1940 was first of all marked by intensive work with expositions and comprehensive development of new laws. Secondly, the period was marked by the reformist pedagogy movement, inspired by educators such as the American John Dewey, the German Georg Kerschensteiner and the Austrians Elsa Köhler and Carl and Charlotte Bühler. This pedagogical reform was not, to any great extent, practiced in the classroom, but was an inspiration for those who introduced the educational policy and the national curriculum in 1939.

Teachers as reformers

In 1939, the same year as the new national curriculum was to be introduced, World War II broke out. The next five years involved a state of emergency, because of which the so called "1939 plan" was not introduced until 1946. After the war, a new era of rebuilding and optimism began. Already in 1945, all the political parties were unanimously in agreement that the whole educational system, on all levels from primary school to university, had to be renewed. With a spirit of cooperation and unity, all segments of the educational enterprise and all the political parties were unanimous in proclaiming that any further developments in education ought to be based on experimentation with new school types and forms.

In 1947 a twenty-one member committee was constituted, called the "Coordinating Committee for Schooling". It was given the task of reviewing the situation with regard to the different school types, teacher education, school administration, and revisions to the law that might be necessary to achieve coordination. In the next five years nineteen different reports were submitted, dealing with every facet of the school system. In its summary report issued in 1952, the committee went far beyond its mandate and looked ahead an extra decade. The committee's prophesy was a common school for all youth. In the fall of 1955, three municipalities were designated to experiment with a two-year comprehensive program beyond the seven-year "folk school". Two years later, seven additional municipalities joined in, and 1400 pupils were involved in the experiments.

During the following decade more and more municipalities all over the country became involved in the experiment with this kind of schooling. In 1969 a new education act for a nine-year basic education was passed, and in 1974 a new national curriculum for a nine-year comprehensive school was introduced. For the first time in the history of the Norwegian educational system, the curriculum was to be the same for children all over the country, no matter whether they lived in cities or in rural areas.

Development of curricula since the 1970s

Not only were the framework and organisation changed. The content was also renewed. There was at that time a general trend of opposition and radicalisation all over the world. The students' revolts in the US and in Europe made an impression, and the awareness of oppression and participation had risen. This was internationally the women's decade. The rights for minority groups were discussed all over the world, and there was a strong belief in local solutions. All these influences were reflected in the new curricula.

The law concerning special schools was amended in 1976, and a new, common law for all children was passed, including the principle of individual adapted teaching. In the curriculum of 1987, local freedom was strengthened. Research had shown that national curricula tended to focus on the national and central culture, and therefore did not always serve the districts in a proper way. Throughout the 1970s and the 1980s lots of young people from rural areas, especially from the north of Norway, had moved to the central south-east region and to Oslo. The new curriculum should, to some extent, counteract this development, by giving the schools an opportunity to make closer connections to the local environment and stimulate the local identity.

Another major change in the 1987 reform was the way the subject content was reconstructed. For the first time, there was no specific content for each level. Instead, the subjects were organized in blocks of three years (1-

3, 4-6 and 7-9). This local freedom can be seen as a part of a central policy where *management by objectives* was an important part of the ideology. The Ministry of Education was no longer to make rigid rules. Local schools and teachers were given the responsibility to run the schools in ways they thought were best, and they were expected to make local plans with aims and objectives, central and local content and assessment systems. This curriculum, however, did not have a smooth start. Some school politicians were critical because it seemed to be a plan made for schools in rural areas, and not for the urban areas. Teachers were critical of the work load. Since the new way of thinking gave them too much work, and since the name of the curriculum was *Mønsterplan* (*mønster* = pattern), it became a joke among teachers to call it the *Monster Plan*. There was also a critical attitude among many researchers towards the focus on local content. They feared that the national perspective would decrease.

The national standards in L-97

When the next curriculum reform process started, the aim was to focus more on knowledge and a common, national content. Moreover, children were to start one year earlier, at the age of six instead of seven. This means that Norway introduced 10 years of compulsory education from the autumn of 1997. More knowledge, a common national content and cultural heritage were main areas of focus. The curriculum had an ambitious general part (core curriculum) which was published as early as 1993. For the first time, a common platform for primary, lower secondary, upper secondary and adult education was presented. The basic values of the core curriculum were expressed through six idealistic portraits:

- The spiritual human being
- The creative human being
- The working human being
- The liberally-educated human being

- The social human being

- The environmentally aware human being

- And as the results of them all:

- The integrated human being

Figure 7.1

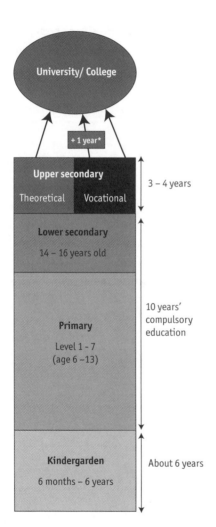

The system is consistent until upper secondary school, but even when choosing different programs the young students are parts of the same school. Kindergarten is not a part of the compulsory system, but it has been an important aim for the last governments to give room for all children.

* A number of the vocational programs give direct access to university

This metaphorical way of describing values and visions, together with a flourishing linguistic genre, has given the first part of the curriculum the nickname, *the poetry part*. Rumour has it that the Minister of Education at the time, Gudmund Hernes, wrote this part all by himself. *The integrated human being* brings together and fulfils all the other values and aims, even if they seem contradictory. The description ends like this: *The ultimate aim of education is to inspire individuals to realize their potentials in ways that serve the common good; to nurture humaneness in a society in development.*

New curriculum in 2006 – what changed?

The Minister of Education in 1997, Gudmund Hernes, belonged to the Labour Party. The minister in 2006, Kristin Clement, came from the Conservatives. Her new curriculum was called "Knowledge promotion", a notion with strong symbolic power. Had knowledge been too blandly communicated in the previous curricula? It is interesting to observe that in spite of this turn, there was consensus in the parliament on one important point. No one wanted to touch the core curriculum from 1997 with all its ambitious values. But the new reform obviously included new trends, some of which were in disharmony with those presented in the core curriculum. The subjects would now be measured through *learning outcomes*, formulated as the final status. The educational researchers who criticised the document, called it too instrumentalistic. Solid tools to develop the knowledge were seen as necessary, and *basic skills* were emphasised – in *all* subjects. The basic skills are listed as follows:

To be able to

- express yourself orally
- express yourself through writing
- read with understanding
- use numbers and calculate
- use digital tools

This means that reading is an important skill also in mathematics, and that digital tools also play a part in language and arts. The content, however, was once again in the hands of the teachers. The rhetoric signalled more local freedom, but with more weight put on control and *accountability*.

Zigzag school?

When Margaret Thatcher presented her school reforms in Britain in the eighties, she was criticised for finding her educational ideals in the past, emphasizing discipline and specific knowledge. While most sciences develop forwards, it often seems that in school the best practices are found in history, especially when the system is threatened. The accusations that Norwegian schools have been more social and therapeutic places than learning institutions should probably not be the debate. We need schools that combine discipline and freedom, knowledge and emotional well-being. The best learning environment is when the whole person is taken care of.

After the PISA tests in 2006 combined with bended results in the new national tests, the two-year-old "red-green" government has to show muscle. While the teachers' union asks for a "reform break", the politicians work on changes. At the beginning of 2008, the Minister of Education is talking about a national, centralised curriculum with a common content. A group of "selected topics" has also been presented. These are not new or surprising. According to the Minister, Norwegian students are to read and dance and be clever entrepreneurs.

It is a little bit like Winnie the Pooh's milk-and-honey answer. And perhaps that is the best solution for now, and then we can forget PISA and tell ourselves that we do not have to score highest in the world. In my opinion, we should remember and implement the ideals of the child-centred and democratic school which our foreign visitors still seem to admire.

Chapter 8

Norwegian Politics

By Kjetil Børhaug

The Norwegian state has its origins in medieval times. The Norwegian kingdom lasted around 400 years - depending on how one defines and assesses its founding at the end of the Viking era. In 1380, Norway joined Denmark in a union and later on became a Danish province. In 1814, Denmark had to cede mainland Norway – but not the ancient Norwegian possessions of Iceland, Greenland and the Faroes. This year also brought a Norwegian Constitution and established political institutions. In many respects the national political system was re-established in 1814 even though the king was Swedish and Sweden controlled the foreign policy of the union. In 1905 the union with Sweden ended and Norway became a completely sovereign nation state.

Since 1814 the Norwegian political development has led to a modern nation-state. The Norwegian political system is in many respects similar to the political systems in other European countries. Norway is a multiparty democracy and national elections are held every four years to the national assembly called Stortinget. The government depends on support in Stortinget. At present, seven parties are represented in the national assembly. Norway is a constitutional monarchy in which the monarch only has symbolic powers. The Prime Minister is the head of government in terms of real power.

Like most European states, Norway has a national governmental level, a regional governmental level and a local governmental level. Local and regional governments are headed by elected councils that stand for election every four years. Local governments dispose a very large proportion of government resources and play a key role as a provider of education and welfare services. Most public sector employees work for the regional or the local government.

Activists demonstrating outside the Norwegian parliament – Stortinget.

The Norwegian government intervenes in most sectors of society through regulations, legal frameworks and various programs, services and infrastructure development. Government spending is substantial.

Norwegian society is heavily integrated with the outside world economically, culturally and technologically. Major challenges to Norwegian politics are international problems such as environmental degradation and migration. Norway is therefore, like any European country, deeply involved in international political co-operation in many areas.

Norwegian politics are also different from its European counterparts in many respects. In this chapter we will point out some of these characteristics that Norway does not share with many others. We will consider political institutions, the political parties and the political controversies.

A Democratic Monarchy?

As a monarchy, Norway belongs to a shrinking minority in a Europe of republics. Even within the small number of constitutional monarchies Norway distinguishes itself by having a monarchy with democratic aspects. Although present day European monarchs have accepted the ideas of democracy, monarchy itself is historically the opposite of democracy.

Crown Princess Mette-Marit is the wife of the future king of Norway, Crown Prince Haakon.

Many leading democrats in Norway wished to abolish the monarchy when the union with Sweden ended in 1905. However, in an attempt not to provoke the European great powers – in particular Britain – the Norwegian establishment decided to maintain the Norwegian throne. The problem was that there was no royal family. The Swedish king was asked if one of his sons would be King of Norway, but the Swedish king was so insulted by the Norwegian decision to leave the union that he refused the offer. The Norwegians then turned to the Danish king who also had a surplus of sons. He approved of the idea, and one of his younger sons, prince Carl, was given the task of establishing a Norwegian royal dynasty. Because Carl was not a very Norwegian name he changed his name to Haakon, which was also the name of several Norwegian medieval kings. Carl was a good choice because he was married to the daughter of the British monarch. Their son had to change his name as well, from Alexander to Olav, another name from medieval royalty.

Haakon could not legitimize his royal authority by belonging to an ancient Norwegian royal dynasty. What makes Haakon a different king is first that he insisted that the Norwegian people should approve of his position in a referendum, which they did with overwhelming majority. This gave the Norwegian monarch a new legitimacy which was in accordance with democracy instead of tradition. No other royal house today has such a mandate from its people. Furthermore, compared to the other European monarchies, the Norwegian royal family is materially speaking very modest and does not dispose of vast fortunes and estates. Nor is it closely connected to the nobility because there is no nobility in Norway, it was abolished in 1814. Instead, the Norwegian royal family has attempted to symbolize Norwegian ideals of equality and closeness to the people. The most prominent symbol of this is a photo of the Norwegian king taking the subway during the oil crisis in the early seventies, and insisting on paying his fare like everybody else. His son, the present king, married a common woman in 1968. Their son, the crown prince, married a single mother who will be the next queen.

The Political Parties

Political parties reflect the major social groups and conflicts of society. Because group alignments and conflicts differ from one society to the next, so do party systems. The multi-party systems of the world therefore offer a confusing variation of political parties. The Nordic countries differ from the rest of Europe, but they all have a core of political parties which are quite similar. Some call this the Nordic party model. It is made up of a large social democratic party, a small left wing radical socialist party, a conservative party, a farmers party and a liberal party. In a European context, and even compared to the other Nordic countries, Norway and Sweden are distinguished by the dominant position of their social democratic parties. The Norwegian Labour party was some years ago metaphorically called "The eagle among Norwegian political parties". It took over government in 1935, stayed in power to 1940, led the exile government in London, and stayed in government from 1945 until 1965. Since 1965 there has been more alternation, Labour being in power 1971-72, 1973-1981, 1986-1989, 1990-1997, 2000-2001, and 2005-2008.

A Norwegian invention in the area of political parties is the Christian People's Party which was established in 1933 as a protest against the secularization of Norwegian society. Over time, it has gradually developed a strong profile on solidarity with the poor countries of the world. When it comes to social policy, the party is close to the Labour party. The Christian

Kjell Magne Bondevik served as Prime Minister of Norway from 1997-2000, and from 2001-2005, making him the longest serving non-socialist Prime Minister since World War II.

People's Party soon established itself as a party with 8-10 % of the votes. It is not a broad alliance of church, rural interests and business interests like the continental Christian democrats. It is based in a conservative Christian missionary movement outside and in opposition to the established Church of Norway, which is considered to be too liberal. In positions of power, whether at the national, regional or local level, the party has been willing to compromise and cooperate with both left and right. As a result of this, the party has played a key role in Norwegian politics and has held the prime minister position twice. Similar parties were established in Denmark and Sweden in the post war period, but they have not experienced the same success except for shorter periods in recent decades.

The Progress Party was a Danish invention established in the early seventies. This right wing populist part was immediately copied in Norway and later on, for a brief period, in Sweden. The Norwegian copy was founded by a man called Anders Lange. He called it "The party of Anders Lange for the reduction of governmental taxes and regulations". Following Lange's death, the party changed its name to the Progress Party. It has gradually become a bigger voter success than its Danish originator. At present, it is the largest opposition party in Norway, second only to the

Siv Jensen is the chairman of the Progress Party, the largest opposition party in 2008.

Labour Party presently in government. Its profile is a blend of anti-elitism, objections against the shortcomings in the welfare state system, neo-liberalism, privatization policies and finally objections against immigration from third world countries. There are right wing protest parties elsewhere in Europe, but the Norwegian Progress Party distinguishes itself by its strength and by having retained such a strong position for a long time.

The Progress Party identifies itself as a non-socialist party and has argued for the establishment of a broad alliance of the non-socialist parties. Until now, the other non-socialist parties – with the partial exception of the Conservatives - have refused to establish a government alternative or an alliance with the Progress Party. This has split the opposition against the present government and made it difficult to envision a new majority that may replace the present majority of Labour, left wing socialists and the Center party (former farmers' party).

In the aftermath of the student protests in 1968, radical left wing groups were formed all over Western Europe. They engaged in protest groups and various interest organizations. They also made their voices

heard in the political parties and sometimes formed new political parties. In Norway this development was different in some respects than in
other countries. A major faction of the left wing radicals established a
revolutionary party called AKP m-l (The Workers Communist Party – the
Marxist-Leninists). It was a party which accepted Marxism and Lenin-
ism, but it was deeply skeptical to the Soviet Union. In their view, Maoist
China, the Pol Pot regime in Campuchea, and Albania were more in
accordance with Marxism-Leninism than the Soviet regime was. AKP m-l
had secret party meetings and prepared for a coming revolution. Following Leninist doctrine, they believed in strict party discipline. When the
party decided that its members should leave the universities to become
part of the proletariat as blue collar workers, many did so for several
years. The Maoist party became a focal point for young radical activists,
not least among the students.

AKP m-l never had great success at the polls, but they were well organized. Even if they were few in numbers, they played a major role in a broad
range of protest groups, interest organizations, trade unions, at the universities and in the public debate. As many AKP m-l activists later on conquered key positions in society – as university professors, top bureaucrats,
journalists and editors in the major newspapers – they were confronted
with their previous approval of Maoist China and the Pol Pot regime in
Campuchea. How could people who had supported such ideas, even wanting to topple the Norwegian political order, be trusted to sit in key positions? Most of them excused their former political views by arguing that
they had a genuine desire for change and solidarity that motivated them.
Some of them published their confessions in books or other writings, and
most of them have been accepted in their elite positions. It has been said
that this overbearing attitude towards the young radicals of the seventies
is a sign of tolerance and strength in the Norwegian democracy. Some revo-
lutionaries stuck to their old convictions, even if they revised some of their
points of view. In 2007, AKP m-l merged with some other radical groups to
form a new political party called "Red". They hope to be represented in the
Storting after the next national elections.

Women and politics

In 1981, Norway got a female Prime Minister for the first time. Her name
was Gro Harlem Brundtland, leader of the Labour Party. She did not keep

the post for long; in September 1981 she had to resign because Labour lost the national election. In 1986, Gro Harlem Brundland formed her second government after 5 years of opposition. This time, almost half the Cabinet members were women. Even though there had been female prime ministers elsewhere in the world, including Margaret Thatcher, Golda Meir and Indira Gandhi, such a large proportion of female Cabinet members had not been appointed before in any country. Pictures of Gro, as Norwegians call her, and the Cabinet on the day of their appointment by the King circulated world wide. Later Cabinets have stuck to a rule of having at least 40% women. This 40% rule has become a principle for governmental commissions and advisory committees and most political parties also feel obliged to this principle. However, female representation in parliament has had difficulties passing the 40% threshold. After the 2005 elections, there are 37.9% women in the national assembly.

Is this relatively high female representation in political institutions a sign that Norway has realized the goals of equality between men and women in a better way than other societies? Equality in terms of equal formal rights is obtained in most Western countries, but equality in terms of actual distribution of resources and power is another matter. There is a quite broad agreement in Norway that equal representation is important in politics, in the labor market and in various power positions outside government. But outside the representative political institutions, Norwegian women are not equally represented. There are few women in executive positions in governmental agencies and in private enterprises. A new law will require that there must be at least 40% women in the boards of major enterprises. This will improve the representation there, but not at the executive levels. In the total labor market, gender differences are also noticeable. Norway has a quite segregated labor market, with women dominating in many low pay, part time jobs.

The politics of the Sami

The Sami are the indigenous people of Norway. The non-Sami people who settled in Norwegian territories over the last several thousands of years co-existed with the Samis for a long time, but gradually the Sami retreated to the mountains and to the north. With the development of the nation state, the Sami came under increasing pressure of assimilation policies. Their religion, language and music were forbidden. When compulsory schooling was introduced, the Sami were forced to send their children to Norwegian schools. Assimilation policies continued well into the 1960s. Many Sami suppressed their cultural origin and were indeed assimilated, especially in mixed communities where Sami co-existed with Norwegians. Only in a few villages and areas in the north did the Sami retain their dominance. It is in these few and remote areas that the Sami culture survived, with the traditional way of living and herding reindeer.

The 1970s and early 1980s saw a dramatic change in how the Sami were considered. Norwegians increasingly came to accept the cultural, social and economic rights of the Sami. What caused this change? The bitter protests against the building of hydro-electrical facilities in some of the core areas of the Sami people united them. Of equal importance was the forming of broader alliances between the Sami, left wing radical groups, and the environmental movement. This protest movement facilitated the recognition of the Sami people, their rights and the value of their culture. Sami traditions and lifestyles were being favorably portrayed in popular culture, such as in the film *Budbringeren* (The messenger) and through the music of artist Mari Boine. A result of this renaissance of Sami culture, lifestyle and rights was that important reforms regarding Sami issues were made in the national government. A Sami council was established, where all Sami have the right to vote when the councilors are elected every four years. The Sami Council elects a President who is the highest ranking spokesperson for the Sami people. This council has its own budget and holds direct control of cultural policies. More importantly, it is an institution which gives the Sami interests a voice in Norwegian politics. In the educational system, Sami schools use their own language in classes and in textbooks, although not at in the higher level educational institutions. Another major change is that the Sami council has raised the issue of the rights of the Sami people to the vast areas of land in the Sami areas. These claims to land rights conflict with the claims of Norwegian coastal communities and the claims of the government which is a major owner of the land the Sami people still use for their reindeer.

The institutionalization of Sami rights in a council elected by the Sami people, legal rights concerning cultural and land use issues, and the general acceptance of Sami traditions has been controversies. In a global context, it is still quite extraordinary that such institutions have been established for a minority group. In most countries similar groups do not have these rights and institutions.

The territory

A state is also defined by its territory, and the Norwegian territory is in some respects different from that of most European states. Not because it is relatively large in size with few inhabitants due to the harsh climate, but because some Norwegian territories have a special status in international law. Norway has a history of Arctic and Antarctic imperialism, and it is one of the states which lays territorial claims on the Antarctic continent. Norway even tried to occupy Greenland during the interwar years, but accepted an international court decision that Greenland should remain Danish.

Norway also claimed sovereignty of the Svalbard archipelago, Spitzberg. In an international agreement from 1920, it was decided that Svalbard should be under Norwegian jurisdiction. Citizens from other states should have the same rights to settle there and to engage in commercial activities as Norwegian citizens. As a result of this, there is presently a large Russian settlement at Svalbard. If citizens from other nations wanted to settle there, they would be equally entitled to do so. Svalbard is therefore both Norwegian territory and open territory.

Norway has sovereignty over a sea area that is bigger than Norway itself. In the 1970s, international conventions decided that the coastal states would have control over all resources as far out at sea as 200 nautical miles. These sea areas are of vital importance to the Norwegian economy, which largely depends on income generated by the oil and natural gas industries, as well as from the fisheries. When major economic interests are involved, conflicts of interests often arise. The sea areas surrounding Svalbard are subject to such a conflict. Norway has claimed its right to regulate fisheries in a 200 nautical miles zone surrounding the archipelago. No other state has accepted this claim. Norway also has a dispute with Russia concerning where the economic zones of the two states meet at sea.

The Political Agenda

Many political issues that are being debated and fought over in Norwegian politics resemble what is being debated and fought over in other European countries. Problems relating to how increasing demands for welfare services should be met, problems concerning how our educational system performs compared to the educational systems elsewhere, problems relating to immigration and multiculturalism, increasing socio-economic differences and economic development are being debated in Norway as in other countries. But some of the controversial issues in Norwegian political debate are special to Norway.

The language problem

Referring to the AKP m-l and their revolutionary program, it was said by an observer that before there could be a revolution in Norway, we would have to agree on how to spell it. There are two standards for how correct Norwegian should be written: The New Norwegian (nynorsk) and Danish-Norwegian (bokmål). The latter developed from the old Danish standard. Although New Norwegian is used only by a minority, its proponents have obtained quite strong legal protection of it, as explained elsewhere in this book. These legal protections include that national broadcasting should use both languages because governmental agencies are obliged to use both standards. Further more, students using bokmål are obliged to take classes in New Norwegian and they have to pass a mandatory exam in New Norwegian in order to graduate from compulsory lower secondary school and upper secondary school.

This situation of New Norwegian being a minority with strong legal protection has been stable for more than 100 years. One would perhaps expect that Norwegians adjusted to this situation and gradually came to see it as a cultural variation that enriches the national culture. But many do not, even if tensions are not as harsh as they were. The language question still leads to heated debates where strong emotions are mobilized and deep seated identities are at stake. Most Norwegians have quite tempered opinions about the issue, and attempts to alter the balance between the two languages are met with fierce resistance.

The European Union

Even more heated than the language question is the question of how Norway should relate to the European Union. The Norwegian government had negotiated an agreement for entering the EEC in 1973, together with Britain, Denmark and Ireland. But the proposal to join the EEC was rejected by the people in a referendum in 1972 even if the majority of the Norwegian political elite was strongly in favor. The struggle prior to the referendum was very bitter and several political parties experienced deep divides in this issue, including Labour. The oldest party in Norway, the Liberal Party, was split into two different parties by this struggle. Although they merged again a few years later, the Liberal Party has never regained the strength it had before the split in 1972. Because of the bitterness of the 1972 struggle and because of the dividing effects the issue had, not least in Labour, the European question was a non-issue for more than 15 years. It was only with the Single European Act and the decision to implement the single market by 1992 that the Norwegian political establishment felt forced to raise the issue again in the late eighties.

Just like in 1972, the government negotiated the entry conditions with the European Union and then the people refused once more in a referendum in 1994. Once again it was a hard struggle but a little less so than in 1972. Norway is the only country which has refused to enter the EU, not only once, but twice. According to the opinion polls, the majority of Norwegian voters have remained negative to joining the EU ever since. Unless an unexpected event forces the Norwegian government to raise the issue once more, it is not likely that the EU question will be on the political agenda before opinion polls show a change in favor of membership.

What are the reasons for the Norwegian refusal to join the EU? It is sometimes argued that Norway is different because it is a new state in a Europe of old states. Yet a very large proportion of European states are not older. There is a large group of European states that were formed in the 19th century and the early 20th century as they broke away from multinational kingdoms. Greece and Romania developed out of the Balkan wars in the early 19th century. Finland, Poland, Hungary, Yugoslavia, Czechoslovakia and Albania all established themselves on the ruins of World War I, well after 1905. Ireland is not a very old state either. Iceland became independent in 1944, and the Baltic states only in 1991 – although they had a short period of independence from 1920 to 1939. Let us also note that Italy and

Germany were created in 1861 and 1871, respectively. The reason obviously cannot be found here.

The reason is not that there is something special about Norway and all Norwegians that make all Norwegians refuse the EU. Similarly, it is not the case that all citizens in the member states endorse the EU. Rather, in Norway – as in many EU member states – there are arguments in favor and arguments against. There are social groups who think they will benefit from membership and other groups who think that they will not. The difference is that in Norway the social groups who think they will not benefit are relatively stronger than in most other European countries. Very important in this respect is that people in the regions that depend on fisheries and agriculture have been strongly against EU membership. This has to do with the fact that Norwegian farmers cannot compete with European farmers due to climatic conditions and small farms. Communities depending on fisheries realize that once inside the EU, it will be necessary to allow boats from other member countries to catch more fish in Norwegian waters, whereas Norwegian fishermen will not gain much by fishing in EU waters. These waters are already heavily overexploited and not as rich as the Norwegian waters. To many groups, EU membership does not seem advantageous simply because there is no sense of crisis in Norway. Unemployment is very low, and the Norwegian economy is going very well. There are not many who think that EU membership is needed in order to end some sort of economic and social crisis.

The EU question is not debated constantly. But it is a major issue in Norwegian politics and it has surfaced regularly with a lot of noise. It will reappear again. Even when it is not on the agenda it is always present in the background. The current government is made up of two parties against membership and one party in favor, with a large internal majority against membership. A part of their coalition agreement is that EU membership will not be brought up. If the issue were to be revived, the government would fall as a result of internal disagreement.

The oil income problem

One of the main controversies in Norwegian politics is what the government should do with all its money. The Norwegian state is not burdened by debts and the combined governmental incomes from mainland economic activities and offshore exploitation of oil and natural gas are very large, not least due to heavy taxation of the offshore activities and to the fact that the Norwegian state also is an owner of parts of the oil fields.

The problem is that if all these government incomes were invested and consumed in the national economy, it would lead to inflation, serious shortage of manpower, wage increases, and even more inflation. In the process, Norwegian mainland industries and services would become less and less competitive. There is no disagreement about this in general terms. The Norwegian state therefore channels a major part of its surplus revenues to a fund which is now one of the biggest investment funds in the world. The resources of this fund are invested in enterprises all over the world. Actually, the fund is by now such an important actor in the international finance markets that its ethical guidelines have an impact. It is serious for an enterprise to be blacklisted by the Norwegian investment fund, as the reactions from the American company Wal-Mart when they were blacklisted demonstrated. The Norwegian government is about to discover a new tool in its foreign policy.

The disagreement concerns the question of exactly how much can be spent domestically and how much should be set aside for the investment fund. How much money can the Norwegian economy absorb without damaging the mainland economy? There is no exact objective and correct answer to this. Various experts set the limit slightly differently. Careful public spending may be provocative to all those citizens who feel that government services are inadequate, who feel that the care for their old parents is not good enough, who do not get public day care for their small children, who have to wait for hospital treatment, or those who feel they pay too much tax. To them, it is difficult to accept such inadequacies while the government has large financial reserves. Whoever says that it would not make much of a difference if we spent just a little bit more will find an attentive audience among dissatisfied Norwegians. The Progress Party in particular has argued along these lines, ridiculing the other political parties for believing that a little bit more would make a difference. The Progress Party has also argued that some problems could be solved by spending money abroad to the benefit of Norwegians. Buying medical equipment abroad does not overheat the Norwegian economy, nor would it overheat if more retired people were placed in institutions in Spain. That spending would heat the Spanish economy instead.

The other parties may agree that some more spending would perhaps not damage the economy too much, but they fear that if the limits are stretched a little bit again and again, things will eventually get out of hand and serious economic problems will result.

Related to the question of how to spend the oil fund is the question of how to maintain national production and incomes once the exploitation of oil and natural gas ends. These are non-renewable resources, and due to climate problems it may be that the use of such resources will have to be reduced in the future. A major question is whether the oil fund can be used in ways that will lead to productive activities in Norway in the future. Could some of these resources be spent on developing new technologies that do not threaten the climate? But again, such spending would also create pressure in the economy. How to maintain the national income in the future is perhaps a more important issue than how much may be spent now, but unfortunately this issue is less seriously debated.

The State-Church Relation

In a global and in a European context the Norwegian system of having a confessional state and a state church is quite rare. The Constitution of 1814, which is the second oldest operative constitution in the world, states that Lutheran Christianity is the religion of the Norwegian state. The majority of Cabinet members must be members of the Norwegian Church and the very same Cabinet appoints the bishops. Church institutions give advice, but the Cabinet decides. Prior to the introduction of parliamentarism in 1884, this right of appointment belonged to the king. Today it still does – formally – but the Cabinet makes the actual decision. Nevertheless, the king remains a symbolic head of the Church of Norway in which a large majority of Norwegians are relatively passive members.

Historically, there have been strong tensions between state and church in Europe, particularly Catholic Europe. The protestant reformation was in some respects a device for princes and kings to loosen the churches in their states from Rome and bring the churches under control. The strictest form of such control was the state church arrangement which Norway has retained to this day whereas in most other countries state and church are separated in terms of formal authority.

The state church arrangement presumed a very homogenous population concerning religion. This is no longer the case in Norway. With increasing pluralism, it becomes more difficult for the state to make one religious position the official one. Sweden, which had a similar arrangement, has ended it. Norwegians have been discussing whether it should be reformed here as well. A key to understand this debate is the tension between conservative and liberal theology. Many, including Labour and the present government, favor the liberal wing in the Church of Norway and wish to keep the Church under governmental control in order to avoid that the conservative wing gets stronger. A main argument for supporting the liberal wing is that this will keep the church open to all. Dividing issues between the liberals and the conservatives include homosexuality and female priests. Those in support of the conservative wing in the church, mainly the Christian People's Party, have been split. Most leaders and spokespeople belonging to other religious communities have argued that the state church arrangement should be ended.

The present situation illustrates several aspects of the state church arrangement. First, that the government actually uses the arrangement in order to influence what the Church should hold as the will of God. Second, the government and the political parties decide, not the Church itself. That is what a State Church implies.

How different?

While being a quite typical Western state, Norway also has its peculiar traits and special features. Some of the institutional arrangements are special, such as the state church, the Sami institutions, aspects of the monarchy and the various types of territorial sovereignty. Some aspects of the party system are special, and so are some of the most heated political issues and controversies in Norway. At other points, such as gender equality, Norway is perhaps less different than what Norwegians like to think.

Chapter 9

Norway in a Global Context

By Kjetil Børhaug

Former Prime Minister Lars Korvald has often been ridiculed for having stated that "Norway is a tiny country in the world". He was made fun of because he made a point of the obvious. Laughing at this remark says more about the weak position of Korvald's 1972-73 government – few governments have had weaker support in parliament – than anything else. Of course, he was right. Norway is a tiny, and in most respects quite marginal country. Its role in an international perspective has often been a matter of how Norway could position itself in a difficult international context in a way that would allow Norway to stay independent, to develop and prosper.

At the same time, ever since its independence in 1905, there is evidence that Norway has aimed at more than just adapting. There is a desire to influence and to make a difference. Norway wants to contribute to a positive, international development and to deter and prevent negative trends. It is a very common phrase in Norwegian foreign policy that Norway wishes "to make its contribution". In this chapter both aspects will be highlighted.

A Tiny Country Adjusting to Great Power Politics

Norway was a Danish province that Denmark had to cede to Sweden in 1814. In this process, Norway and its citizens was an object that was being dealt with as it suited Great Power interests. In this case, Britain and its allies had to reward the Swedes for their support against Napoleon. Norwegian points of view played no role in that decision.

Norwegians could only adjust and exploit the room for manoeuvre that they perceived they had. In the absence of effective Danish authority, they made a constitution in 1814 and established almost all the political institutions of a modern state from scratch. Once these were in place and the Swedish king did not want to provoke his newly won Norwegian subjects, the constitution and the political institutions survived.

In 1905, when Norway left the union with Sweden, it was clear to all Norwegian decision makers that such a move was not for Norway and Sweden to decide on their own. If the European great powers did not approve, the situation for the new state would be precarious. Norway managed to mobilize British acceptance for the independent state, and in the following years, Norway considered Britain as a supportive power in case of a crisis. But no military alliances were made with the British.

As a newly independent nation, Norway decided to pursue a foreign policy of neutrality. This was an era of intense rivalry among the European great powers Britain, Germany, France, Russia, Italy and Austria. The Norwegian aim was to stay out of these conflicts and rivalries. During World War I, neutrality was difficult to maintain. Both Britain and Germany profited from trade with Norway and both parties put Norway under pressure to cooperate more closely with them than with the other side. Still, Norway managed to stay neutral through the war, but suffered heavy losses of men and ships. Norwegian merchant ships often passed through war zones and many were sunk by German submarines.

Norwegian neutrality policies seemed to have worked relatively well during World War I. Norway stayed on this course during the interwar years, and also when World War II erupted in 1939. The dangerous balance among the great powers did not succeed in 1940. Germany invaded Norway on April 9th, 1940, and Norway remained occupied until May 1945. By this time, almost all territories that had been controlled by Nazi Germany had been re-conquered by Allied forces. Norway was still under German control, occupied by more than 300 000 German troops. Only in the northern parts of Norway had Soviet forces driven the Germans back and occupied parts of the region. A peaceful German surrender was negotiated for the rest of Norway.

World War II experiences led to a reassessment of Norwegian foreign policy. The dominant view was that Norway would need allies. At the same time it seemed important no to alienate the Soviet Union, who came out of the war as one of the dominant powers of the world. The Soviet Union held a lot of sympathy in Norway; not only for its important role in defeating Germany, but also for its liberation of Finnmark in 1944 and its voluntary withdrawal from Norwegian territories in 1945. At first, the Nordic coun-

The German attack on Norway on April 9th 1940. German troops marching on Karl Johan street in Oslo.

tries discussed the possibilities for establishing a Nordic military alliance. It was concluded that such an alliance would not have the necessary military credibility to deter an aggressor. The idea was deemed not viable, and the Nordic countries had to seek other solutions.

The Western powers were planning an Atlantic alliance, and after some hesitation Norway and Denmark both approached this alliance. Because the Nordic countries were close to the Soviet Union, such an alliance was a delicate matter. Both the Western powers as well as the Soviet Union had strategic interests in the Nordic region. The solution became what is sometimes labelled the Nordic balance. Denmark and Norway became NATO members, while Finland signed a treaty with the Soviet Union. This treaty obliged the two countries to consult each other in case of international crisis, and the Soviet Union had military bases in Finland for some time. Sweden remained a neutral buffer between Finland on one side and the Nordic NATO members on the other. With this arrangement, Norway had a firm footing in the Western alliance. However, it remained a major concern in Norwegian security policy not to provoke the Soviet Union. Because of this concern Norway has not had its defensive forces in the North stationed near the Soviet border, but several hundred kilometres further west and south. Norway has not accepted nuclear arms on Norwegian territory and it has refused to let its allies have military bases in Norway.

Great power rivalry in the post World War II era was structured by the conflict between the USA and the Soviet Union. In this struggle, Norway lined up on the US side and stayed a loyal NATO member. The military guarantees from NATO, and consequently from the USA, became the core of Norwegian security policies.

Following the dissolution of the Soviet Union, Norway again finds itself among great powers, and new questions about how to align in this field arise. There are those who reject that there is a need for basic changes. They argue that NATO is still there and the alliance with NATO and the USA is and remains the core of Norwegian security. Another perspective is that because the Soviet Union is no longer a global rival to the USA, the USA is less interested in securing Norway and the ocean outside Norway. The security guarantee is less secure, it is argued. At the same time, the EU is slowly taking on a larger responsibility for European security. The EU will remain close to the USA but it will take over some of the burdens of securing Europe. US military presence in Europe is consequently reduced in recent years. In such an arrangement European security is decided upon bilaterally between the USA and the EU and Norway is left out because EU does not cover Norwegian security needs. According to this line of reasoning, Norway should realign itself internationally and join the EU which in the future will be the key ally for USA in Europe. The counter-argument to this line of reasoning is that the EU does not have the will or the military capacity to act militarily on any scale. It is only the USA who has the capability to provide a credible military deterrence. Close ties with the USA is therefore still a vital interest for Norway, especially due to its closeness to Russia.

Russia also plays a role because on one hand, Norway has major interests at sea in the north. Cooperating with Russia would be very beneficial to these interests. This concerns fisheries, oil and natural gas, and not least environmental problems related to commercial and military activities in Russian regions close to Norway and related to international shipping along the Norwegian northern coastline. Norway needs to be on good terms with the Russians, but Russia remains a potential military threat. In this triangle consisting of Russia, the EU and the United States, Norway might be forced to redefine its position. Doing so confronts Norwegian decision makers with difficult dilemmas.

Norway has adapted to shifting great power alignments, strategies and interests. But it would be wrong to reduce Norway's relation to the outside world to adaptation only. Norway has also quite consequently attempted to contribute to building stable, international cooperative arrangements, and Norway has attempted to contribute elsewhere in the world in order to promote peace and development.

Adapting to international power structures, contributing to the development of cooperative institutions and intervening in areas where there are serious problems are three aspects of Norwegian foreign policy that are interrelated. There are spill-over effects between these three areas, but hopefully these distinctions make the complexities of Norway's relationship to the outside world more comprehensible.

Building Institutions for International Cooperation.

It is sometimes said that during the first decade after 1905, Norway tried not to have a foreign policy. The first foreign minister of Norway once stated that the best foreign policy is not to have one. But this referred to foreign policy in terms of playing in with great power rivalries. Norway attempted to stay out of these. What Norway has not stayed out of is attempts to establish international frameworks for cooperation and peaceful conflict resolution. Being a tiny country, vulnerable to great power abuse of power and strongly dependent on foreign trade and international shipping, Norway had strong interests in a systematic arrangement of international relations. At the same time, there is also a large portion of idealism behind this aspect of Norwegian foreign policy.

The commitment to stable and ordered international relations is already evident in the strong Norwegian commitment and support to the League of Nations that was established in Geneva after World War I. The League failed to act effectively against Italy in Ethiopia and Japan in Manchuria and this led to its breakdown and demise well before World War II. Norway, however, remained a strong supporter of the league for as long as it could.

After 1945, this policy has been continued. First and foremost by a strong Norwegian commitment to the United Nations, whose first Secretary General was Trygve Lie, a Norwegian. Norway has served several terms in the

Security Council and relative to its size, Norway has contributed more with financial support and with peacekeeping forces than most other states.

Beyond the UN commitment, Norway has entered a very broad range of international conventions and organizations. Norway has been active in establishing arrangements that facilitate trade, and it has tried to contribute to international agreements concerning environmental problems. A willingness to make and to join committing international institutions has been a main priority in Norwegian foreign policy. There are, however, some notable exceptions where Norway has had reservations. First, as discussed in the chapter on Norwegian politics, Norway has twice declined to join the European Union. Second, Norway has had reservations concerning the International Whaling Commission. According to Norwegian beliefs in institutionalized international cooperation, Norway has joined the commission. But Norway has been a whale hunting nation for a very long time, with a policy of allowing whale hunting at a sustainable level of species not endangered by extinction. The majority of the commission members have for periods been in favor of banning whale hunting completely irrespective of whether a species is endangered or not. This has led Norway to reserve itself against commission decision to stop whaling. Norway has kept up a modest level of whaling. Third, even if Norway is one of the largest oil exporters in the world and has profound interests in the price level for oil it has not been willing to join OPEC. There have been occasions when Norway has adjusted production levels in accordancce with OPEC production regulations aimed at influencing price levels, but Norway has mainly left this task to OPEC.

The Nordic cooperation has been of particular importance. Norway and Sweden were prepared for war in 1905. Nordic history is one of rivalry, wars and territorial conquests. With this background, it is all the more remarkable that the Nordic countries have come to cooperate so closely, especially in the years following 1945. The Nordic Council is a main institution for Nordic contacts. By means of regular meetings in the Council, extensive informal contacts and negotiations, various cooperative arrangements and agreements have developed. Passport controls were abolished in the 1950s among the Nordic countries. The airline company SAS is a joint Scandinavian venture and the Nordic countries have often taken common positions in international affairs. As Sweden, Denmark and Finland are now members of the EU while Iceland and Norway are not, the Nordic cooperation is no longer very dynamic. This has been

one of the arguments in favor of Norway joining the EU, as it would facilitate a continued Nordic cooperation.

Contributing to international cooperation is clearly in accordance with
Norwegian small state interests. But it also reflects ideals of peace, tolerance, cooperation, and international solidarity. However, such ideals are
perhaps even more visible in the field of development assistance, humanitarian aid and in peace building. The Norwegian efforts and motivation
has been so ambitious in this field that some suggest that even if Norway is
a tiny state in many ways, it is a "humanitarian great power".

Development Assistance, Humanitarian Aid and Peace Building

Organized governmental development assistance appeared for the first
time in 1952, when Norway was still a receiver of American development
assistance (the Marshall program). But there were strong historical prece-
dents for Norwegian idealism and solidarity in relation to the conflicts
and poverty in the outside world. Christian missionary activities started in
the mid 19th century and Norway became one of the countries that sent the
highest number of missionaries relative to its own population. Christian
mission is controversial and there are different views as to how legitimate
it has been and on the effects it has had. But it seems plausible that it represents a current of religious motivation to come to the aid of those in need
and a senior Norwegian scholar and specialist in Norwegian development
assistance, Olav Stokke, argues that this is still one of several motives for
development assistance and humanitarian aid.

Another crucial precursor to later Norwegian ambitions in aid and
development assistance is the large scale humanitarian relief program that
was organized in the newly formed Soviet Union in the early 1920s by the
Norwegian hero and celebrity Fridtjof Nansen. In the aftermath of the
unrest and civil war in the Soviet Union the humanitarian situation was
desperate. The Nansen program went on for several years and made a difference for many. A historical irony is that one of Nansen's assistants was
Vidkun Quisling, who betrayed his country during World War II and was
shot as a traitor in 1945.

The first major Norwegian development assistance project was launched
in Kerala, India, in 1952 and went on for many years. Actually, Norway gave

India development assistance into the 1990s although at a limited scale. The Kerala project was a fisheries development project. From the start, Norwegian development assistance has focused on both productive activities as well as on welfare services. During the first decades, Norwegian development assistance often took the form of large scale projects over many years in sectors where Norwegians felt they had special knowledge; such as in fisheries, shipping, fertilizers, roads and forestry.

From the early 1960s, African states gained their independence. As these countries were very poor, Norway soon made Africa the main recipient of development assistance. Tanzania, Botswana, Zambia, Kenya, Mozambique, Namibia and to some extent other countries such as Malawi and Zimbabwe received substantial amounts of development assistance. In some countries, such as Tanzania, Norway became one of the major donors in a very donor dependent country. As a result, Norway found itself in the unusual role as a powerful actor in international relations.

Even if idealism played an important role in the establishment of Norwegian development assistance it is also related to Norwegian small state interests in international cooperation and regulated international relations, peace and stability. Norway had received and effectively benefited from the American Marshall aid and believed that this success could be reproduced in Africa and contribute to stable development there, to the benefit of all.

Norwegian development assistance has changed over the years. In the beginning, aid was given as large scale projects where Norway provided technical experts, management, funds, various commodities (Norwegian boats, Norwegian fertilizers or Norwegian machinery). The Norwegian Agency for Development Co-operation (NORAD) organized it all in liaison with the authorities of the receiving country. These projects were seldom very sustainable, because they were not integrated in the governmental structure in the receiving country. Consequently, when NORAD pulled out, these projects tended to experience severe difficulties. Over the years, NORAD tried various strategies in order to integrate the projects better locally and nationally. Today, Norway does not run and manage many projects by itself. As a main rule the recipient government must be responsible for this while reporting how money is spent and progress is being made.

A major component in Norwegian development assistance today is to improve the functioning of the governmental apparatus in the receiving country. This implies assistance to fight corruption, to improve tax administration, to develop administrative infrastructure (equipment, buildings, and vehicles), and to develop better management practices and planning. It also involves democratization. Norway assists in organizing elections and it supports civil society organizations. For instance in Tanzania, Norwegian development assistance funds a non-governmental organization which works to inform people of the rights they and their children have to education. It is called Haki Elimu which means "Right to Education" The organization helps organize local groups that put pressure on local governments and schools, and Haki Elimu is also active in the public debate as a critical corrective to the government.

A special instance of Norwegian assistance to the democratization of Africa is its support to the opposition in apartheid South Africa. Norway was a part of the broad, international anti-apartheid front, but in addition, Norway also funded both the ANC and other opposition groups. This had to be done secretly and funds were channeled by the Norwegian embassy in South Africa via the Norwegian People's Aid to the ANC and other groups.

Along with the other Nordic countries and sometimes the Netherlands and Canada, Norway is one of the "soft donors". All donors offer both grants and credits, and as a soft donor Norway offers a large proportion of its assistance as grants. Norwegian development assistance is never linked to arms and military purposes. The support to South African opposition groups is perhaps a partial exception. Being soft also implies that Norwegian development assistance has for a long time insisted that projects to the benefit of the poorest sections of society and women should have priority.

Repeatedly, there are discussions about the effectiveness of development assistance. Development assistance being to a large extent a moral issue in Norway, it is difficult to discuss these questions in a balanced way and the debate is often heated. Considering how effective single projects are, it seems clear that the results are variable. There are some projects that do not have many positive effects and there are many projects which have meant a positive contribution to people and local communities that have been directly involved in the project. However, many projects with positive effects are not sustainable when Norway pulls out. But development assistance has higher ambitions than to make a positive contribution. There has been an ambition, like in the Marshall program, that well targeted development assistance should have a stimulating effect on the overall social and economic development in the poor countries. It should fuel and accelerate a general development process. It is difficult to measure such effects but accelerated, broad development has hardly occurred in those countries that have received most Norwegian assistance.

Parallel to the establishment of governmental development assistance, private, non-profit organizations have also proliferated. Long before 1952, the missionary organizations worked in many developing countries. The Church of Norway has not been involved in missionary activities but is has established its own organization for humanitarian relief, Norwegian Church Aid. There were also humanitarian organizations such as the Red Cross, Save the Children and Norwegian People's Aid which is connected to the social democratic trade union movement. These organizations raise funds on their own, but they are increasingly funded by the Norwegian government. Since the early 1980s, these organizations have been seen as valuable partners. As more government money is channeled through such organizations, many more new such organizations have been founded. In a recent evaluation report, it is estimated that more than 100 private organizations are partially funded this way.

The oldest and largest private organizations – those that are mentioned above – were previously mainly involved in humanitarian relief to refugees and to communities hit by drought or other natural disasters. They still are, even if they also have become channels for long term development assistance. The Norwegian government is also a major actor in humanitarian relief and has developed an advanced system that is able to react quickly if needs arise. Such humanitarian relief operations are often coordinated by the UN, through the UN High Commissioner for Refugees (UNHCR).

Peace Building

As pointed out above, Norwegian foreign policy in the years following 1905 emphasized the importance of peaceful cooperation and conflict resolution. As early as the years around 1905, leading Norwegian politicians and scholars viewed working for international peace as a moral duty for the country. The active support for the League of Nations and later on United Nations supports this idealistic commitment to peace. The longest serving foreign minister Norway has had, Halvard Lange (1945 to 1965), stated in a presentation of Norwegian foreign policy that:

"The entire Norwegian foreign policy tradition makes it clear that we have no other wish in our participation in international politics than to contribute to peace and co-operation among the peoples of the world."

Norway has hosted to the Nobel Committee since 1901. Its members are appointed by the national assembly, Stortinget. This is also a part if the idea that Norway has a special moral duty to work for peace among nations. The ambition to work for peace is an important reason why Norway has worked for the development of international institutions for cooperation and exchange. In recent years, however, Norwegian efforts for peace have been renewed and important innovations have been developed. The signing of the Oslo accords between Israel and the PLO in the early 1990s is the most visible and symbolic expression of the renewed commitment to building peace. However, the peace building concept is complex and has several components.

A key component is to organize and advise in negotiations between the conflicting parties. In order to achieve this, it is necessary to provide substantial resources. A great deal of patience and willingness to work with the conflicting parties and issues over longer periods of time is required. A condition is that Norway as a mediator has no interests in the conflicting area itself and is not seen as closer to one side than to the other. This will more often be the case for a small state than for a larger one, which is one of the reasons why Norway sees itself as suited for this task.

It may take time to build confidence on both sides. In the Palestinian conflict, a Norwegian presence in Gaza and the West Bank over some time was important in order to achieve the confidence of the PLO. The Norwegian Labour party had long-lasting, close relations with the Israeli Labour Party and thus had a reservoir of goodwill on the Israeli side too. Often this long-term work of building confidence is done by non-governmental aid organizations. In the case of the Palestinian conflict, a key actor was the research institute of the biggest Norwegian trade union. This institute worked in the Palestinian communities for several years, mapping and analyzing living conditions and the consequences of the conflict on ordinary people.

In the case of Guatemala it was Petter Skauen, national representative for Norwegian Church Aid, who had developed networks, contacts and trust with the different parties in the conflict there. Measures to increase the trust between the two opposing sides are important, such as bringing them together outside the arena of conflict for longer periods of time, allowing them to get to know one another and develop personal trust.

Once a peace settlement or a stable cease fire is reached, it is necessary to aid in the establishment of a viable, non-oppressive governmental structure. In order to achieve this, development assistance is channeled to the area. It is important to have a working administrative system, reliable police forces, budgets to pay decent salaries to public employees so that corruption does not undermine trust in the authorities and it may be necessary to give general budgetary support to make the government work and demonstrate that peace brings progress. It may also be necessary to rebuild physical infrastructure such as roads, bridges, electricity and water supplies, as such facilities are often destroyed in warfare. In the Palestinian areas Norway and other countries provided substantial development assistance of these various types.

Norway has been involved in several conflicts, not only in the Israeli-Palestinian conflict. In Guatemala, Sri Lanka and Sudan Norway has also endeavored to play a peace building role, in various cooperative arrangements with other states and organizations. Conflicts such as these produce much human sufferings. People lose their income, their homes and many become refugees. As a result of this, it is necessary to organize major humanitarian relief programs. Both the Norwegian government and Norwegian non-governmental organizations work closely together with this. In general, the peace building policies are marked by very close liaisons between governmental and non-governmental actors.

All these measures, combined and in effect for a long period of time, may eventually build peace. But it is difficult, and the peace building policy does not imply that there will not be set-backs.

Norwegian representatives argue that Norway is in a better position than most to organize and coordinate such peace building. First, it requires large resources and civilian staff with experience from work in other cultures and conflict areas. Norway has these resources. Such work can best be led by a country which itself has a tradition for trying to solve internal and international conflicts peacefully. Peace building requires that the mediator does not have any interests in the conflict or on the area of conflict. This will normally be the case for a small country like Norway without a colonial past. Some argue that in this respect it is an advantage that Norway is not a member of the EU. Another reason why small states should do this is that during difficult peace talks a small state does not have the

State sectretay Jan Egeland greets former president Julius Nyerere from Tanzania during a meeting in Oslo in 1996 when Nyerere worked as a peace negotiator in Rwanda and Burundi.

option to "help" the peace process by putting pressure on one or both sides, like the Americans did when the Dayton agreement concerning ex-Yugoslavia was negotiated. Such pressures might provide results on a short term basis, but it may make the peace agreement less viable in the long run, which would be a serious shortcoming.

Norwegian confidence in the peace building approach has been substantial. So has confidence in Norway's special ability and capacity to perform and lead such processes. A key actor in Norwegian foreign policy and peace building, Jan Egeland, has introduced the idea that Norway is a small power in most respects but because of its peace building, development assistance and humanitarian aid Norway is a humanitarian great power. Critical voices point out that Norwegian peace building has not yet brought lasting peace anywhere. It is argued that peace is a matter of the will of the concerned parties or of a third party forcing a solution. In this perspective, Norwegian peace building ambitions are deemed unrealistic.

A Tiny Country with Conflicting Foreign Policy Ambitions

Being small and vulnerable, Norway is forced to adapt to international structures and processes while at the same time trying to contribute to a global development that would suit Norwegian ideals and interests.

Norwegian foreign policy is based on a combination of various motivations, as indicated above. First, there has been a strong historical motive of neutrality. Even if this motive is weaker to day, the wish to stand outside the EU and OPEC is by some attributed to this tradition of neutrality, of wanting to stay out of international high politics. Second, there is a motive of security by means of being a loyal alliance partner. Loyalty to NATO and the USA has been significant; some argue that Norway is far too loyal and that the Norwegian military contributions in Iraq and Afghanistan reflect this. Third, Norwegian foreign policy is often motivated by a belief in international organization and rules for international interactions. This is seen in the UN policy and in support for rules and lower tariffs in international trade. Contributing to development in poor countries is also to some extent a contribution to a stable world of development and peaceful cooperation. Fourth, idealism plays an important role in Norwegian foreign policy. Solidarity with the poor and the Christianity idea of loving one's neighbor are important factors for development assistance and peace building.

It is not easy to assess the effects of Norway's attempts to contribute to a more peaceful world, to development in poor countries or to the development of institutions that may regulate and bring order to international interactions. Such effects are dependent on what happens elsewhere in the world and what other actors do.

Norwegian foreign policy, perhaps especially development assistance and peace building, also has effects domestically. It influences how Norwegians understand themselves and how they view the role of Norway in the world. Professor Terje Tvedt at the University of Bergen argues that Norwegians' understanding of themselves and their country as good and as bearers of high ideals in a cruel world is a major effect of how Norway relates to the world.

Chapter 10

Norway – An Egalitarian Society?

By Pål Repstad

Whatever became of Einar Gerhardsen?

It is often said in public discussions in Norway today that we used to be an egalitarian country, but times have changed, and we have become more similar to other Western countries. Many people seem to think that inequality has been steadily increasing as a social fact, and also that inequality has become more acceptable to people in general. One among many expressions of this sentiment came in 2002 in a popular song, written and performed by Norway's oldest pop star, 76 year old singer and songwriter Odd Børretzen. He had a great success with his thoughtful, some would say slightly nostalgic, refrain: *Hvor ble Einar Gerhardsen av?* – Whatever became of Einar Gerhardsen? Einar Gerhardsen was a Labour Party leader and also prime minister in Norway for almost the whole period from 1945 to 1965. In his time he was a controversial politician, but several decades later, for Odd Børretzen and many others Gerhardsen has become a sort of supra-political father figure, a symbol of a simpler and poorer, but also a warmer, more caring and more egalitarian Norway.

Likhet – a complicated concept

I do not intend to drown the readers of this chapter in quantitative information, but as a social scientist I have to present some conclusions based on harder data than popular song texts. First, however, it is necessary to spend some time considering the concept of equality. What are we

Einar Gerhardsen emerged as the leading politician in Norway during the first 20 years after World War II. He was a symbol of an era marked by economic growth, political stability, solidarity and the development of the welfare state.

talking about? The concept can have different meanings in English, and this is even more the case with the Norwegian word for equality, *likhet*. Many discussions about *likhet* in Norway tend to be fuelled by the fact that people attach different meanings to the word. In Norwegian, *likhet* may stand for both similarity and equality, and *ulikhet* for both differences and inequality. These two kinds of *likhet* are sometimes mixed in public discourse. Both culturally radical, individualist people as well as spokesmen for the extreme right can sometimes reach rhetorical heights by talking about how very grey and boring and social-democratic we are in Norway, where everybody is expected to be *alike*. As one can hear, the criticism includes dullness and conformism as well as distributive aspects. I am not impressed by the intellectual vigour of this kind of criticism. Historically, I would rather think that the egalitarian values in Norwegian politics and society have caused cultural liberation, flourishing and pluralism including most of the Norwegian population. I think that the welfare state has released a lot of resources in people rather than having been culturally restraining.

As I write this article (February 2005), there is a very interesting discussion in two national newspapers, *Aftenposten* and *Dagbladet*, about individualism versus collectivism in small Norwegian local communities, prompted by a novel about growing up in an industrial community in Western Norway, Odda. Author (and sociologist!) Lars Ove Seljestad has written a novel, *Blind*, about a professor in sociology who is very unhappy, having left his class, his family and the local community behind. Seljestad has been criticized for painting a romantic picture of Odda and of local industrial communities in general. One of Norway's most visible younger public intellectuals, Knut Olav Åmås, who is actually from Odda himself, has presented an alternative narrative about growing up in Odda, a story about lack of tolerance towards everybody with ambitions, everybody who is 'different'. Åmås' most important refuge in his youth was Odda's public library, according to himself. There he could get glimpses of a larger world than Odda. In this still ongoing discussion one of the most interesting comments on Åmås' personal testimony came from a trade union leader and Labour politician in Odda, reminding Åmås that the unusually good library probably would not have existed, had not the local political Labour majority decided – collectively – to spend considerable resources on it!

Thoughts about Norwegian egalitarian culture are central in the texts of the internationally known Norwegian social anthropologist Marianne Gullestad (1946–2008). She is worried that our sense of equality also means that we are sceptical and negative to the new and the different. Therefore, she has suggested that, when talking about *likhet*, we should distinguish more consciously between the different meanings of the word. Marianne Gullestad finds the egalitarian heritage well worth keeping, in the sense that we should try to keep the social, economic and political inequalities as small as possible in Norway. At the same time, she underlines the need for greater tolerance of dissimilarities, especially in the face of increasing ethnic and cultural pluralism over the last 30 years or so, mainly connected with increasing immigration.

Gullestad may well be right in saying that Norway has been a small and sparsely populated country, and therefore also quite a homogeneous country, and that as a result, we are not very well adjusted to cultural pluralism. It is true that at least up to the early 1980s the majority had a rather harsh policy of cultural standardisation concerning an old ethnic minority, the Sámi people in the North. But to draw strong causal links between ideals of equality and ideals of cultural homogeneity can be too sweeping and too simple. For one thing, my own general impression from reading survey material is that those Norwegians most strongly in favour of social and economic equality are not the ones most negative to immigration and immigrants.

Even if we ignore the special problems posed by the Norwegian concept of *likhet*, we are still left with a plurality of meanings of the English word equality. It is quite common in sociology and social philosophy to distinguish between equality of opportunity, equality of treatment and the more radical concept equality of outcome or result.

Equality of opportunity means that all people should have the same formal rights in a society. This means for instance that you cannot refuse women the right to do certain jobs, or introduce different rights according to race. The general right to vote, for women as well as for men (introduced in Norway in 1913), was an important breakthrough for equality of opportunity. Still we have some exceptions to this principle. The King cannot vote, and in a more global and perhaps more serious perspective, as in other countries, many rights, for instance to public welfare, are reserved for people with national citizenship, and there are also severe restrictions against permanent residence and employment in Norway for some foreigners (though not for all).

Equality of treatment means that people in the same situation have a right to be treated equally. In Norway, the system of child benefit (*barnetrygd*) is a good example. Child benefit is distributed by the state according to the number of children, not according to whether the parents are rich or poor. Compared to most other countries, Norway has a comprehensive welfare system for redistribution. According to the sociologist Steinar Stjernø, roughly 1/4 of the Norwegian population receives welfare benefits from the welfare state at any given time. Without the redistributive mechanisms of the welfare state, over 30 % of the Norwegian population would have been poor by EU standards. This and similar universalist systems are often criticized for being unjust to the poor and very expensive for the taxpayers. They are however defended by saying that if the benefits of the welfare state are only given to a small selected group of very poor and needy, the general support for the welfare state system will soon wither away. If the middle class and the well to do have no personal gain from the welfare state, they will soon increase their stigmatization of the needy and stop supporting any system of redistribution. The United States is often used as a negative example in this connection.

I mentioned that equality of results is the most radical of these concepts of equality. As long as we practice equality of opportunity and equality of treatment, the end result may still be that people have very unequal standards of living. The classic socialist criticism of equality of opportunity is expressed in the famous French dictum: Bourgeois equality means that the King and the poor and miserable have exactly the same right to sleep under the bridges of Paris. The point is that equal formal rights and equal treatment do not imply any kind of redistribution and equalization. If equality of results is to be obtained or at least approached, society – meaning the political system and the public sector – must treat people differently, unequally. The poor should get the most economic support. Those suffering from the most painful and longest lasting diseases should have most health care. Those with the strongest cognitive handicaps should have most education. Those with linguistic, cultural and material handicaps in the Norwegian setting, for instance refugees, should have extra resources to secure their integration, and so on.

Equality of outcome – a controversial aim

Reaching the goal of equality of outcome is not necessarily a question of time and gradual improvement. Equality of outcome is a very controversial ideal, and it often collides with another principle of equality and justice, which we may call equality of achievement or performance. This principle implies that there should be a reasonable connection between what you achieve and the way you are treated. What you get should be a result of what you do yourself. Over the last 20 years or so liberalist ideas, sweeping over the whole world, have also to some extent left their mark on Norwegian ideals and politics. Consequently, equality of achievement has become a more important idea, and has to some extent marginalized ideas of radical redistribution. In this situation, maybe we should consider some old and new normative arguments for equality of outcome.

The main normative argument against an ethics of achievement, from the viewpoint of an ethics of redistribution, is of course that what you achieve is never fully your own merit. You stand on the shoulders of others, or your freedom of action is limited by other people and by structures. It is therefore ethically just to have some kind of system of redistribution in a society to compensate for such inequalities of real opportunities.

It is often said that the state can only deliver material and economic support. In order to improve meaning and a sense of purpose in people's lives, we have to rely on civil society. In a way it is of course true that we cannot solve every kind of problem by throwing money after people, but this is a dubious statement when it is presented without qualification. Quite a lot of empirical studies in the comparative sociology of welfare stress the great significance of money as a vehicle for social integration in modern society. Cash support from the state turns out to be very significant in keeping people threatened by marginalization, for instance children and parents in financial difficulties, socially and culturally integrated in mainstream society, because this financial support enables otherwise poor people to take part in everyday activities in society and thus to some extent prevents loneliness and disintegration.

Another part of current conventional liberalist wisdom tells us that help from the state creates only helplessness. This point of view can be met by counter-arguments with some empirical sociological grounding. There are some sociological studies that cast doubt on the widespread assumption among liberal economists that generous public support removes people's work motivation. A lot of social and cultural factors, some of them not unconnected with the Protestant work ethic, seem to be relevant for people's choice – provided that there is a real room for choice. Often the freedom to choose between work and unemployment is very limited, as rational choice theory tends to overlook. The risk that the welfare state may, through its generosity, create a so-called culture of dependency, is grossly exaggerated, not least in current American debates on social policy. Comparative studies of European countries show that there is no clear statistical patterned co-variation between how generous a welfare state is, and the profile of the work ethic in the same country. Norway may actually serve as an example: The country has relatively generous social insurance benefits, and at the same time a high level of work motivation. Cash transfers may therefore also be seen as a means of keeping people inside the general culture, with its traditionally high regard for achievement values.

Furthermore, small economic differences stimulate social integration and contribute to preventing social conflicts and the development of mutual stereotypes. Recent data from The European Social Survey show that people in the Nordic countries have more trust in each other – and in political institutions – than people in most other European countries. This is relevant for the issue of efficiency in society. According to the Norwegian sociologist Knud Knudsen, the Nordic countries have an important comparative advantage here, as the transactional costs of social and economic exchanges are low, because of this high level of mutual confidence.

The situation in Norway

Let us move on to a more descriptive approach. What is the situation in Norway with respect to different ideals of equality? A very short answer is that we have to a large extent equality of formal opportunity. We have to a somewhat lesser extent real equality of treatment and to a much lesser extent equality of outcome – although social and economic inequalities in general are smaller in Norway than in most other countries, in the West or globally speaking.

What about trends over time? Are we going in the direction of a colder society? This temperature metaphor is often used. We can probably interpret it in the sense that in a colder society, people are more selfish and more materialist, and that inequality becomes more widespread and also more accepted in society. Let me say at once that there is no fixed and neutral way of measuring this kind of temperature in society. As we shall see, social scientists too present different answers to the question. We have no well-developed thermometer for social life and social structures.

Let us first pay a visit to a Norwegian social scientist, Ottar Hellevik, for many years a central participant in a research project called Norwegian Monitor. This project includes representative surveys repeated over a period of close to twenty years, and with the same questions, so that comparisons over time are possible. On the basis of several answers in the surveys, Hellevik divides the Norwegian population into four categories, which in the 1980s were roughly of the same size. We have the modern materialists. They are oriented towards short-time consumption, they are enthusiastic about new technology (always first with the new cell phone), they have little sense of tradition, and they put their own welfare and interests first. Secondly, we have the modern idealists, representing equality between the sexes, anti-authoritarianism, caring, tolerance and individual self-realization. Then there are the traditional materialists, focusing upon material security and economic growth, but much more culturally conventional and traditional than the modern materialists. Hellevik's last category is the traditional idealists, committed to patriotism and traditional values, often including respect for the Christian heritage.

As most four-fold tables in sociology, these categories are ideal types, pedagogical caricatures. But Hellevik shows from his rich data material that a
surprisingly large part of the Norwegian population fits into one of the
four categories without too much friction.

A reasonable assumption would be that the poorest are the most materialistic, because they have to be concerned most with their economic situation. This is not the case, according to Hellevik. The materialists are
about as well-to-do as the idealists, but they want more, and they are also a
little less happy with their life than the idealists. The four types are quite
evenly spread out in Norway geographically, but otherwise there are some
variations. Women are more idealistic than men, and level of education
has some significance. There are relatively more modern idealists among
people with higher education, and relatively more traditional materialists
among those with less education. Young people are more modern, and a little more materialistic than older people. There is one exception here, as
the young ones are more involved in environmental and ecological questions. On the whole, the correlation between social position and value profile is not very strong, according to Hellevik.

Knud Knudsen has recently presented some results from an international survey of people's perceptions of and attitudes to economic inequality. Not surprisingly, the inhabitants of Scandinavia stand out as the
most egalitarian. They can accept a difference of two average industrial
workers' incomes as the maximum legitimate difference between high and
low status jobs. Given this way of measuring legitimate differences, Norwegians accept only half as large income differences as people in the US.
According to Knudsen's analysis men can accept more inequality than
women, the well-to-do more than the poor, and older people more than the
young ones. Some of these results seem to confirm Hellevik's analysis of
the social distribution of materialism versus idealism, while others do not.
The differences may have something to do with the fact that neither the
independent nor the dependent variables are completely identical (for
instance income versus education, attitude to economic inequality versus a
whole battery of indicators of materialism/idealism).

What about changes over time? Changes can occur in two ways: People
can change as they grow older, and new generations can enter society with
a new profile. Both mechanisms seem to be present from the 1980s until
today, according to Ottar Hellevik's analyses. He concludes that there were
more modern materialists among us around the turn of the millennium

than 15 years earlier. There are also fewer traditional idealists. The relative number of traditional materialists and modern idealists seems to have been constant in the period.

We must not interpret this too dramatically. Not all Norwegians have become modern materialists, as Knudsen's figures have shown us. But Knudsen finds a similar trend to that of Hellevik. There is an increase in the level of Norwegians' views on "legitimate inequality" from 1992 to 1999. As Hellevik defines modern materialists, the increase from 1985 until the end of the century is from about 1 out of 4 to a little under 1 out of 3. According to him the trend is clearly going in a more materialistic and in some ways selfish direction.

Other Norwegian social scientists have painted a slightly different picture. Willy Martinussen, a professor of sociology, has stated that Norway still is a society with quite a lot of care and solidarity. In several works he and his fellow researchers have stressed that egalitarian values are still more dominant in Norway than in most other Western countries. A large majority still want to reduce social inequalities. Furthermore, popular support for the welfare state is relatively stable in the Norwegian population, and this support has increased rather than weakened during the last 30 years, according to Martinussen's summing up of several surveys. However, initiatives for radical economic redistribution are much more controversial than political measures aiming at securing a minimum level of economic standard of living for everybody. It is primarily the security dimension in welfare policy that enjoys broad support in public opinion. The values of solidarity are crossed or limited by some competing values of achievement. The majority seems to say that above a minimum level of security for all, there should be a connection between what you contribute to society and what you get.

In Norway as in other Western countries we sometimes speak about the two-thirds society, a society where two thirds of the population are comfortably well off, while one third is not. A more precise description (but slightly more bothersome) would be the one-plus-eight-plus-one society. A small segment (actually probably less than one tenth) has a privileged economic situation and significant power over the country's political and economic development. At the bottom end of this class society we have another ten per cent of the population (or probably a little less) with not a very good and secure standard of living and with little power over their own situation. The large majority of eighty per cent consists of people with varying economic conditions, of course. What they have in common is that their standard of living is fairly comfortable, and they have a reasonable degree of control over their own life. Their influence on the development of society is very modest, however.

Struggling for equality – from self-interest to ethical motivations

Many analysts have pointed to a difference in the situation of the poor and marginalized between today and in the years between the two world wars, when the Labour movement and other interest groups were fighting for social reforms. Then the majority was quite poor, and they fought for their own interests. Traditionally, we associate collective solutions and solidarity with the industrial working class. Since 1972 the industrial working class in Norway has diminished. Due to an increase in part-time work, the working class has also gone through a process of fragmentation, while the middle class has increased in number, both objectively and on the level of subjective class identification. Today the majority of the population is quite well off. One consequence is that it is probably psychologically more difficult to be relatively poor when you are part of a small minority than in a situation where most people are poor. Furthermore, a political implication of the one-eight-one-society is that most people have little immediate self-interest in improving the conditions of the poorest tenth of the population, especially if the result will be increased taxes for themselves. The consequence is that reforms in a political system with a majority rule must be decided and implemented more through appeals to the majority's ethical sensibility than through appeals to short-term self-interest. So, whether you think redistributive reforms are possible in Norway depends on your optimism concerning people's potential for solidarity and altruism.

Towards new forms of inequality?

Some say that all kinds of talk about class societies are obsolete, or that new class divisions have replaced the old ones. Today we can sometimes read in the papers that the new divisions in society go between those with and those without higher education, or between those with or without

Industrial magnate Kjell Inge Røkke is one of the richest persons in Norway and an example of a capitalist who is not afraid of displaying his wealth. His holiday home in Oppdal (south of Trondheim) has been used as an example of "conspicuous consumption".

access to the internet. However, I think a good many sociologists will agree with me that both education and internet competence tend to follow old class divisions, based primarily on what kind of work situation you are in.

There is a need for certain nuances in the class analysis of modern Western countries like Norway, though. A well-known Norwegian media personality for nearly ten years has been the industrial leader Kjell Inge Røkke. A former fisherman with little formal education, he now owns large companies, he is immensely rich, and he is often in the media displaying what the Norwegian-American sociologist Thorsten Veblen over a hundred years ago called conspicuous consumption. Røkke drives fast cars and large boats, dates rich and beautiful women and has a number of countryside estates, one of them reportedly with over 30 bathrooms and with a living-room so big and long that a popular joke is that you can trace the curve of the earth's surface indoors.

For some, Kjell Inge Røkke is a symbol of the development in Norway towards greater acceptance of showing that you are rich. The historian and left-wing political leader Berge Furre, now approaching the age of 70, recently said in a newspaper interview that when he grew up, it was not considered decent to show your wealth, while today you are admired for displaying how rich you are. Maybe Røkke also is enjoying some credit for living up to the Ashlad myth from ancient Norwegian fairy-tales, a happy-go-lucky person with considerable upward, social mobility. But it is also interesting to note that several popular reactions to Røkke and other conspicuous consumers vary from laughter to moral indignation. Max Weber noted that to be financially well off did not mean that you had high cultural prestige in society. He pointed to the difficulties of *les nouveaux riches* in gaining acceptance and being included in the established cultural and economic elite. In a more systematic way the sociologist Pierre Bourdieu has constructed an analytical framework with two core concepts. In addition to economic capital, meaning more or less the same as in the Marxist tradition, Bourdieu also uses the concept of cultural capital. By cultural capital Bourdieu means knowledge and competence from the formal educational system, cultural competence of a more informal kind that you have to be socialized into more or less from your birth, and thirdly good, smooth communication skills in your segment of society.

The standards of cultural capital, and accordingly the hierarchy, are probably much more visible and fixed in Bourdieu's home country, France, than in the more culturally democratized Norway. But his analytical framework is no doubt relevant in Norway as well. According to Bourdieu, in the private sector the elite group tend to have much economic capital and little cultural capital. It is the other way around in the public sector elite. Some years ago a Norwegian newspaper columnist raised the very blunt question: Why are Norwegian business leaders so foolish and uncultured? There may be good reasons for posing that question, but it certainly also tells a tale about some cultural power struggles and antagonisms in Norwegian society, struggles between different elites, in Bourdieu's terms. One of the more curious expressions of these tensions is a daily column in a large newspaper directed towards the business sector, *Dagens Næringsliv*. Every day a journalist calls a business leader, asking which books he has on his (more seldom her) bedside table. And almost every day the answer is very short, usually because there are no books there, at least no fiction.

This presentation of tensions between cultural and business elites has taken us a long way from more basic, material inequalities. Therefore it should be added that as a main rule, there is often still in Norway as elsewhere a concentration of economic, political and cultural privileges and power in society. The main exception to this rule is to be found in political life. The development of the Norwegian welfare state is an illustration that in a liberal, democratic society, the number of people and their ability to organize themselves for common causes can be a stronger and more decisive power than economic power in the hands of a minority.

A short conclusion

Before this rather sweeping journey comes to an end: Norway has been characterized by more equal patterns of distribution and a more egalitarian popular opinion than most other Western countries. The reasons for this are probably manifold: a sparsely populated country has created a necessity for co-operation and close networks among people. The topography of the country has made it difficult to build up great fortunes in the past. A strong egalitarian and ascetic value system is connected both with strict low-church revivalist movements and with a strong labour movement. The *bedehus* (prayer-houses) and *Folkets Hus* (the labour movement house) in many local communities have both been expressions of egalitarian cultures, and they have also strengthened this cultural trait.

Today these egalitarian traditions are challenged and to some extent weakened by global structural and ideological forces, aptly named globalization, capitalism, liberalism and individualism. We are not that special in Norway; to say that would be to nurture stereotypes. Nevertheless, according to statistics and surveys, still quite a lot of the old egalitarianism remains in this country. So listen carefully, Odd Børretzen, the spirit of Einar Gerhardsen may still be around. What the future will bring is not for a sociologist to predict. We should stick to interpreting the past and the present. That may be difficult enough in itself.

Chapter 11

Minorities in Norway – Past and Present

By Eva Maagerø and Birte Simonsen

Norway for Norwegians! Unfortunately it is possible to find graffiti like this painted on walls in Norway. Generally, it is believed that extreme right wing groups are the culprits, which is probably true. But what can be said about the more silent attitudes among the rest of the people? Is it true if we present Norway as an open and friendly country? The answer will differ according to the perspective of those replying. Probably people belonging to the majority would answer yes, while people belonging to minorities would feel more in doubt. In official documents, there is a significant development towards a better understanding of multiculturalism, but in practice it still seems to be difficult to put these good intentions into practice.

This chapter tells the story of how Norwegian society has met and meets people who do not belong to the majority, both from inside and outside Norway.

Including strategies

In the behaviour of the majority towards minority groups we can identify different strategies. The three main strategies are: *assimilation, integration* and *ghetto building* (or *segregation*). These concepts require clarification:

The Latin word *assimilation* means to make similar. The notion is borrowed from biology, from the theory of photosynthesis. Socially and politically, this strategy implies that there is a dominant norm for people to follow in order to be accepted as a member of a given society, and this strategy therefore signals that some people have to change to be like the main group.

Integration has its origin from Latin too. *Integer* means untouched or whole. This strategy differs from assimilation by stating that society consists of different, equal groups who are supposed to live together in mutual respect. In an integrated society, diversity and multiculturalism are viewed as positive and stimulating.

The term *ghetto* was first used to refer to the special Jewish quarters in European cities. However, it now commonly labels an urban area where people from a specific ethnic background live together as a group, e.g. "China Town". Ghettoes can be viewed from different perspectives. Initiated by the majority group they can be a way of excluding other people. But sometimes they can also be preferred by the group itself. If people fear they may lose their identity, they feel safer if they are physically close to people with the same background. The other word used to describe the same strategy, segregation, means that something is split.

These strategies can be found both in Norwegian history and in the present day situation. As we shall see, the official policy in Norway has moved from assimilation to integration, while other European countries, e.g. France, still follow a strict policy of assimilation. French law, which does not allow the use of the hijab (the traditional scarf) in schools, would not be a realistic, political project in Norway, because of the ideal of integration.

From assimilation to integration

Texts written about Norway in the decades before and after World War II often present Norway as a mono-cultural society. In retrospect, it is obvious that this was a political programme more than a description of reality. The founders of the modern social democratic state seemed to prefer that the inhabitants were identified as *Norwegians* and nothing else. Later history and analysis show a more diverse picture. The story of the forced assimilation of the Sámi people and different national minorities is a black spot in Norwegian history. Consequently, in recent decades, much effort has been made to underline the change to an official integrative attitude. The present-day viewpoint is that it is important to build bridges, not barriers. But while this is easy to say, it is more difficult to implement. There seems to be the problem that when active assimilation stops, total invisibility may be the result. There is no longer any direct oppression, but there is no real participation and power yet either.

What caused the change from a policy of assimilation to a policy of integration? To generalize, the sixties and the seventies were decades of political radicalism; the students' revolt, the protests against the Vietnam war, the hippie era, the fight for women's liberation, and the campaign for nuclear disarmament. To sum up this period, it can be characterised by words such as protest and solidarity. As a consequence, diversity and consciousness of people's origin became more natural, even an ideal.

Minority and majority as basic concepts

The notions *minority* and *majority* have been used several times already, but they require elaboration. *Minor* is Latin and means less, while *major* means bigger. In the first place they are neutral words, just saying something about size or numbers. But in a social perspective, these words also contain dimensions of power and position.

When a majority oppresses minorities, the oppression may take place in the fields of language, religion, educational opportunities and culture. We will present the following three minority groups within Norwegian society:

- Indigenous people
- National minorities
- Cultural and language minorities

The world's indigenous people

Indigenous people are sometimes referred to as *native people* or *first people*, indicating that they have lived in a certain area prior to colonization by outsiders. Since 1982 the United Nations has developed international standards for the treatment and rights of such people. Indigenous groups are protected by ILO Convention no.169, which was ratified by the Norwegian Government on June 20th 1990. This was a turning point for the Sámi population, the only group in Norway to have indigenous status. Indigenous people elsewhere include the Aborigines in Australia, Indians in America, Inuits in the Arctic region and Maoris in New Zealand.

The decade from 1994 to 2004 was named The International Decade for Indigenous People by the United Nations. During this period work connected to the protection of rights, ownership of land and development of education was emphasised, which has resulted in a significant increase in the self-esteem of the people involved. In late December 2004, the General Assembly of the United Nations proclaimed a Second International Decade of the World's Indigenous People. The main goal of the current decade will be to strengthen international cooperation in resolving problems faced by indigenous people in areas such as culture, education, health, human rights, the environment, and social and economic development.

Many indigenous populations are dependent on hunting, fishing and natural food gathering. These are not only additional ways of getting food in an economically sustainable way; they are far more a platform for cultural and social identity. Therefore we will find national discussions and conflicts connected to almost every indigenous group in the world. One organisation, Arctic Climate Impact Assessment (ACIA), works especially with the consequences of modern life style for the indigenous people in the northern areas of the globe.

Sámi people – the Norwegian indigenous people

The Sámi population is in fact one "nation" living in four countries: Norway, Sweden, Finland, and Russia. The people had settled in this region before the national borders of Scandinavia were fixed. The size of the Sámi population in Norway is 30–50,000, with the greatest numbers in Finmark (in the north of Norway) and in Oslo. Within the population language, culture and life style will differ. Even though those that move around with their reindeer (flyttsamer = moving Sámi) tend to dominate as a prototype and a symbol, the picture is much more diverse.

A brief look backwards

The assimilation policy in Norway, both before WWII and in the 1950s and 1960s caused many difficulties for the Sámi people. Children were only allowed to use Norwegian as their school language, and it was forbidden to present the Sámi culture through songs, religious acts, fairytales and clothes. Their natural life style was interfered with by laws being passed, and the Norwegian majority controlled much of their land. As a consequence of this bad treatment, many Sámis still want to "forget" the past and hide their origins.

The Sámi parliament

In 1989 a special Sámi Parliament (*Sámediggi*) was established. 39 representatives from different parties and groups meet in the parliament building in Karasjok. Elections are held at the same time as for the Norwegian national assembly, *the Storting*. A president is in charge. The parliament handles special issues relating to the interests of the Sámis. Special rules apply in order to be registered as a Sámi, but they are not very exclusive. In the end it is enough to "feel like a Sámi". The purpose of this broad definition is to encourage the younger generation to participate even if their families have been hesitant to show their origin. The number of people who vote in the parliament elections is increasing. During the last election, in 2003, 10,000 people voted. The effect of the Sámi having their own parliament has been discussed, since the *Storting* still is looked upon as the *real* parliament. There is no doubt, however, that for the Sámis, the parliament and the administration connected to it, have a great symbolic effect. Finland and Sweden also have Sámi parliaments similar to the Norwegian one.

National day, national song and flag

Since 1993, February 6th has been national day for all Sámi people. This particular day has been chosen in order to commemorate a historical event; the first Sámi meeting in Trondheim in 1917. For the first time Sámi people from different countries came together to discuss common affairs. At a conference in Sweden in 1986, a song written by Isak Saba in 1906 became the official Sámi "national" anthem.

1986 was also the year when the Sámi flag was created. The colours in the flag are blue, red yellow and green, inspired by the Sámi costumes. A circle in the middle represents the sun and the moon, because an old poem states that Sámis are sons and daughters of the sun and the moon. The artist Astrid Båhl designed the flag, and it is used especially on February 6th and August 9th, when the parliament session is opened.

This indicates that there are two official flags in Norway. It is however interesting and a bit depressing that there still are some tensions between the Norwegian majority and the Sámi minority. In 2005 the question was raised whether the 17th of May procession in Oslo only should have traditional Norwegian flags in red, white and blue.

In the Norwegian government there seems to be greater sympathy for indigenous people abroad than for the group inside Norway itself. The leader of SAIH (Norwegian Students and Academics International Assistance Fund), Kathrine Sund, in April 2005 criticized teacher education and the school system for not taking into account that Norway has an indigenous group inside its borders. The power of assimilation has come to an end, but invisibility is also a kind of power, she writes. She points out that few children in Norway are aware of the fact that their country has *three* official languages (*bokmål, nynorsk* and *Sámi*) and that most Sámi people live in Oslo without reindeer.

An important turning point: "The Alta affair"

In 1978, when the national parliament in Norway decided to build a big dam in the river Alta in Finmark, many people protested and demonstrations were arranged at the actual scene in Alta, in front of the *Storting* and in the streets of Oslo. This was a turning point in the Norwegian majority's understanding of the situation and the position of Sámis. The fight against the building of the dam did not succeed. The project was realised in a smaller scale, but in a way the new, growing consciousness was a victory in itself.

The interest of the Norwegian government conflicted with those of the Sámi population in connection with the development of a huge dam in the Alta river. The Sámis wanted control of the pastures for their reindeer, while the government needed cheap hydro-electric power. Here is a group of Sámis during a hunger-strike (sultestreik) outside the Storting in 1979.

Upbringing and socialisation in a Sámi context

Today the differences between Sámi and Norwegian family life are not very big. People in Sámi districts have the same access to media as people in other parts of Norway, and their houses have the same facilities. But if we go only a couple of generations back, there were not many similarities between them. While an upbringing in urban areas was connected to social norms and good behaviour, the upbringing of Sámi children concentrated on survival. With winter temperatures down to minus 40° C, it was necessary for the children to learn quickly from the adults how to adjust to the harsh environment. But this did not mean that they missed out on childhood. In spite of the hard natural conditions, playing was an important element in their socialisation process. The content and the character of the games however, were inspired by the adult life they would live later, closely connected to real life.

Anton Hoëm(1978) describes the Sámi society as rural and simple, in contrast to an urban and more complex society. The Danish painter and anthropologist Emilie Demant-Hatt (1913) visited several Sámi families about hundred years ago. She describes the children as having both freedom and rights, but she did not notice any direct upbringing, like being told how to behave. It seemed that Sámi parents did not punish their children either. Demantt-Hatt described the relationship between parents and children as a sort of equality – a mutual respect. In a theoretical perspective this could be called situated learning, or indirect upbringing. The parents functioned as models, and the children were very much aware of how important it was to imitate them. But this freedom and equality were not absolute. There was a strong social control you could not avoid. It was a "we-society", ruled by the parents' and grandparents' natural authority.

Asta Balto(1997) points out that there were significant differences between boys and girls in the upbringing situation. They were both offered the same freedom and close contact with parents' work. But they were normally trained in different skills. Girls were kept near the house or the *lavvo* as participants in cooking and handicrafts, while boys were hunting, making tools and taking care of the reindeer. The women had a strong position, because their activities were as necessary as the men's for the survival of the family.

School could be a challenge

In the Sámi societies, school did not normally have first priority. Working and being able to master nature was seen as the most important. The children were used to taking care of themselves and coping, while the parents were concerned when sending them to boarding schools that they would forget important skills. The government, on the other hand, wanted to convert the "undomesticated" Sámi children to Norwegian "standards". The freedom and lack of direct training in respecting social rules were often a problem, and the shift of context and culture in school made the children feel unsure. Consequently they often reacted by being too noisy or too quiet. It did not help knowing a lot of different words for reindeer! The situation for the teachers was of course difficult too. Only a few of them were able to understand the Sámi language, and they also lacked knowledge about the culture. One of the cultural differences that certainly must have created problems is the Sámi way of dealing with *time. Time is a ship that never casts anchor*, according to a Sámi proverb. Time and nature are closely connected. Time does not pass by, time comes, as the saying went. It is like the cycles of nature. The hours and minutes and seconds are not significant; you have to take the whole situation into account. In the summer when there was sunshine all night, the children were used to sleeping when they wanted to, and even to playing in the middle of the night.

Curricular reform

The ratification of the Indigenous People's Convention had important consequences for the Norwegian school system. The school reforms of 1997 and 2006 have special editions for the Sámi schools and classes. Since 1989 it has also been possible to train as a teacher in Kautokeino, at the smallest state-run institution of higher education in Norway, with a student capacity of about 300. The college has developed a series of courses specifically adapted to Sámi students, which can be taken either as part of teacher training or as post-teacher training.

Not many countries in the world have a school subject called *reindeer husbandry*. As a nation with indigenous people living inside its borders, the Norwegian parliament has to provide content in the curriculum that strengthens the Sámi identity and at the same time develops knowledge and understanding among the Norwegian pupils, a so-called Sámi dimension. The typical handicraft *doudji*, and the traditional Sámi song style *joik*, must according to the curriculum, be familiar to all Norwegian children.

Traditional yet modern

All traditional cultures in the world are threatened by urbanisation and the ideal of individuality. The collective societies (we-societies) are often seen as old fashioned, and the younger generation reject the values of their ancestors. Older people among the Sámi complain that their grandchildren lack important life skills. The sustainable way of living by using all resources is not necessary today, but that does not mean that it should be abandoned. The Rio Declaration establishes that indigenous peoples and their societies play a vital role in the management and development of the environment, due to their knowledge and traditional practices. In Norway this perspective is promoted through a special Sámi LA 21 project. The project has raised the Sámi Parliament's aspirations in the sphere of environmental protection policies, and the government will take the Sámi perspectives into account in its future processes and efforts for sustainable development.

Sámi culture all over the world

The indigenous cultures influence all kinds of art, all over the world. Amerind culture has, over a long period, been a part of modern music and art. But also Sámi artists have been well known. Mari Boine became famous all over the world when she presented her album *Gula Gula* – about what our mothers tell us. The author Nils Aslak Valkeapää describes in *Vindens veier* (The ways of the wind), from 1990, how man, nature and culture are linked together in his culture. Perhaps the most significant Sámi artist today is Nils Gaup. Many people have seen his film *Veiviseren* (Pathfinder), and even more people will go to the cinema to see another of his films, *The Kautokeino Revolt*, from 2007. To allow all kinds of indigenous peoples to meet, many festivals are arranged. One of them is located in Kåfjord in the north of Norway every year, kalled *Riddu Riddu*.

National minorities

Not only indigenous people were victims of assimilation processes. The increased awareness of origin and identity all over the world made more injustice to minority groups visible as well. The concept, *national minority*, was established to express this reality. We find examples of oppressed groups in many other countries in Europe; the most obvious is the treatment of "Gipsies", officially called Rom people.

International agreements

The EU Parliament has passed resolutions on a lot of programmes, both educational and social, to support national minorities. In Norway this has also been a field of priority in the latest national research programme. The European Council drew up a framework convention in 1998 to protect national minorities. The main operative part in the convention is section II, containing specific principles on a wide range of issues, including : the prohibition of forced assimilation; the promotion of the conditions relating to the preservation and development of the culture and the preservation of religion, language and traditions; access to and use of the media; the use of the minority language in private and in public as well as its use in connection with administrative authorities; the use of one's own name; topographical names in the minority language; learning of and instruction in the minority language.

The Framework Convention also draws attention to the Convention of the Rights of the Children, article 30: *In those States in which ethnic, religious or linguistic minorities or persons of indigenous origin exist, a child belonging to such a minority or who is indigenous shall not be denied the right, in community with other members of his or her group, to enjoy his or her own culture, to profess and practise his or her own religion, or to use his or her own language.*

The Norwegian national minorities

In Norway there is great pride connected to the signing of our first national constitution in 1814. Every year, the 17th of May is celebrated to remember this event when we severed the connection to Denmark after 400 years of colonization. But from a minority perspective, there has been no reason to celebrate. The Constitution declared that Romany people, foreign beggars, monks, Jesuits and Jews were *persona non grata* in Norway. These paragraphs in the law were not used very actively, and they have gradually disappeared. The so-called "Jew paragraph" prohibiting Jews to immigrate was abolished in 1851.

According to the European Framework Convention, Norway has five main national minority groups:

- Romany (travellers, in Norwegian *Tatere*)

- Roma (gipsies)

- *Skogfinner* ("Forest-Finns" – a population of Finnish origin, who settled in the eastern part of Norway near the border to Sweden

- Kvener (population in the north of Norway, also of Finnish origin)

- Jews

These groups have different historical backgrounds. However, what they have in common is that, because of language, religion or culture, they have needs which differ from those of the majority population in Norway.

An example of a national minority

Let us consider Romany people as an example. Up to the 1950s they travelled from place to place by means of horses and boats, doing jobs where ever they could. The government did not support their lifestyle, and about 1950 government officials started to take their horses away from them, split the families and send the children to special institutions. A lot of women were sterilised in an attempt to stop the population from growing. New historical documents have given us more knowledge about this dark period. At present, members of this group are doing a lot of work to raise the self-esteem of this minority group. For example, they have home pages on the Internet where people can try to trace their familiy roots. Also, there is a museum, Glomdalsmuseet, that has a special department showing the history of this people.

Why were minorities treated like this? Were Norway and other European countries ruled by cruel politicians? Political documents from the same period show another side of the story. The work is often mentioned as a *hygienic* project. The intention was to "save" these people and to help them to be a part of modern society. However, in spite of good intentions, the project was morally wrong. Norwegian politicians have realised this, and the official approach is now to apologise.

Development in educational issues

The languages of the national minority groups have not been accepted in the school system in Norway. But things are changing. Whenever practically possible, families can choose their minority language as their first language. To meet these needs, some teacher education institutions in the north of Norway offer courses, for example, in *kvensk* language.

Cultural and language minorities

The third group belonging to *minorities* in Norway is more diverse than the two previously mentioned. This group consists of immigrants from all over the world. Some of them need more support and adjustment than others, since this category also includes Danish and Swedish immigration, people with a very similar language and culture to the Norwegian population. Normally *real* immigration in Norway is said to have started around 1970. Of course people had moved to Norway before this, but after 1970 the number of immigrants and refugees increased, and the situation and the challenges became clear for the political authorities. In the 1970s there was a demand for workers in Norway, and the borders were open for *guest workers*, mostly from Pakistan and India. First of all it was family fathers that came, and then wifes and children often followed.

Immigration stop

But soon attitudes changed. There was a fear that too many would choose Norway as their new home country, and that the number of immigrants would be too high. The politicians therefore decided in favour of an *Immigration stop* in 1975. But this did not mean that the borders were totally closed; refugees, asylum-seekers and family members could still apply for visas in accordance with international rules. So, despite the immigration stop, the number of immigrants increased every year. In addition, as a member of the European Economic Area (EEA), Norway now has a new type of guest worker arriving. People from the EU countries, especially after the most recent enlargement, use the free labour market to find jobs here. This situation raises new types of inclusion questions, for example the right to have the same salary as Norwegians.

Integration in schools

Teachers play an important role in achieving integration. However, there seem to be different positions on the matter among the teachers. The important question is how they view the situation of having different nationalities and different languages in their classrooms. Some will look upon it as a problem, some as a challenge, and some as a real enrichment. Probably the last group create the most interesting educational situation, both for minority and majority students – and for themselves as teachers.

Marie Louise Seeberg shows, in a comparative study between a school in the Netherlands and a school in Norway, that Norwegian teachers seem to be less flexible than their colleagues in the Netherlands when it comes to including foreigners in the classroom. Perhaps one explanation can be that the multicultural situation does not have a very long tradition in Norway. Starting from 1970, the main developments in multicultural classrooms may be described as follows:

- 1970-1980: "The novice period". Teachers were slightly shocked by the situation, and the tendency was to choose one of the following solutions: either immigrant children were kept by themselves in special rooms, or they were just left to sit in the class room listening to a language that they did not understand.

- 1980-1990: The immigrants' "problem" was defined as foreigners not knowing the Norwegian language. Consequently, they were taught outside the classroom until the "problem" was solved, and they could master the language well enough to follow the lessons. The question was how long this would take.

- After 1990: The perspective has changed slightly in the sense that diversity is now looked upon more as a resource and not only as a problem. The value of the mother tongue has become more visible. But in parallel with a more skilled teacher attitude, society has turned in a more neoliberal direction, where "soft" values are on the wane. New international tests also seem to create new challenges for integration.

The rights

The normal principle of suitably adapted education for each child also gives certain rights to the students from language minorities. L 97 states that: *In order to meet pupils' different backgrounds and abilities, the school for all must be an inclusive community with room for everyone. The diversity of backgrounds, interests and abilities must be met with a diversity of challenges. Suitably adapted education is a necessary and prominent principle in the compulsory school.* As a consequence the students with a mother tongue other than Norwegian have the right to be taught their mother tongue and the right to have Norwegian as a second language. In paragraph 2.8 of the Education Act, the right to special training is stated: *The Ministry issues regulations concerning the obligation of municipalities to provide special tuition for pupils from language minorities.* The official definition of a minority student in Norway is: *Students in primary and secondary school, who do not have Sámi or Norwegian language as their mother tongue, and who do not learn Norwegian before they have contact with society outside the family.* But in spite of all these formal rights, it is obvious that minority pupils often fail in the educational system compared to ethnic Norwegian pupils.

The challenges connected to the national and international tests can easily result in a new type of exclusion and stigmatisation. When school heads try to find explanations for the low ranking of their schools' results, the temptation to blame minority children is obvious. Lovleen Kumar Brenna, Indian born and leader of the national parents' organisation, has warned strongly about this. She should be listened to for at least two reasons. Firstly, there is no research giving evidence to support the claim that immigrants lower a school's educational level. Secondly, such a focus will make the integration process go more slowly.

Schools do not become multicultural just by using flags from different countries and by serving exotic food now and then. In an attempt to give schools some help in their integration efforts, a national centre, NAFO, has been established at Oslo University College. The sole mission of the centre is to take care of multicultural issues in schools. In an integrated society it is not only the duty of minorities to change. The majority population has to adjust as well. Ann Magritt Hauge, the leader of NAFO, argues in favour of describing schools as being *common cultural* rather than *multicultural*, because the diversity and the mixture of cultures create something quite new, a new diverse culture. A really integrated school, according to Hauge, should not make differences between the majority and minorities by talking about *us* and *them*.

Table 11.1   Attitudes, 2002–2004

Attitudes towards immigrants and immigration, in percentages		
Statement	Agree	Disagree
Most immigrants make an important contribution to the Norwegian work life	66	24
Most immigrants abuse the system of social benefits	40	48
Most immigrants enrich the cultural life in Norway	70	21
Most immigrants represent a source of insecurity in society	45	44
All immigrants should have the same opportunity to have a job as Norwegians	83	13
Immigrants should make an effort to become as simiar to Norwegians as possible	54	39

Source: www.ssb.no/english

What is real integration?

Shabana Rehman, a Norwegian stand-up comedian (originally from Pakistan), replied once in an interview that she only feels totally integrated when she wears a red anorak, sitting in an outdoor dry toilet with no running water, located near a cabin up somewhere in the mountains. If this is to be described as being a true Norwegian value, it certainly will cause alienation. Most Norwegians never use an outside dry toilet.

Marianne Gullestad (1946–2008), a Norwegian anthropologist, has written a book where she pointed out that Norwegians still seem to suffer from a sort of xenophobia (fear of the unknown) and that there is an obvious lack of reflectivity in the way people meet changes in the population structure. She analysed the ongoing official debate, and she found a lack of reflection in all groups of society, not only among right wing politicians, but even among researchers in social sciences.

Gullestad wanted to challenge what she called "the national order" and to redefine what *Norwegian* should mean today. She wanted to make it possible for many opinions to be heard and many perspectives to be considered. In a modern society it is more relevant to talk about the many small truths than about the one big truth.

Chapter 12

Trends in the Development of Norwegian Childhood

By Ann Christin E. Nilsen

How to raise children is an important question in all societies. Every community has certain values and norms that are passed on from one generation to the next, usually in a slightly altered form. Impressions of "well raised" and "badly raised" children exist, and these impressions are based on the extent to which a child behaves according to what is expected.

In spite of the contemporary demographic picture in Norway, which shows a declining portion of young people compared to the middle-aged and the elderly, children and young people form a relatively powerful group. Their needs, opinions and ways of life are acknowledged and often taken into consideration in policymaking. As a consequence, it has been claimed that we live in a society that favours youth for age. It is a recurring topic in the public debate in Norway whether today's children are spoilt and ignorant or reflective and self-aware.

In this chapter I will discuss the role of children in contemporary Norwegian society from a social scientific perspective. The intention is to give the reader an insight into some important tendencies and discourses that contribute to the construction of present-day childhood in Norway. Which different values and ideas about childhood prevail? How do different societal conditions have an impact on how the child's role is regarded? And in which ways does this context have an influence on how Norwegian children are being socialized?

The relativity of childhood

The idea of childhood is something that we rarely question. People in a society tend to have a shared knowledge about the concept of childhood, both in a biological, judicial and social sense. Children can easily be distinguished from adults based on criteria such as physical appearance and behaviour. Furthermore, in most societies children have specific rights and duties that are not identical to those of adults, and these norms are determinant of what is expected from children. The norms, however, vary according to the values and attitudes that predominate in the society in question. The child's role can therefore be considered as a product of the expectations of the surroundings – how the surroundings value certain forms of behaviour, and reject others. In other words, what is regarded as appropriate child behaviour depends on the context, the surroundings in which this behaviour is being acted out. As a result, the idea of childhood as a phenomenon is relative to time and context.

The French historian Philippe Ariès depicts how the concept of childhood has developed in history; from the medieval idea of children as "minor adults", who could take part in the same activities as adults and be exposed to the same reality as adults in terms of work, family life and even sexuality; to the idea of children as "incomplete" human beings, in need of education and upbringing, which developed in the Renaissance; and to the most recent idea of children as equals to adults, characteristic of the modern era. Thus, the present understanding of the uniqueness of children is the result of a long process in which the idea of childhood has been negotiated. Studies on childhood in different cultural contexts show a similar variety. In a study of children in a rural Zimbabwean village, Pamela Reynolds illustrates the different notion of children and adults with reference to burial rituals. In the society studied deceased children were buried further away from the village than adults, indicating their belonging to the "wild" in contrast to the adults belonging to the "domestic". Although less explicit, similar notions about children occur in modern Norwegian society as well, under headings such as "the mysterious people" or "child nature". The most recent turn in the debate on the role of children, however, is towards a greater focus on children's innate competence, which I will return to later.

In the following section I will focus on some characteristics of the Norwegian context and the impact of this context on the perception of childhood.

How much time do parents spend together with their children (hours pr. week)?			
	Women	Men	Total
Norway	24,1	15,1	39,2
Netherlands	25,2	9,2	34,4
Denmark	13,1	7,3	20,4
Italy	13,2	5,3	18,5
Great Britain	14,3	3,9	18,2
Poland	13,4	4,7	18,1
France	13,1	4,5	17,6
Austria	12,5	3,3	15,8
Finland	8,9	4,8	13,6
Sweden	8,0	5,1	13,2
Spain	9,5	1,8	11,4
Germany	6,9	2,5	9,3

Source: European Working Conditions Survey

What characterizes the Norwegian context?

Contemporary Norwegian society is often defined as a modern society (although some thinkers claim that we have entered an era of post-modernism). The concept of modernity refers to a specific era of time, and the ideas and values that are predominant in this era. Modernity is often understood as the result of a process of modernization, and is linked to the development which has taken place in most western societies since the beginning of industrialization, and which is still taking place. The modernization process in Norway accelerated in the 1950s with the rebuilding of the country after World War II, and the development is still in progress.

Values and ideas that are connected to modernity include a strong belief in industrialization and technological progress, a decline in the adherence to religion and religious practices, and an increased focus on the individual and on individual rights. In other words, the introduction of modernity marks the end of more traditional ways of life, characterized by a stronger sense of belonging to a specific social group (e.g. the family), a more hierarchical organization of social institutions, and a stronger emphasis on religion and tradition. Integral in this process is an increased awareness of the importance of knowledge and competence, as society demands more from the individual as an independent social actor. The future becomes less determined, which leaves more open to the individual's choice. Thus, modern society is accordingly often referred to as the "knowledge society".

One of the most apparent features of the modern society is individualization, the increasing awareness of individual rights and possibilities. This tendency, which in its very essence distinguishes modern societies from more traditional ones, is also referred to by some thinkers as individuation. This concept implies that the individual is regarded as an independent unit who can claim certain rights and responsibilities as a member of society, regardless of social situation. This applies to children too. In other words, researchers and politicians share an interest in studying children and children's lives independently. This marks a change from former policymaking where the well-being of the child was considered to depend more on the functioning of the child's closest network of family and kin. Still, family and social networks are considered to be the major benefactor to the child, and concepts such as "family policy" and "family studies" are consequently still widely used with reference to children. However, in addition to this there is a stronger child orientation in both research and policymaking. This implies that the social position of the child is being reconstructed.

With the world's first ombudsman for children, a spokesperson for children's rights and welfare, Norway has gained international recognition for its focus on children. And Norway places itself as one of the most child-centered societies in the world. *The World Values Survey*, which among other things collects data from countries all over the world on values related to socialization and family affairs, shows that Norwegian parents are far more likely to provide their children with help and support than to assist their own parents. Compared to countries in other regions of the world, the Norwegian respondents differ greatly in this respect. One explanation may lie within the expectations of the welfare state when it comes to caring for the elderly. Today the welfare state has taken over many of the functions that formerly used to be in the hands of close family, such as care for the elderly population. Other welfare arrangements, such as universal child benefit, paid leave and cash benefit for parents who stay at home with children under 3 years of age, contribute to promoting this child-centeredness. As a consequence, there is a strong tendency for Norwegian parents to prioritize children. This can be illustrated by the birthrate, which compared to other European countries is high, at 1.83 in 2004. The fact that the educational level of Norwegian women is high in spite of this birthrate indicates good welfare arrangements that allow women to choose both to extend their family and to have a professional career.

Child-centeredness is in other words a distinct trait of contemporary Norwegian society. Another trait worth commenting on deals with changes in the life-phase formerly defined as childhood, and which can be grasped in the concept of the "knowledge society". As this label indicates education is vital in modern society. Within one generation the "educational wave" has brought about significant changes in people's life-course in most western societies. The period during which the main activity is learning has extended at both ends, with high enrolment rates both in kindergarten and at university. Children today start their educational careers at a younger age than ever before, and remain learners for a longer time. It is often claimed that childhood as a life phase is being shortened, while adolescence is being extended. Whereas childhood formerly referred to the life phase before adulthood, people today identify an intermediate life phase, known as adolescence or youth. With the introduction of adolescence as a separate life phase childhood has a shorter duration. Early exposure to the adult world through media and commercial marketing is often considered to contribute to this shortening of childhood. However, media and commercial marketing may also be regarded as important ingredients in contemporary childhood, and as such essential in the construction of childhood.

The question of interest here is how these tendencies are reflected in the understanding of childhood and contribute to influencing the socialization goals – the values and ideas that are favoured in the upbringing of children. I will devote my attention to this question in the following.

Trends in Norwegian socialization goals

Within social sciences socialization refers to the process whereby the individual becomes part of society by learning and adapting to the norms and values that are predominant in the given society. It is commonly understood that socialization goals are products of the ideology that predominates in the context. Some researchers consequently explore variations in socialization goals with reference to gender and cultural context.

Three concepts are particularly relevant for a discussion of contemporary Norwegian childhood and socialization; professionalization, democratization and institutionalization. I will base my discussion on these concepts.

Professionalization

Professionalization refers to a process that has accelerated in recent years, and deals with a change in the parental role. The concept is also used with reference to the increased presence of professionals in children's daily lives, a tendency which I will return to later. With reference to parents the concept suggests a more professional approach to the parental role, and it implicitly challenges the idea of parenting as a competence you gain by doing, a competence that most people are disposed to and have the potential to develop. The recent growth in the market for handbooks on parenting and increasing media coverage of parent-child relationships indicate that there is a substantial readiness among Norwegian parents to approach child rearing more professionally. The media, which weekly devote large quantities of columns and time to the latest advice in child rearing and child welfare, can serve as an illustration. Parenting has in other words become an activity that demands certain skills and knowledge which has to be learnt through other means than experimenting, or "trial and error". As a consequence children interact with adult caregivers who are skilled, conscious of and even strategic- minded about the way in which they parent. This professionalization of the parental role is connected to the modern, liberal development that allows adults to choose whether, when and how they want to become parents. Having a child is in most cases a planned and well-considered event.

As children and parents have complementary roles, a change in the parental role consequently involves a change in the child's role. The question of interest, then, is why do parents have to be professional. The complementary answer of the question is because the children are. One may of course object to the concept of professional children, as it is not a matter of professional skills. However, some researchers have introduced concepts such as "the competent child" or "the dialogical child", indicating that children have an innate social competence that extends former images of the child as a "tabula rasa" that can be formed and raised to fit into a given context. As a consequence children are on the one hand allowed to play out their personalities to a larger extent, while on the other hand children are met with higher expectations. The implication is that the parent and the child interact on more equal terms. This leads us to the concept of *democratization*.

Democatization

The modern family is often described as a symmetrical family consisting of equal and autonomous members. The most common family unit is the nuclear family, consisting of a mother, a father and children. However, as a consequence of the increasing number of family break- ups new family structures are emerging. Data from Statistics Norway show that in 2004 75 % of children lived with both parents, where the great majority of the parents (60 %) were married. 20 % of children lived in a single-parent household (where 17 % were headed by the mother), whereas the remaining 5 % of children lived with one biological parent and a step-parent. In 2003 more than 20 000 children witnessed their parents' separation. Although the short-term consequences of family break-ups for the children seem to be less serious than feared, there is concern about the long term consequences of family break-ups among child psychologists and social scientists.

The feminist movement of the 1970s paved the way for a more equal relationship between men and women by rejecting the family hierarchy which was structured according to the top-down principle of "father, mother, child and cat". Today's families are far more symmetrical, although one may question whether child-centeredness has resulted in a new family asymmetry in which the children are those in charge. Some critics even claim that a family hierarchy has been replaced by family anarchy. Nevertheless, most researchers agree that the modern family is a symmetrical and democratic institution, in which most agreements are reached by means of negotiation between the family members. Norwegian sociologist Ivar Frønes consequently refers to the modern family as a "negotiation family". Family life is constantly being negotiated and renegotiated, with the overall goal of ensuring all family members' rights. The following extract from an essay about personal involvement in work, which was written by a Norwegian girl aged 14, may serve as illustration:

> At home I do a lot of chores (...) I hate housework, and get far too little payment. If I had been paid properly it would have been all right. I think it is fair that children do some housework, because parents working full time are old, tired and have little time. But I want more money for doing it.

Norwegian parents seem to appreciate child participation and tend to encourage their children to adopt democratic behaviour. According to the *World Culture Report* Norwegian parents rate values such as independence and responsibility highest when asked which values they would like to pass on to their children. These values correspond well with democratic ideals. Norwegian respondents do not diverge much from respondents in other Western European countries in this respect, but compared to countries in other regions these values are given greater esteem by the European respondents.

Democratic behaviour implies an ability to reflect, to make personal judgements and to develop personal opinions. Reflectivity is consequently a virtue which has gained in recognition and today stands as one of the most valued abilities of a child. Along with the increased focus on reflectivity, there has been a decline in religious adherence and religious practices, and a tendency to reject moral imperatives. "You shall..." has been replaced by "may I advise you to...", and respect has gained a more universal connotation and refers less to authority. The aim is for children to develop both self-consciousness and social awareness; to express their individuality in harmony with their surroundings. The Norwegian author of children's books, Torbjørn Egner, has captured this principle of reflective behaviour in a phrase that is almost inbred for Norwegians, known as "The cardamom law":

> You shall never bother others,
> You shall be both fair and kind,
> And whatever else you do I shall not mind.

The same appreciation of reflectivity and democratic behaviour can be found in the Norwegian core curriculum, in which the promotion of holistic education, reflection and self-consciousness is emphasized. This can be illustrated by the following extract:

> Education has a number of seemingly contradictory aims: (...) – to overcome self-centeredness and a belief in the right of the strongest – and to inspire strength to stand alone, to stand up, to dissent and not to knuckle under or cave in to the opinions of others

The educational objective is to encourage in children individual thinking, in addition to social adjustment. Democratic practices, such as school-democracy, is regarded as significant in order for children to learn democratic behaviour.

Institutionalization

Family and school are considered to be the most important agents of child socialization. Nevertheless, there is a strong tendency for children to take part in a range of organized activities in addition to school and family life. Ivar Frønes refers to this as *institutionalization*. The development in kindergarten enrolment rates may serve as an example. At the beginning of the 1970s, about 2 % of Norwegian pre-school age children attended kindergarten. By the end of 2003 the percentage was 69.1 % for children between 1 and 5 years of age. In the age group 3 to 5 years, which is the demarcation line for receiving cash benefit for a parent staying at home with the child, the enrolment rate was 85 % by the end of 2003. In addition there is a black market of unregistered nannies. These numbers show that there has been an enormous growth in the demand for professional child care. It is not by coincidence that this coincides with mass female entry into the labour market.

But it is not only pre-school child care that has witnessed a growth in enrolment rates. Also after-school arrangements organised by the school and other organised leisure activities, such as sports, scouting and voluntary organization work, have been subject to increased popularity. As a result children spend less time on free play and more time on organised activities. There is of course a great learning potential in such activities, and most children enjoy activities where they can improve their skills and play with their peers. However, some critics claim that this development involves a deteriorating child culture, as children have fewer opportunities to define their own days and interests. Others object to the development by referring to children's well-being. When children's daily lives are too packed there is a risk of developing stress, as they do not get the chance to relax. Furthermore, institutionalization involves a tendency to

Children spend increasingly more time on organized activities. The photo above is from a time when children spent more time on free play.

increased homogenization. As children's daily lives gradually become more structured and defined by kindergarten, school and organised leisure activities, children all over the country more or less follow the same daily rhythm and perform the same activities. This homogenization of life forms is believed to be strong in Norway compared to other countries, and can be further illustrated with reference to the school system referred to as *enhetsskolen* or The Unity School and the state broadcasting corporation (NRK), which broadcasts children's programmes. The idea behind *enhetsskolen* is that children are entitled to the same educational opportunity, regardless of social background and locality. Hence *enhetsskolen* provides a common standard, and contributes to the construction of shared references. Similarly, the NRK TV programmes for children, which are broadcast at 6 pm every day, "prime time" for most Norwegian children under a certain age, provide children with the same frames of reference.

Despite this tendency towards increased homogenization it is acknowledged that there are significant differences between children in different situations. Children's living conditions vary, as do their school performances. These variations follow a pattern which indicates that some groups

*The use of cell-phones has created a
new arena for communication between
adults and children.*

are more vulnerable than others. The increased awareness of child poverty,
which especially affect children of immigrants, the unemployed and single
parents, shows a willingness to come to terms with conditions that cause
such differences.

Criticism of the increased institutionalization is mixed, and it can easily be argued both for and against. One consequence, however, can not be
questioned. As school, kindergarten and organised leisure activities
increase in importance, the role of the family is being altered. The family
is no longer the sole socialization agent, but has to fulfil this function in
close cooperation with the other socialization agents. The family is thus
confronted with new challenges, among which lack of control may seem to
be the most important. However, many parents seem to cope with this
challenge by adopting some aspects of their children's ways of life. In a
study of young people's use of cell-phones, it was found that parents, especially mothers, occupy the role of coordinators. By means of sms they have
frequent contact with their children, and are informed about where they

are and when they can be expected home. In other words, the cell-phone works as a "security-line" between the children and their parents.

The three concepts discussed in this section cover some of the essential trends in Norwegian socialization goals. What these trends have in common is that they presuppose the modern ideals of individualization, individuation, and reflectivity. Contemporary Norwegian childhood is consequently often referred to as "modern childhood".

Conclusive remarks

This article offers a social scientific perspective on the construction of Norwegian childhood and on some trends in Norwegian socialization goals. The Norwegian context is characterized by an adherence to the modern ideals of scientific faith, secularization and individualization, a marked child-centeredness and substantial welfare conditions that enables a strong child focus. This context is reflected in the socialization goals, where three trends are particularly important; the presence of skilled adults who seem to approach child rearing more professionally than intuitively (professionalization), a negotiable and democratic attitude towards children (democratization), and new arenas for child socialization, which includes a stronger emphasis on peer socialization (institutionalization).

Norwegian childhood can on the one hand be described as a secluded life phase characterized by protection and receiving. On the other hand, Norwegian childhood can be described as a dynamic life phase characterized by active participation and contribution to society as well as development of the self.

Part 3

Culture

Chapter 13

The Norwegian Language – Democracy in Practice?

By Eva Maagerø

Only 4.7 million Norwegians and two written Norwegian languages, a lot of dialects which have such a strong position that they can be spoken even from the speaker's platform in the parliament, and no standard spoken language which children are taught in school. Do you think this is peculiar? This is what the Norwegian language situation is like, and it is rather special compared to most countries. Language and culture are always intertwined. Language is a meaning-making system developed in a culture, and the language situation of a society always says a lot about the culture and about values and ideology in that particular society. When we study the language situation in Norway, we will discover that a strong ideology of equality is important. Equality characterises Norwegian society in many ways, and is therefore discussed in several chapters of this book, including this chapter.

In order to present the language situation in Norway, we will start with a brief introduction about the relation between language and landscape. Then we discuss the two written Norwegian languages and look at the differences between them, where we find them used, why we have them (which takes us into the history), and what the influences of the language situation are in school and society in general. We will also present the spoken language situation. In the last 30 – 40 years there has been, as in other Western European societies, a wave of immigration to Norway, above all by refugees from conflict areas of the world. This increase in the population has made Norway, where traditionally Sámi and Finnish have been the only minority languages, a more heterogeneous language society than before. This development will also be briefly touched upon in this chapter.

Language and landscape

Norway is a rather large country with a small population. It consists of about 386 975 square km, which on average means only 11–12 people to every square kilometre. One should also bear in mind that most people live in and around Oslo and the Oslofjord, along the Southern coast and in and around the cities of Stavanger, Bergen and Trondheim. The areas in the middle of Norway, the Western and Northern coast and also the inland area in the North have very few inhabitants. In this long and narrow country with an extremely long coast broken up by many fjords and with mountains and valleys in the middle, communication has always been a challenge. If you could turn Norway around, it would reach as far south as Rome. In early times ships were the best means of travelling. Crossing the mountains in the middle of the country was much more complicated than communication along the coast, and normally only possible in summer. The more urban parts of Norway like Oslo, Drammen, Kristiansand, Stavanger, Bergen and Trondheim are all on the coast and in the southern part of the country. In the rest of Norway small concentrations of houses or rather isolated farms dominate, which means that the distance to the next town for many Norwegians has been, and still is, long. The railway, which traditionally connects different parts of most countries, is of course important in Norway too. There are, however, not so many railway lines partly because of the complicated geographical conditions and partly because of the low number of inhabitants. For example the railway network stops in Bodø in the northern direction, which means that most of the northern part of the country is without this kind of communication, and must rely on buses, boats and planes. This is sometimes complicated when the weather is extreme, which often happens in this part of the country.

The small population, the size of the country and the rather complicated geographical and communicative conditions are important to keep in mind in order to understand the language situation. For example these can explain the large variety of dialects which we have in Norway. Let us, however, start with the written Norwegian languages.

Communications have traditionally been difficult in Norway because of the rather awkward geographical conditions. This, to a large extent, explains why Norwegians speak a large variety of dialects.

The two written languages *bokmål* and *nynorsk*

In this country with only 4.6 million people there are, as mentioned above, two official Norwegian written languages living side by side. They are called *bokmål* (Book Language) and *nynorsk* (New Norwegian). The majority of the Norwegian population uses *bokmål* – about 85 % – and the rest – about 15 % – uses *nynorsk*. *Bokmål* is therefore the clear majority language. In 1885 the parliament (the Storting) decided that the two languages should have an equal status, and they were both declared official languages, which they still are today. In many countries there are several official languages, for example in Switzerland German, French, Italian and Rhaeto-Romanic, in Canada English and French, and in Finland Finnish and Swedish. In these countries the official languages are, however, linguistically distinct languages, which means that they are so different from each other that they have to be learned as foreign languages. Finnish and

Swedish, for example, even belong to different language families (Finnish Ugrian and Indo European). In Norway, however, Norwegian and Sámi are official languages and as different as Finnish and Swedish, but in addition there are the two written languages *bokmål* and *nynorsk* which both are Norwegian and so similar that they can both be understood by all Norwegians without any problems. Actually, the differences between *bokmål* and *nynorsk* are so minimal that it is linguistically difficult to talk about these two written realisations of Norwegian as two languages; therefore the notion 'written norms' is often used instead.

How different are *bokmål* and *nynorsk*?

The small differences between the two written norms we find above all in the following areas:

- In the lexicon (but not very often), for example *erfaring* (*bokmål*) and *røynsle* (*nynorsk*) which means 'experience', or *veileder* (*bokmål*) and *rettleiar* (*nynorsk*) which means 'tutor'.

- In the grammar (for example the morphology), for example *biler* (*bokmål*) and *bilar* (*nynorsk*) – 'cars', *penere* (*bokmål*) and *penare* (*nynorsk*) – 'more beautiful' and *kommer* (*bokmål*) and *kjem* (*nynorsk*) – 'comes'.

- In the use of prefixes and suffixes which originally are not Norwegian or Nordic but come from, for example, German influence in the Hanseatic period. In *bokmål* these elements of foreign origin are accepted, while they normally are not accepted in *nynorsk*, for example *kjærlighet* (*bokmål* – with the German suffix –*het*) and *kjærleik* (*nynorsk* – with the Norwegian suffix –*leik*) – the noun 'love', *anmerkning* (*bokmål* – with the German prefix *an*-) and *merknad* (*nynorsk* – without a prefix) – the noun 'remark' and *behandle* (*bokmål* – with the German prefix *be*-) and *handsame* (*nynorsk* – without a prefix) – 'treat'.

- In the phonetic system which also has an influence on the orthography, for example in the adverb *hvorfor* (*bokmål*) and *kvifor* (*nynorsk*) – 'why', and in the adverb *ikke* (*bokmål*) and *ikkje* (*nynorsk*) – 'not'.

There are also some differences in the syntax and in the style. It is often said about *nynorsk* that it has a more verbal style and is closer to spoken language than *bokmål* is. The reason for this you will see when we look briefly at the history.

The following text extract from *Det vokser ikke hvitløk på Skillebekk* (Garlic doesn't grow in Skillebekk) by Iben Sandemose, first in *bokmål* and then in *nynorsk*, will give some idea of how similar the two written varieties of Norwegian are:

BOKMÅL	NYNORSK
I det svarte, gamle huset med vill og skrikende blåfarge hadde vi ikke andre dyr enn bestemoren min. Hun var ganske liten, litt krum i ryggen og med svært raske, spenstige ben. Munnen var stor og rød, øynene svarte. Håret krøllet hu med krølltang som ble varmet på platen, da lignet hun en liten løve. Derfor kalte vi henne Simba.	I det svarte, gamle huset med vill og lysande blåfarge hadde vi ikkje andre dyr enn bestemora mi. Ho var ganske lita, litt krum i ryggen og med svært raske, spenstige bein. Munnen var stor og raud, auga svarte. Håret krølla ho med krølltong som blei varma på plata, då likna ho ei lita løve. Derfor kalla vi henne Simba.
Simba sov med sov-i-ro i ørene og våknet sjelden før utpå dagen. Da var hun som regel litt kvalm og spiste noen vommeletter. Det er små, hvite piller som smaker som tørr bomull. Jeg passet godt på å ikke bli kvalm.	Simba sov med sov-i-ro i øra og vakna sjeldan før utpå dagen. Da var ho som regel litt kvalm og åt nokre vommelettar. Det er små, kvite piller som smakar tørr bomull. Eg passa godt på å ikkje bli kvalm.

Source: *Arne Torp et.als: Språklinjer*

Where do we find *bokmål* and *nynorsk*?

Bokmål is mainly used in the cities and in the areas with the largest concentration of population. In addition to this the population in all the eastern part and also in the northern areas of Norway use *bokmål*. *Nynorsk* is used in the western part of Norway, on the coast, along the fjords and partly in the mountain areas. In Sogn and Fjordane county, which is a central part of western Norway, nearly all the inhabitants use *nynorsk*. The two written norms are connected not only to geography, but also to identity and culture. *Bokmål* is often associated with urban culture and an urban way of life. It is also in most cases the language of advertising, pop music, fashion, entertainment, and young people's culture. It is the language of the weekly magazines and the big newspapers, and also of the commercial world and the world of technology. People living in the *nynorsk* regions, but identifying with urban culture, will probably choose *bokmål*.

Nynorsk is often associated with traditional and national values and with regional or local culture. Writing *nynorsk* might be a signal that your identity is more related to local values than to urban style, and that your local roots are of great importance to you. *Nynorsk* might therefore be used by local banks and businesses, and is also to a certain degree the language of primary industry (farming, forestry and fishing). In addition there are of course *nynorsk* writers in the more urban areas of Norway too, people who have moved from the rural districts, but still want to keep their language identity, or people who might have lived in a town all their lives, but still want to show that their identity is more related to rural values than to urban values. *Nynorsk* also has a strong position in the academic world, especially in the humanities. Authors write in both languages, also modern authors, and one publishing house in Oslo, *Det norske Samlaget*, only publishes books in *nynorsk* while one theatre, also in Oslo, Det norske teatret, only uses manuscripts in *nynorsk*. There are some regions in Norway, for example Trøndelag in the middle of the country and the valleys in the more eastern areas, where both *bokmål* and *nynorsk* are used in the local communities.

The use of *bokmål* and *nynorsk* therefore shows a colourful picture, of which it is not always easy to gain an overview, and the choice of written language is, as we have seen, really related to cultural values and to a person's identity. The distribution of the two written norms has been constant for many years. *Nynorsk* experienced its largest growth during World War II. In 1944 34.1 % of the population wrote *nynorsk*, and perhaps this high figure partly can be related to the national values important during the war. *Nynorsk* is seen by many as more Norwegian than *bokmål* (see the history of *bokmål* and *nynorsk* below).

After the war, though, the number of people using *nynorsk* soon decreased again. In the efficient modern Norwegian society many have prophesied, however, that *nynorsk* would disappear. Till now this has proved to be wrong. *Nynorsk* is certainly the minority written language, but it has shown for many years that it is capable of survival and important for many people in Norway, and therefore also of importance for Norwegian society and culture.

Why *bokmål* and *nynorsk*?

The reason for having two very similar written Norwegian languages is to be found in the history of Norway. As already mentioned language and society always interact with each other, and sometimes the general devel-

The Vikings brought new ideas to Norway. One of the most important was The Latin alphabet. This drawing by F. Bau depicts a Viking community in Kaupang in what now is the county of Vestfold.

opment of a society has a strong influence on the language. This is the case in Norway. Let us briefly go back to the Viking age. At that time Norway was a free country with a king as leader. Contact with Europe was strong, and cultural influence from other countries in Europe was significant. The Latin alphabet was introduced to Norway about 1000 AD, and a written language was developed. A lot of texts were written in the old Norse language, which was used in Norway and Iceland in the Viking age. Especially in Iceland literary activities were visible through sagas and poems and also through the work of the great author Snorre Sturlason. In Norway the king's court was always important for the development of the written standard. First the king lived in Nidaros (today Trondheim), then Bjørgvin (today Bergen) and then Oslo, and the written language was flavoured by the spoken language of the different places. When the plague (the Black Death) came to Norway in 1349, Norway had had a well developed written language for more than two centuries.

The plague was a catastrophe for Norway, as it was for so many other countries in Europe. Reading and writing skills in the Viking age can in most cases be related to the church and the monasteries. As a result of the plague many priests, monks and nuns died because they took care of the sick, and became infected themselves. Consequently literacy nearly disappeared. At the same time Norway also suffered an economic depression, which weakened the position of the country for many years.

Politically, however, it was an exciting time. The Norwegian king, Håkon VI, who had married the Danish princess, Margreta, died in 1380, and consequently Margreta became queen of both Denmark and Norway. As a result a union between the two countries was established, with Denmark as leader. In 1397 Sweden became a part of the union, called the Kalmar union because the agreement between Sweden and Denmark- Norway was signed in the Swedish town of Kalmar. Sweden left the union, however, in 1523.

The union with Denmark lasted for more than 400 years, till 1814. In the early years Norway had a fairly strong position in the union with its own state council able to make important decisions for the country. After some years, however, Norway's status was reduced, and the country was treated as any other Danish region. As mentioned above, language and power always belong together, and this political situation had a strong influence on the language. The Danes, who had the power in this situation, never had to learn or use the Norwegian language. All important positions in Norway were held by Danes, who used Danish when they spoke, and everything they wrote was of course also in Danish. In the early years after the union laws and letters among, for example, farmers were written in Norwegian, but as every year passed the position of Danish as a written language was strengthened. After a while Danish had taken over as the written language in Norway, and Old Norse as a written norm had disappeared.

In the process of strengthening the position of Danish in Norway three things in particular were of great importance. First there was the art of printing. In 1462 Johan Gutenberg succeeded in inventing a printing press so that books could be mass produced. Till then books had been hand- written on calf skins. This took a long time and was expensive, and only a few people had books. Now books were spread out to a larger part of the population. The books which were produced in Denmark-Norway were all in Danish, which helped Danish as a written language to gain ground among the people in Norway. Second, there was the reformation of the church. In 1536 it was decided that the Lutheran and not the Catholic Church should be the church of Denmark-Norway. In the reformed church generally Latin was abandoned in the services, and the Bible and other religious books were translated into the national language of the different countries so that people were able to understand the holy texts. In Norway's case the Bible and other religious texts were translated into Danish and spread among the population, and the services in the Norwegian churches were held in Danish by Danish clergymen. This of course also strengthened the position of Danish as the written language in Norway. Third, in the 18th century it was decided that young people should have a better education in connection with the confirmation of the promise given to the church on their behalf at their baptism. They were to know more about the Bible and the church, so they would know what the promise comprised. In 1736 it was decided that all young people should learn to read and write in connection with their confirmation. The language they learned to read and write was Danish.

When we enter the 19th century, Danish was therefore the written language in Norway. No Norwegian written languages existed any more. Even the laws were written in Danish, for example Kristian V's statute book from 1683 and 1687. All literature, prose and poetry, written in these years were in Danish. Norwegian authors like Petter Dass (1647–1707) sometimes used Norwegian words in their texts in order to create a local colour, but still the language was Danish.

1814 is an extremely important year in the history of Norway. This was the year Norway left the union with Denmark and entered into a union with Sweden, which lasted till 1905. The reason for this was that Denmark had been on Napoleon's side in the Napoleonic War while Sweden had fought against Napoleon. Denmark, being on the losing side, had to give Norway to Sweden, on the victorious side. Many Norwegians, however, hoped that this would be an opportunity for Norway to become a free nation. 112 men (no women) from all parts of Norway met in Eidsvoll north of Oslo in order to give Norway a constitution and establish a parliament. The Danish prince Christian Fredrik was invited to Norway as the future king. The men of Eidsvoll managed in a short, hectic time to write a new, rather progressive constitution for Norway and to establish a parliament (the Storting), but not to avoid union with Sweden.

In these years when the dreams for freedom were strong, it was very embarrassing for Norway to have Danish as a written language. Most people in Norway at that time spoke a Norwegian dialect, but all those who could write wrote Danish. Language is often seen as a symbol of a people and of a nation. When people fight for freedom, they often also fight for their language. This can be seen in the history of many peoples of Europe, but also for example when Africans fought against the colonial powers, when Indians fight for their rights in America today, or when minority populations fight against the power of a majority in Asian countries. It was important also for Norway to have a written Norwegian language even though Norway was in a new union with Sweden.

Ivar Aasen (1813–96) is the father of nynorsk.

In the language discussion two ways to get a Norwegian written language were pointed out. One way was to make Danish Norwegian, step by step, by integrating Norwegian words and expressions, grammatical elements and syntax in the existing Danish language. Danish is a Nordic language close to Norwegian, and therefore this was seen as a linguistically possible and also pragmatic way of doing it. It would take some time, but this would give people an opportunity to change their language habits gradually. This point of view was supported and also developed by the author Henrik Wergeland (1808–45) and later by the teacher Knud Knudsen (1812–95). In practice Peder Christian Asbjørnsen (1813–82) and Jørgen Moe (1812–85) followed this pattern when they collected and wrote down Norwegian folktales and myths in the 1840s. This language became *bokmål*. The other way of making a Norwegian written language was developed by Ivar Aasen (1813–96) and supported by Professor P. A. Munch (1810–63) at the university in Kristiania (Oslo from 1925). Aasen believed that Danish could never be changed into Norwegian. In his opinion this would be too unsystematic. He wanted to collect information about the dialects from all parts of Norway and build a new Norwegian written language based on them. Where it was difficult to make a choice between different dialects, he would take into account Old Norse from the Viking age. Aasen did this work himself. For four years he travelled around in Norway on foot and collected information about the dialects, and then he constructed a new

Norwegian language which was introduced through a dictionary and a grammar, and also through fiction, drama and poetry that Aasen wrote himself. This language became *nynorsk*. The Norwegian parliament decided in 1885, as already mentioned, that both written languages should be official written languages in Norway.

Over a long period in the 20th century *bokmål* and *nynorsk* were brought closer to each other by means of intensive language planning. This work has, however, stopped, and from about 1980 they have developed as two parallel written Norwegian languages (or written norms). The authorities have supported the idea that they are both important linguistic and cultural resources in Norway, and that they therefore should have equal status. Every individual should have the right to use each one of them. Because *nynorsk* is used by fewer people, the official policy is that *nynorsk* must be positively discriminated through extra measures implemented by the state. One example is the Nynorsk Competence Centre, which was opened in 2005. This centre will give information about *nynorsk*, give advice to schools about *nynorsk* education and also do research connected to *nynorsk* language.

The two written languages in school

Both written languages have, as already mentioned, an equal, official status, which means that both have to be learned by children in school. When children start school at the age of six, they choose one as their main language, which, for example, will be used when they are introduced to reading and writing. Pupils normally choose the language which is mostly used where they live. However, if as many as ten pupils want to have the other written language, the school will have to organise an extra class for them. The language chosen in the first year will normally be the written language the pupils continue to have in and outside school in the following years and for the rest of their life. The other written language the children will meet through different kinds of texts like stories, essays, articles etc. in primary school. This is stated very clearly in the curriculum. In lower secondary school, however, the students will learn the other written language more actively; they study the grammar, and they use it as a working language, which means that they write texts in the other language too. The other written language should not be handled as something strange and different, but as a positive resource and as a variety of Norwegian. The focus should be on the similarities, and not the differences. Before finishing their compulsory education (10 years), the students have exams where they demonstrate their competence in both written languages. If they continue to upper secondary school for three more years, as many young people in Norway do, they continue with both written languages if they choose subjects that lead to further studies at university. For these students the exam in Norwegian is in both *bokmål* and *nynorsk*. A student in teacher education must master both *bokmål* and *nynorsk*, and the same is demanded of students studying Norwegian as their mother tongue at university.

All school textbooks in all subjects in Norway are published in two parallel editions, one in *bokmål* and one in *nynorsk*. The parallel editions must appear at the same time so that all students have equal access to good learning material in their particular language. This is expensive for the publishers, and therefore there have been experiments with books having one chapter in *nynorsk* and another in *bokmål*. The evaluations of these books, however, have not always been positive.

There are of course many discussions among students and their parents and teachers whether so much time should be used to learn two rather similar written languages in school. Some think that the time could be used to develop, for example, better genre competence, greater insight into literature and better orthography in the main language. Some find that it is sufficient to read texts written in both languages, but that it is unnecessary to learn both actively. Others emphasise that the situation with the two different written languages is so significant for Norwegian culture and therefore should be a part of the syllabus in school. Learning both written languages gives students the chance to explore the rich potential of Norwegian.

Bokmål and *nynorsk* outside school

Official languages must also be represented in the official Norway: that means in all official bodies like state and regional administration, state health care, the educational institutions, the police and the postal services. All those who work in institutions like these must be able to write both *bokmål* and *nynorsk*. All official documents from these institutions are in both written languages. That means that everybody can choose whether they want their diploma from university, tax forms or their wedding certificate in *bokmål* or *nynorsk*. Some years ago a man refused to accept a fine for exceeding the speed limit, because the police did not have the relevant document in *nynorsk*. Documents and forms in the post offices and the health stations are also available in two versions. On bank notes the name of the country can be written in two ways, *Norge*, which is *bokmål*, or *Noreg*, which is *nynorsk*. The same can be seen on stamps. In Norway there are two television channels and several radio channels run by the state, and they are therefore a part of the official Norway. Films and other programmes are subtitled in Norway, not dubbed. The subtitles are written in both languages, and it has been decided that 75 % of the texts must be in *bokmål* and 25 % in *nynorsk*. Newscasters and anchors responsible for programme overviews in radio and television must also use both languages.

Spoken Norwegian

The dialects

As mentioned above, people in Norway speak dialect, and there is no standard spoken language taught in Norwegian schools. There are many dialects in Norway, and one important reason for this we can find in the relation between the Norwegian landscape, the small population and the communication conditions (see above).

In modern Norway many means of communications have been developed, and people move around much more than they did before; sometimes because they want to go to school or university in more urban areas, sometimes because they have got a new job in another part of the country. People have more contact with people from other places, and when people meet, different ways of speaking meet. The small differences between local neighbouring dialects have therefore disappeared, and larger dialect areas, so-called regional dialects, have developed. The regional dialects are strong in Norway, and you can nearly always hear from which area a person comes. Most people appreciate hearing other people say, for example: "I can hear that you come from the South" or "Aren't you from the Trondheim area? I can hear it from the way you speak." Their dialect reveals a person's geographical identity, and roots like these are important in Norway. It is said, for example, that Norwegians ask where a person comes from before they ask for the person's name. The linguistic differences between the dialects are not so great that this causes problems in communication between people from different places in the country, and this makes it easier for people to keep their dialect also when they move to a new place.

The dialects are in general looked upon as valuable in Norwegian society, and they can be used and are tolerated in all situations, also in official situations like in the parliament, political meetings, academic contexts, speeches, job interviews and television programmes. Many Norwegian prime ministers have used their dialects while in office, which has given them a homely touch which may even have been a positive element in the elections. Professors may use their dialects when they give lectures, and dialects are used on the stage in all the regional theatres in Norway.

Some people might, however, have reasons for bringing their spoken language closer to written language; that means that they use, for example, grammatical elements which can be found in *bokmål* or *nynorsk*. Some also have the spoken language in the west of Oslo as an ideal. This is, however, always an individual choice, made consciously or unconsciously by each individual. A person can have many reasons for making a choice like this. The language they use always says something about them, and a person may want to associate with an urban life style by speaking the language of the capital, or giving a serious impression by keeping close to the grammar and the wording of the written language. Young people who want to live and work in the place they come from seem more likely to use the local dialect than young people who dream of a life in Oslo or in a big city in another country.

No spoken Norwegian standard language

In many countries students have to learn a spoken standard language when they come to school. The dialects are looked upon as language for private and informal contexts while a standard language is for communication in more formal and official situations in society. The spoken standard language has in many societies developed from the spoken language in the capital. The capital is a centre for power, money and culture, and all these things together give the language of the capital prestige. However, Norway is different on this point. For many years Copenhagen was the capital (see above), but Copenhagen Danish could never be a linguistic model for the population in Norway. Since 1905 Oslo has been the capital, but it takes time to develop the status of a standard spoken language. Even though the spoken language in Oslo may be considered by some people as having a high status, it has never been accepted by the population as a spoken standard for everybody. Here the strong value of equality is important. Why should the Oslo way of speaking be better than any other dialect? Why should my way of speaking not be good enough? The French sociologist Pierre Bourdieu once said that if you invest in a standard language privately or in school or both, your investment should give you a profit of increased cultural capital. But if your investment does not give you this profit, why should you invest? This seems to be the case in Norway. Most people find that they do not need to make this investment effort. They live well with their dialect.

In school all children therefore speak their own dialects, and the use of dialects must be promoted. Educational legislation says that the pupils can use the language they speak at home also in school, and the teachers, in their choice of words and expressions, must show consideration for the pupils. Teachers cannot correct children when they speak their dialect or express negative attitudes about a student's dialect. The curriculum emphasises that dialects are people's primary language, and all dialects must be tolerated and treated with respect. Already in primary school pupils must learn about other dialects and become aware of differences in the dialects, and in secondary school the pupils must learn about changes in dialects over time, and also about internal and external developments causing changes in spoken language. In addition to this they must learn about the language situation and language policy. This tells us that the use of dialect, the primary language, is supported by the authorities in school policy and in the curriculum in Norway.

Minority languages in Norway

Traditional minority languages

As mentioned above, there are two traditional minority languages in Norway, Sámi (or Lappish) and Kvensk (close to Finnish). The Sámi language has always existed in Norway, because the Sámi people have been in the country as long as the Norwegians have. Their language is very different from the Nordic languages. It belongs in fact to another language family called the Finnish-Ugrian language family, together with languages like Finnish, Estonian and Hungarian. The rather small Sámi population (ca. 60–70 000) lives in large areas in Norway, Sweden, Finland and Russia (about 40 000 in Norway), and their language differs considerably from place to place, so much that we can talk about different Sámi languages and not dialects. The Sámi people in the middle of Norway can, for example, hardly understand the Sámi people of the north and vice versa. Today it is said that the largest group of Sámi people in Norway live in Oslo.

In Norway the Sámi people have not always been treated respectfully. Policy for a long time was hard towards the Sámi people; they should be assimilated in Norwegian society as effectively as possible. Their language and culture were suppressed, and there was a law that you had to be able to speak Norwegian in order to own land in Norway. In school the children had to learn Norwegian, but not as a foreign language. They met Norwegian in all subjects from the very first day; their teachers spoke only Norwegian, and it was forbidden to speak Sámi in the breaks or even sing the traditional Sámi songs (joik) in school. Only in the 20th century was the assimilation policy changed, so that the Sámi children today have their own curriculum in school, where all subjects are taught in Sámi and Norwegian is taught as a foreign language. The Sámi people in Norway have also had their own parliament since 1989, and here especially the work promoting language and culture has been important.

Kvensk is a language quite close to Finnish. It has been regarded as a Finnish dialect, but in 2005 it was given the status of a language. It has been a minority language in Norway since the 18th century. Finnish people immigrated mainly to the north of Norway and to the forest areas on the south-eastern border with Sweden. The Finns in the North were called kvener. Their reason for coming to Norway was often lack of food in the northern part of Finland. Kvensk has been the mother tongue of rather small groups of people in towns like Vardø and Vadsø in Finmark in the north. In Finnskogen, a forest area in the south-east, the Finnish language has now disappeared. Kvensk was treated badly, like Sámi, by the Norwegian authorities for a long time. Today, however, children can study it in school in Finmark, and its status as a language and not a Finnish dialect might support the development of kvensk language and culture in Norway in the future. Still there are people who think that a border between kvensk and Finnish has been drawn by recognising kvensk as a language, and that this border destroys the natural contact between the two languages.

The new minority languages

Since the 1960s Norway has experienced a wave of immigration like most Western European countries. Approximately 360 000 immigrants from mostly African and Asian countries live in Norway today. This means that about 120 different languages are in use in Norway at the moment. This is a new and interesting situation, which represents both a resource and a challenge. It is a resource because the immigrant population has a language competence which covers a large number of languages in the world. This competence consists of their mother tongue, which millions of people may speak (for example Arabic, Urdu, Farsi, Spanish, Russian etc), and in addition to their mother tongue many immigrants speak several other languages too. For example a Somali may speak Somali as his or her mother tongue, Italian because of the colonial power and Arabic because of religious reasons. This language competence can be of great importance, for example, in international cooperation in business, culture, technology and academic matters in the continuously globalising world, but till now Norwegian society has not managed to exploit this resource. The many languages are also a resource in school. Comparison of languages both lexically and grammatically can give the students a strengthened linguistic consciousness and knowledge, and insight into other language situations and other people's culture is important in a world with many conflicts. This has, however, not been exploited very much either.

The many languages are also a challenge for Norway. Immigrant children and adults must learn Norwegian satisfactorily in order to become active members of society, and to be able to influence their own situation. In addition to this it is important that all immigrants can keep and develop their mother tongue. This language competence makes it possible to have contact with the society they come from, with relatives and friends and with their original culture. This is not seen as mainly a private responsibility in Norway, but also as a task for society. Mother tongue teachers are therefore important in school in order to develop the mother tongue to a high level, and also to create a 'bridge' between the home culture and the Norwegian culture. Teachers with a minority background can also offer new, important knowledge in all subjects by bringing other cultural perspectives into the lessons. In this way it is possible to develop a multicultural content in school.

Summing up

In this chapter the language situation in Norway has been described and discussed. It has been important to show that language and culture belong together, and that language also is related to power. The language situation says a lot about a society, about values and ideologies and also about tolerance and respect. On the other hand it is impossible to understand the language situation of a society without knowing about the history and development of the society. It has been emphasised in this chapter that equality is an important value in Norwegian society, and in chapters 1 and 2 it is explained why this value is so important. In relation to language this value, or ideology, means that also the approximately 15 % of the population using *nynorsk* must have the same rights as the 85 % using *bokmål*, and that dialects as the primary language for every individual are considered by most people as positive and appropriate in all situations. For a long time equality did not include the Sámi and Kven population. In modern Norway, however, their situation has clearly been improved. With regard to the new language minorities, it takes time to understand and exploit their language competence as a potential in society in general and in school. Many are, however, of the opinion that it is important to provide good opportunities for everybody to develop their mother tongue. In chapter 11 you may read more about the general situation of traditional and new minorities in Norway.

Chapter 14

Norwegian Myths and Tales

By Elise Seip Tønnessen

Myths and tales are at the same time universal and culturally unique. They are universal because the topics and plots know no national borders. The stories have been following mankind describing and explaining their life experiences through generations in a collective form of storytelling that has grinded and refined the form. At the same time these stories have been given shape and flavour and cultural garments from the local setting in which they have been told. Depending on the alleged relationship to historic reality, we distinguish between myths, legends, and folk tales. While folk tales are considered pure fiction, the legends [and sagn] claim some kind of connection to historic persons, events or places. Myths, on the other hand, are rooted in prehistoric times when the distinction between fact an fiction was not drawn as sharply as we have seen later.

Pre-Christian mythology

The myths of the old Norse culture are older than the national borders, and thus in many ways common to the Nordic countries. The Norse mythology represents stories and beliefs connected to old German paganism, where the Nordic variety is among the best preserved versions. These stories stem from oral sources dating back to preliterate ages, and were written down in the flourishing aera of sagas in Iceland and Norway. They convey beliefs about the way the world came to be, how it is organised and how it will eventually come to an end,. The stories of the old Norse gods feed on the religion of the Vikings from before Christianity became the dominant religion around the turn of the first millennium. Today they are read mainly as stories expressing and explaining some central values, parallel to the myths of old Greek and Latin culture. They share the interest in explaining the place of mankind in the world, placed on a timeline between creation and apocalypse.

Our knowledge of these myths is based on fragments in written sources from around 1220, when beliefs in the old gods were already left in the past, though they still played a part in literature. Snorre Sturlason gave an overview accompanied by examples in *Edda*, or *The prose Edda*, his book teaching the art of skaldic poetry. Another collection of poems about the old gods was found and probably written down later. But these poems were believed to be a result of a long history of oral transmission, so they have been among the sources Snorre based his work on. This is why this *poetic Edda* was given the name "the older Edda". After the collection was given to the king of Denmark the latin term "Codex regius" was more commonly used. It was kept in Copenhagen until 1971, when it was returned to Iceland.

World view

According to the myths, the world as we know it was created from the remains of the giant Ymer, who in his turn was shaped out of the encounter of the cold ice and the hot fire. His blood became the sea, his flesh the land, and his bones turned into mountains and cliffs. Grass and trees came from his hair, and his scull formed the sky above us. The old Norse myths taken together tell us a meta-story about the rise and fall of a culture, from creation to the end of the world at Ragnarokk.

In the eyes of the Vikings, the world was shaped as a flat, circular disc, divided into concentric spheres. The gods lived in their castle, Åsgard, at the centre, the giant trolls or 'jotner' in the periferi, and mankind were placed in-between. This worldview was not merely geographical; it characterized human beings as "god and troll within the same body" (Bringsværd and Hansen-Krone 1991:16). This leads to interesting and sometimes amusing stories about encounters between gods and humans, or between gods and trolls. These interactions create new problems and conflicts, and also result in offspring that make the clear division into three species more and more complex as the meta-story evolves.

A family of gods

Just like in the Greek and Roman tradition, the gods were not divine in a modern sense. They did not represent the eternal good as opposed to the absolute evil. Rather the opposition in this mythological world was between order and chaos. The gods lived with love, jealousy, hate and intricate family relations. The most prominent family of gods was led by Odin. He was the king of warrior gods, called æser, the one who had created the world together with his two brothers Vilje (Will) and Ve (Woe).

The stories about Odin reveal characteristics worthy of a king and creator: He is wise, he is a great warrior, he can perform magic and he can see what is happening all over the world. Magic animals and items surround him: His horse, Sleipner, has eight legs, and can run faster than any other horse. He has got two ravens, Hugin and Munin, who fly all around the world to collect news for him, and his pets are two tame wolves. His spear will hit any target, and he has got a magic ring, giving him eight new golden rings every ninth day. Odin is easily recognised because he has got only one eye. His other eye was sacrificed to the giant Mime in order to get access to the well of wisdom.

Tor is the son of Odin and the strongest and fiercest of all the gods. His mother is Jord (Earth), the daughter of Night; perhaps hinting that she has supplied the dark sides to her son's personality, in addition to the practicalities of being deeply rooted in 'Earth'. When Tor drives across the heavens in his cart drawn by two goats, he produces thunder and lightning – a metaphoric description of his temper. He keeps getting involved in fights, and in his possession is a magical hammer, Mjølner, the most dangerous weapon in the whole world.

Balder is the son of Odin and his wife Frigg. He is handsome, friendly, and most beloved by all the gods. In short, Balder is too good for this wicked world, as his tragic story reveals. The poetic story about his death is one of the most popular of the Norse myths. It reveals a softer side of the warrior gods, where the whole world agrees to Frigg's plea that no one should hurt Balder. All except the little mistletoe, which seems too small and insignificant to give such a promise. Eventually Balder's weak spot is found by the unpredictable Loke, and he has to travel the sad way to Hel in Nivlheim, the underworld of the dead. An attempt to get him back is done by his brave brother Hermod. He rides all the way to Hel to negotiate Balder's return from the dead. Hel agrees to let him go on one condition: that the whole world weeps for Balder in order to prove that he was loved by every creature on the surface of the world. And the world is covered with tears for Balder, by everyone except Loke. He uses his magical powers to change appearances into an old woman, Tokk. She claims that her eyes are dry after too much crying, and rejects the idea of crying for anyone. Consequently Balder has to remain where he is until the end of the world.

Included in the family of æser there are some representatives of another family of gods, *vaner* that once challenged Odin's power. They are the gods of farming and fruitfulness in every sense of the word. Frøya and her brother Frøy came to Åsgard as hostages, but gradually became included, adding new values to the harsh life among the gods in Åsgard. Frøya is the goddess of love, the most beautiful and attractive of all the gods. Ironically, she does not experience real love for herself. Her beloved Od leaves her, and every time she thinks of him, she cries, and her tears turn into gold. Still, this gives her an independent and powerful position among the gods, in contrast to most of the other goddesses, who earn their position primarily in their roles as mothers, wives and mistresses to the mighty gods.

Loke is an outsider, originally coming from the trolls in Jotunheim. But after mixing blood with his good friend Odin, he becomes one of the gods. Loke is constantly changing, in appearance as well as in mood; you never know when to count on him. He is connected to magic and fire, a trickster type, involved in most of the dramatic episodes in the world of the gods. He is married to the goddess Sigyn, but has also been breeding with the trolls. This becomes fatal, when he becomes the father of three mythological figures that play a vital part in this whole mythological world coming to an end. The wolf *Fenre* kills Odin in the end. The serpent *Midgardsormen* grows so huge that it surrounds the whole world, and eventually kills Tor, who kills him in the same instance. And *Hel* becomes the ice-cold queen of death, and leads an army of the dead fighting the gods in the end.

The conversion from Norse mythology to Christian faith has been dated to the year 1030, when the later Saint Olav was defeated in a battle at Stiklestad in Mid-Norway. In reality the changes took place over a period of 150-200 years. As the old Norse gods were forgotten, some of the mythological creatures, such as giants, elves and dwarfs were integrated in folk tales in the form of leprechains and trolls. In modern everyday culture we find Norse mythology reflected in a number of names of places, such as *Torshov* in Oslo or *Frøyshov* in Setesdal; places that were once used for worshipping Tor and Frøy. The remainders of Norse mythology are also found in the names of the days of the week: tirsdag (Tuesday; Tyr's day), onsdag (Wednesday; Odin's day), torsdag (Thursday; Tor's day) and fredag (Friday; Frøy's day).

The last decades have seen a renewed interest in the myths about the old Norse gods, for various reasons. In global popular culture some of this mythological material has been included, for instance in J.R.R. Tolkien's *The Lord of the Rings* where Midgard plays a central role as the land of the mortals. The reuse of these stories in popular film has opened up to the inclusion of elves, dwarves and giants in the flourishing fantasy genre in modern fiction. In the Norwegian context Tor Åge Bringsværd has urged modern readers to re-conquer and re-interpret the old myths, along with contributing with his presentation of new versions of the old stories in modern picture books (see chapter 16 on Children's literature). A very different motivation may be found in groups that see the myths as an ideological background for modern death metal music. Whatever the motivation; the myths are back in the school curriculum, ready to be reinterpreted by new generations.

Folk tales

Political as well as cultural changes led the Norwegian people into new contexts in the Middle Ages. Through the four centuries under Danish rule the cultural elite was situated in Denmark, and this was were the written literature was published. Among ordinary people in Norway stories and poetry were mainly transferred orally from generation to generation. These traditions became particularly important when the new nation started its search for national identity after 1814, bridging the gap between the proud past of sagas and skaldic art, and the national awakening.

However, the focus on "the people" was not specific for Norway. The romantic belief in the people representing a kind of organic unity with a common consciousness was well known from the German ethnologist Johann Gottfried Herder (1744-1803), who has given us concepts such as *Volksgeist* and *Volksseele* (the spirit and soul of the people). Following these ideas, well educated people developed an interest in collecting the old tales and committing them to writing.

The best known collectors of folk tales in Norway were Peter Christen Asbjørnsen (1812-1885) and Jørgen Moe (1813-1882). They met at a private school, and were to become known as an inseparable pair in their work to collect folk tales and give them a written form reflecting the genuine Norwegian *Volksgeist*. The first part of their collected work was published in

Th. Kittelsen's illustration:
The Ashlad and the Troll

parts from 1840-1844. A second and complete edition followed in 1851-1852. As the work progressed they had become more aware that their aim was to present their contribution to the national literature of Norway. They wanted to preserve the aesthetic dimensions in the folk tales as well as present the genuinly Norwegian aspects of the narratives. Asbjørnsen continued the work for the rest of his life, turning towards legends and popular beliefs. Moe wrote in a broader range of genres, including stories for children as well as religious poetry. He gave up the collectors work after he became a member of the clergy. In 1865 he left his collections and notes to Asbjørnsen. Moe ended his career as bishop in Kristiansand (1875-82).

Magnus Brostrup Landstad (1802-1880) spent part of his childhood in Telemark, and also as part of his working life in the clergy Telemark was an area where the folk tradition had been well preserved. The old ballads were still sung by old people in Seljord and Kviteseid, but Landstad noticed that their role in public life was declining. He cooperated with Olea Crøger, the daughter of the minister in Heddal in the heart of Telemark, who had collected texts and melodies from the traditional ballads. Together they published a collection of Norwegian ballads in 1853. Apart from this collectors work, Landstad is most widely known for his hymns, which also integrate elements from the folk tradition. His name is known from the first Norwegian hymnal after the period of Danish rule, *Landstads salmebok*. It was first published in 1869 after two decades of collecting and editing. In a revised version it remained the main hymnal for the Church of Norway for almost a century.

One aim for the folklore collectors was to (re)construct a kind of national identity, based on the traditions handed down by the people through generations. Asbjørnsen and Moe were inspired by the German brothers Grimm in their ambition to retell the stories in the language and narrative form used by ordinary people. In the Norwegian case, this was a particular challenge, since there was a great distance between the written Danish language and the Norwegian spoken by farmers and simple people in rural areas. The solution they chose was to have an impact on the future linguistic development of the new nation. Asbjørnsen and Moe gave the folk tales a written form that was basically Danish in spelling, but still tinted by spoken Norwegian in the vocabulary and partly also in syntactic constructions. This was the beginning of a gradual change of written Danish towards the spoken vernacular of Eastern Norway, which ended up in what we today know as *bokmål*.

Asbjørnsen and Moe collected most of their tales in Eastern Norway, around and north of Oslo. This is why Norwegians today still regard the typical landscape of the folk tales to be like the wooded hills and slopes of Eastern Norway. The trolls as we know them from the superb illustrations by Theodor Kittelsen and Erik Werenskiold have also taken their form from this landscape. They are shaped as giants, resembling big rocks or snow-covered trees. The main characters are typically rooted in this rural society, with the sympathy always leaning towards poor and simple people. The typical protagonist, Espen Askeladd, is the youngest of three brothers. The two oldest, with the biblical names of Per (Peter) and Pål (Paul), are always the first ones to begin a task or try to solve a problem, and they always fail. And they never believe that little brother Askeladden (the Ashlad) will succeed, as he is the one who has never achieved anything, but spent his days fooling around with the ashes in the fireplace. What distinguishes Askeladden from his brothers, is that he is open and generous to other people, and creative and observant under all circumstances. This is how he performs the tasks given by the king, and ends up winning the princess and half the kingdom. The king is portrayed as the richest farmer in the area. He may hold on tightly to his power and possessions, but he always ends up keeping his promises. The bad guys in these tales are people with official power: the bailiff and the clergymen.

The author and teacher Regine Normann (1867-1939) presented a different kind of folktales in her two collections from 1925 and 1926. Her stories were collected from school children in Northern Norway, and they display a landscape and a mentality quite different from the well-known tales collected by Asbjørnsen and Moe in Eastern Norway. The main character is often a young child, who has to take up responsibilities not common to his/her age. The characters belong in coastal Norway, where the protagonist may be turned into an eagle or a raven. The mythological creatures are also connected to the wet, wild and dangerous ocean, and they may seem more scary than the more stupid and sometimes good-tempered trolls of the eastern woods. Regine Normann published several novels, and was an important personality in contemporary culture. But today she is primarily remembered because of her collections of tales.

The simplicity of the folk tales, with one main hero, stylized characters and repetition typically in threes, meant that they were initially regarded as simple stories for children and ordinary people. But they soon were accepted and respected as the cultural heritage that represented the true soul of the Norwegian people.

Chapter 15

Norwegian Literature

By Elise Seip Tønnessen

In the world of school text books the history of Norwegian literature starts quite abruptly in 1814. That is, of course, for historical and political reasons. In actual fact, the connection with the Danish field of literature lasted well into the second generation after the constitutional break with Danish rule. Authors went on writing in Danish, with a gradual shift towards accepting words and expressions from the Norwegian vernacular in written discourse. And even two generations after political independence in 1814, great Norwegian writers like Henrik Ibsen and Bjørnstjerne Bjørnson published their books through Danish publishing houses, gaining the advantage of a broader public.

This article will present some trends and some of the main authors in the two centuries leading up to modern Norwegian literature.

Searching for national identity

During the first decades of the new nation, the cultural connections with Denmark lived on, and were more or less taken for granted. It was only when the first generation of writers and artists of the new nation reached maturity that the debate about national identity came to the surface. The big issue in the 1830s was whether the best strategy would be to maintain a continuity from Danish literature and culture. This was the view of the poet and philosopher Johan Sebastian Welhaven (1807-1873). He claimed that Norway as a young nation could only become a civilized society and build a culture of its own if we recognised the centuries under Danish rule as our heritage. In fierce opposition to this view, Henrik Wergeland (1808-1845) claimed that as a new nation, we should build a cultural and national identity on genuine Norwegian ground, founded in the insights and stories of ordinary Norwegian people.

This does not by far tell the whole story about Henrik Wergeland, a person and a writer out of the ordinary in a multitude of ways. His collected works fill 23 big volumes in a broad range of genres, written through 18 short years before he died in 1845, only 37 years old. His writings can be connected to European romanticism, especially the British and French tradition. But at the same time, he was influenced by the ideology of the enlightenment and rational thinking from the 18th century. In spite of his international orientation, his cultural programme considers the Constitution of 1814 (signed, among others, by his father Nicolai Wergeland), as a new start in the effort to establish a Norwegian national identity.

The long lasting opposition between Wergeland and Welhaven and other intellectuals associated with them is remembered by every student in Norway, mainly because of a spicy intrigue caused by Camilla (Wergeland) Collett (1813-1895). Camilla Collett was Henrik Wergeland's younger sister, and she was romantically involved with Welhaven. This was no secret, since she published her memoirs from this period, including part of her personal diary. Squeezed between the two, she leaned towards Welhaven's classicist view in ideological matters. After her love affair with Welhaven was over, she married one of his associates, Peder Jonas Collett (1813-1851). Together they engaged in collecting folk tales in the 1840s, propagating a more refined style in the written version than her contemporaries Asbjørnsen and Moe (presented in the previous chapter). Camilla Collett is well known as a writer in her own right, particularly because she published what is known to be the first novel in Norwegian literature: *Amtmandens Døttre (The District Governor's Daughters* 1854-55) In this story about a family with four daughters she propagates women's rights to follow their heart and decide about their own life in personal matters. In her later years she mainly published essays. Some of them follow up her engagement in women's rights, seen from the point of view of the single woman after she was widowed in 1854. Another major topic reflects on her experiences from travels all over Europe. Thus Camilla Collett lived an unorthodox life for a woman of her time, and used traditional female genres such as diary, letters and commenting essays to express unorthodox views on the life of women in society.

The 1850ies saw a new generation of authors entering the scene, who were to establish what has been known as the (first) 'golden age' of Norwegian literature. A whole group of them met at a private school ("Heltbergs studentfabrikk") preparing aspiring youngsters for university studies. These young men were for some reason or other positioned as outsiders in the cultural system of the capital: some were the sons of government officials in rural areas, some were upcoming intellectuals from previously uneducated classes, and some of them just didn't fit in with the strict system of Latin based schools. This group has been depicted in Bjørnstjerne Bjørnson's celebration of his old school master in the poem "Gamle Heltberg", as well as culturally analysed in Arne Garborg's novel *Bondestudentar* (*Rural students*) half a generation later.

Aasmund Olavsson Vinje came to the capital from Telemark, and remained a representative of rural Norway and an eager user of 'nynorsk' along with the autodidact Ivar Aasen (see chapter 13 on the linguistic situation). Jonas Lie and the slightly younger Alexander Kielland, who both followed their family traditions in studying law, were counted among the 'four great' writers of realistic literature in the three last decades of the 19th century. In the foreground of this group we find Bjørnstjerne Bjørnson (1832-1910) and Henrik Ibsen (1828-1906), a pair extremely diverse in personality and style, still following a parallel path of development in the topics of their writing. They both went through a period of historic interests and were inspired by folklore, before they became the main contributors to the modern breakthrough of realistic literature focussing on the problems of contemporary society. Bjørnson played a major part in public debates; he wrote across the genres of poetry, drama and epic prose, and was awarded the Nobel price for literature in 1903. Ibsen, in contrast, upheld a mysterious distance to the public scene and came to specialize in dramatic writing.

Henrik Ibsen: half a century of drama

Exactly 50 years went by from Henrik Ibsen published his first drama (Catilina, 1849) to his last one (*When We Dead Awaken / Når vi døde vågner*, 1899). During this half century he developed his own dramatic technique and his typical motifs and use of the dramatic space on stage. But at the same time he followed the trajectory of Norwegian literature: He started out in the aftermath of national romanticism, focusing on ideas through motifs from folklore and ancient history. This has been known as the *idealist* period in Ibsen's writing. He reached full maturity as a writer in the period usually known as *realism* – and played a main part in the golden age of Norwegian literature from the 1870s and 1880s. The last phase of his work (from *The Wild Duck* published in 1884) focused more on psychology than politics, mostly occupied with existential questions expressed through *symbolism*.

Henrik Ibsen was born in Skien and spent some of his formative years from the age of 16 to 22 as an apprentice in the pharmacy in Grimstad. This is the background for the claim often made in this area that the dramatist Ibsen was 'born' in Grimstad. This was where he wrote his first play and got it printed with the help of some friends. Shortly after, he moved to Christiania (the name of Oslo at that time) to study for the university entrance examination. But it was when he got a position directing productions at the theatre in Bergen (1852-1857) that he really started learning the craft of dramatic writing. Part of his job was to write a new play every year to be performed on the anniversary of the theatre on January 2nd. These early plays tried out ideas, mostly in historical settings from the middle ages in Norway, or classical times in the Roman Empire.

Inspired by memories from his youth in Grimstad he wrote the epic poem *Terje Vigen*, published in 1861. The story is set in the time of the Napoleonic wars (1807-1814), in the difficult years of famine caused by a drought during the British blockade of Denmark/Norway. The poem tells the story of a young sailor, Terje Vigen, who "proved quite a scamp in his early days". Responsibility for his wife and little daughter changes him, and this is put to test during the famine. Terje rows across to Denmark to get flour for bread for his family. On the way back he is caught by a British war ship and sent to prison for five years. Returning to his home and finding that his family has not survived the famine, Terje Vigen turns into a scary man. Many years later a British ship is in trouble outside the shores where Terje lives and works as a pilot. When he recognises the British lord who once had him captured, bringing with him his wife and daughter, Terje is put to his life's hardest test. Only after forgiving his enemy can Terje Vigen find peace.

Henrik Ibsen's breakthrough in a bigger context, including all of Scandinavia, happened with *Brand* in 1865. The first version was an epic poem, but Ibsen changed it to a drama written in verse. The main character, who has given the drama its title, is a vicar and an idealist who ends up hurting his own family because he is not willing to compromise his high standards. In this play Ibsen constructs a dramatic plot in a way that points ahead to his most famous works. Typical too is the open ending when Brand is caught by an avalanche, as a voice from above says "he is the God of mercy" ("han er Deus Caritatis"). Whether this is to be understood as a criticism of Brand's merciless idealism, or a last act of divine grace offered to Brand, is an open question.

Brand was written after Ibsen left Norway in 1864, disappointed over the fact that his country had failed to help Denmark in the German-Danish war. He stayed abroad, living in Italy and Germany for a period of 27 years, only interrupted by short visits to Norway. Seeing Norway from abroad seems to have triggered his creative powers. His next play, *Peer Gynt* (1867), has become one of Ibsen's most famous works, read and played from a multitude of perspectives through history. Both of these plays were originally meant to be read, not performed on stage. In particular that is understandable for *Peer Gynt*, where the plot moves through Norwegian scenery of a natural as well as a mythological kind, and on to Northern Africa and out to sea. The main character Peer is inspired by a legend about a hunter from the central mountainous part of Norway, given written form by Peter Christen Asbjørnsen in 1848. Peer can be seen as a modern character, a liar and a dreamer, shifting in moods from one context to the next. His father turned into a drunkard and his mother Åse clings to the dreams of the past. Peer is outlawed after he steals a bride from her own wedding. Through five spectacular acts he moves across the mountains, into the hall of the mountain king (*Dovregubben*) and on to dubious business in Marocco. After that he travels through the desert where he is proclaimed a Bedouin chief and a prophet, and on to Egypt where he ends up in the madhouse in Cairo. The act set in Northern Africa is seldom performed on stage, where we usually see a shorter version in three acts.

After all his adventures Peer meets a mythological figure, the button-moulder, accusing him of being nobody when he returns home towards the end of the play. In a famous scene he is compared to an onion: a character with one layer outside the other, but no core. The ethical imperative to mankind in this play is "be yourself". Peer has renounced this token of humanity when he joined the trolls in Jotunheimen. Being a troll is opposed to being human – the trolls only care for themselves ("er seg selv nok"). In the last scene of the play, the only hope for Peer lies in the heart of Solveig, the woman who has loved him through a long life. Only in her love can he hope to find true human identity. The play ends before the readers get to know how Peer's reunion with Solveig comes to pass.

In contrast to Brand and Terje Vigen, Peer Gynt is a modern, divided character, seen by some as a sign of early modernism in Norwegian literature. The play uses plenty of the folkloristic stories and features that were so popular in the search for a national identity around 1850. But at the same time Ibsen plays satirical games with this sense of identity, rooted in history more than in contemporary society. In this respect, *Peer Gynt* represents a farewell to national romanticism and points ahead to the period of realism in which Henrik Ibsen's writing focused on the problems of contemporary society, rather than historical and general ideas. This shift represents the most radical turn in his writing.

Contemporary drama: an instant success

New themes as well as a new way of writing came to the fore when Henrik Ibsen's play *Pillars of Society* (*Samfundets støtter*) was published in 1877. It was an instant success; the following year this play was performed in five different theatres in Berlin. No other play has taken Ibsen so long to complete, with so many rejected attempts. He was searching for a new realistic form of expression. The dialogue was no longer written in verse, and the modern topics required a natural, modern way of speaking.

Two years later Ibsen presented *A Doll's House*, perhaps the most typical example of what has become known as Ibsen's drama technique. The play conforms strictly with the classical unity of time, place and plot, the whole drama unfolding during three intensive days around Christmas. Through three acts we get to know the story of Nora and Thorvald Helmer's marriage. By using his typical retrospective technique Ibsen tells us about how Nora forged her father's signature in the early days of her marriage, in order to obtain money to save Thorvald's health when he was ill. In the drama this fault from the past threatens to backfire on Thorvald, now that he has reached the status of managing director of a big bank. This conflict reveals how Nora and Thorvald have totally different views on the ethics of society and family life. Nora discovers that Thorvald is not the man who can give her "the wonderful", the "miracle of miracles". His priorities are totally different from hers.

The play is condensed also in the orchestration of characters, presenting five main characters that can be seen as two couples reflected in each other, and one outsider (Dr Rank) as commentator. In contrast to the foregrounded couple Nora and Thorvald drifting apart, we experience

Henrik Ibsen (1828-1906) wrote a series of world famous dramas over a period of 50 years in the second half of the 19th century.

another couple finding a new unity after having endured hardship. Krogstad represents the threat to Nora's and Thorvald's happiness as he was the one who lent Nora the money in the past, and will now reveal her faulty morals unless he gets a position in Thorvald's bank. Mrs Linde is Nora's old friend, who once turned her back on her love for Krogstad in order to secure her family financially. This couple reflects how society treats men and women who do not comply with the public norm, but also the strength gained in the end by following the law of the heart. The fifth character, Doctor Rank also plays a part that serves as a comment on the presented conflict. He is willing to make a sacrifice for Nora, at the same time revealing his long-lasting love for her. This is not acceptable by her moral standards because it would mean trading love for money. And with his fatal illness he is also an example of what is believed to happen to the child of a demoralized father.

The title, *A Doll's House*, serves as a metaphor for the conditions women are subjected to in this kind of society. But it also functions as a more concrete setting for the drama to be exposed in. This is typical of Ibsen's dramatic writing from now on. He develops a unity of symbolic and concrete meaning, as we see in the titles as well as the plots of the following plays: *Ghosts* (1881), *An Enemy of the People* (1882) and *The Wild Duck* (1884).

Tragedy and symbolism

The drama that followed *A Doll's House* can be seen as a continuation, according to a comment by Ibsen himself: "After Nora it was necessary to present Mrs. Alving". She represents the older, more mature woman, who in contrast to Nora did *not* leave her husband. She is a woman who wants to be independent, but she is tied down by her sense of duty and her loyalty to society's expectations. The title of the play, *Ghosts*, points to inherited sins that follow the family from father to son. Besides Mrs. Alving, her son Osvald is a central character who falls victim to secrecy and hypocrisy in the past. He comes home to visit from Paris, and meets the servant in the Alving home, Regine. She hopes to go with him back to Paris, but this plan is jeopardized when she learns that she is really the illegitimate daughter of Captain Alving, and thus Osvald's half sister. Mrs Alving can be seen as a tragic hero who tries to abide by high moral standards, but in so doing she fails to give space to the joy of life. *Ghosts* is the first in a row of tragic dramas ending with the death of the main character(s). Another example is *The Wild Duck* (1884) where young Hedvig shoots herself after she learns that her father is not her biological father. Once again we see an innocent victim of parents' efforts to hide their faults in the past. This is the play where Henrik Ibsen presents his famous claim that an average person is not able to live with the unmerciful truth.

Towards the end of his writing career Ibsen's plays return to some of the questions that occupied him as a young writer: The choice between following his calling or seeking happiness, between art and life. A typical motif in these late works is the relationship between a tired old man and a young woman representing fresh life and engagement. At this stage his works reflect concern, not only for his own happiness but also for the price paid by his close relations. The dialogue in *When We Dead Awaken* (1899) between the ageing sculptor Arnold Rubek and his former model Irene in this play is typical of the sense of doubt in these last works by Henrik Ibsen:

> "- When we dead awaken
> - Yes, what do we really see?
> - We see that we have never lived."

A new generation: Knut Hamsun

Knut Hamsun's (1859-1952) entrance on the Norwegian literary stage happened ostentatiously with his novel *Hunger*, published in 1890. This gave the reading public a sense of something radically new, compared to the previous generation of strong writers. Hamsun himself made a point of being different when he criticised his predecessors in a series of lectures the following year: Their characters were shallow, they presented 'types' rather than complex human souls. Hamsun made it his programme as a writer to work like a psychologist, describing the subconscious with its "bizarre phenomena of the soul", "twisted emotions" and "wonderful work of the nervous system" (Beyer 1975: 4; 129).

Hamsun was past thirty at the time of his literary breakthrough, but he had been writing since he was a teenager. His first work (*Den gaadefulde*) was published in 1878 when he was eighteen. After a couple of more tries at writing novels, which are rarely read today, he started off on a period of travelling, surviving on casual work. Two periods in America during the 1880s provided material for articles in journals that indicated the role that Hamsun was to play in Norwegian culture through the coming decades. One was a criticism of the programme of realistic literature aspiring to educate the people. Hamsun demanded that literature should be artistic, not educational or political. These thoughts were further developed in another article about "The spiritual life of modern America". In quite an arrogant way the author propagated an aesthetic attitude that privileged the spiritual and subjective views of the artist in a romantic way. And for the rest of his life he remained critical to Anglo-American culture.

In 1890, the same year that Hamsun published *Hunger*, he wrote an article that presented his ideas about literature entitled "From the unconscious life of the mind" ("Fra det ubevisste sjeleliv"). This was a declaration of a new poetics that underlined the need for psychological refinement in literary characters. Hamsun suggested that literature should be more about "the trackless journeys of mind and soul".

Through the 1890s Hamsun developed his psychological programme as well as his literary style in a series of novels, *Mysteries* (1892) and *Pan* (1894), among others. Both these novels follow up the perspectives in *Hunger*, depicting people who feel estranged in this world. The main character, Nagel, in *Mysteries*, arrives by chance in a small coastal town where he pro-

Drawing from a contemporary magazine after Hamsun's lecture on Norwegian Literature. Hamsun's left foot is placed on Ibsen's head.

vokes the establishment, engages in confused love relationships and dreams about his powerful union with nature.

This is developed even further in *Pan*, a novel about the experiences of the hunter Thomas Glahn and the summer he spent in the "eternal days of the Nordic summer". Like Nagel in *Mysteries*, he reveals very little about his background and where he came from. Like the main (nameless) character in *Hunger* he is a first person narrator who cannot be trusted. His changing moods and biased explanations of what happens and why portray exactly the kind of nervous soul and twisted emotions that Hamsun had promoted as relevant to true literature.

Thomas Glahn in *Pan* is a hunter who lives his simple life in a hut in the woods, apparently close to nature. But his constant awareness of his relations to nature distances him from nature, rather than making him an integral part of it. As the narrator of the story he is always looking inwards, even when telling us about his hectic love affair with Edvarda. Through a few short weeks of summer this love story goes through all the phases of falling in love with sweet sensations, sensibility, doubt and eventually a love-hate relationship as harsh as we see it in his Swedish contemporary August Strindberg's works. The impression of the text as true romanticism is not only due to the love story it tells. The romantic feeling is deeply integrated in the literary form as well as the characters' mentality.

In spite of the strong focus on emotions, there is also a social framework to this story. Edvarda is the daughter of Mack, the mighty owner of the local fishing station. This social setting, including the character Edvarda, appears again in later novels, (*Benoni* and *Rosa*, 1908), about a young widow who is disappointed and unhappy.

Hamsun's radical breakthrough in the 1890s earned him the reputation as the father of modern literature (Andersen 2001: 296), as Isaac B. Singer put it: "The whole modern school of fiction in the 20th century stems from Hamsun". He has inspired the great European modernist generation of the 1920s with writers like Thomas Mann and Franz Kafka as well as Ernest Hemingway and Henry Miller.

More wanderers

After the turn of the century we see a further development of ideas and motifs from Hamsun's first works. He wrote more stories from Nordland, where he spent most of his childhood, depicting small societies dominated by the mighty owner of the fish station. This backdrop, however, never turns Hamsun into a socially aware realist. Rather, he focuses on the dreams and aspirations of ordinary people, struggling with their inner life as well as their position in society.

A typical theme throughout Hamsun's work is the portrayal of the wanderer. This is even expressed in many of his titles: *Under the Autumn Star* (1907), *A Wanderer Plays on Muted Strings* (1909) (the two novels were translated into one volume entitled *Wanderers*) and *Vagabonds* (1927). His characters are restless, always moving, sometimes against the crowd, never really finding their place in the world.

Back to the soil

One novel by Hamsun is unique in its warm and undivided sympathy for the main character, and that was the book that earned Hamsun the Nobel Prize for literature in 1920. *The Growth of the Soil* (1917) presents a wanderer of a different kind, one who wanders into the wilderness to conquer it with his bare hands, and in this he finds peace. Isak Sellanrå can be seen as the incarnation of Hamsun's dream about cultivating the soil, demonstrating the blessings of a simple, primitive life close to nature (Beyer 1975: 169). Isak with his bodily strength and simple mentality is described as "a log with hands, but inside he was like a child". His wife Inger with her harelip, escapes from public shame to the wilderness, and with her hard work and appreciative attitude proves a worthy match to Isak. Both are contrasted to weaker, more restless characters related to those we find more commonly in Hamsun's work. The novel is written against the background of the First World War, when cultivating new soil became vital for Norway. This was also the period when Hamsun himself tried out farming besides his writing, first in Hamarøy in Nordland, and later at Nørholm in Grimstad.

The Growth of the Soil stands in sharp contrast to most of Hamsun's other works, because of its warm sympathy with its main character, and a lack of the irony that is otherwise so characteristic of Hamsun's work. Still it is connected in a pessimistic perspective on industrialization and modern life. Ironically Isak's heroic work to conquer the wilderness brings modernity into the simple life that he loves.

The typical Hamsun wanderer based his vitality on spontaneity, moods and erotic power. That may be one reason why Hamsun experienced some problems in writing as he grew older. The novels he wrote after the First World War are pessimistic and sharply satirical against modern society. But once again Hamsun found a way to renew his writing. He did so by introducing a new type of wanderer in the trilogy about August (1927-1933), the *vagabond* – which is also the title of the first of the three books. These novels present less despair than the early wanderers in Hamsun's writing, and more charm and playfulness. August comes from nowhere and can go anywhere. Hamsun presents him with deep ambivalence: The moralist narrator is deeply critical of this gambler bluffing his way through life. On the other hand the imaginative narrator reveals a weakness for the charm and fantasy that August spreads around. Primarily he is seen as the product of urban, capitalist and industrial developments in society.

A political postlude

As we have seen, Hamsun was deeply sceptical of the development of modern society and of the influence from Britain and America in particular. Culturally he always leaned towards Germany, where his work had been well received and appreciated. This has been pointed to as one of many reasons why Hamsun came to support Nazi Germany and the German occupation of Norway 1940-1945. This immediately changed his position in the public sphere. After the war Hamsun was detained in the old people's home in Grimstad, after a legal process involving a psychiatric examination that concluded he had permanently impaired mental faculties.

The debate about how to view Hamsun's position during the Second World War seems to have no end as far as public opinion is concerned. On the one hand some would claim that Hamsun was an old man at this point, isolated and hard of hearing. But the view that his political standpoint was the result of a weakened mental capacity in old age was firmly contradicted when he published his own reflections on this period of his life *On Paths Overgrown* (1949) at the age of 90.

On the other hand there are voices that claim that Hamsun's Nazi sympathies can be traced all through his work. These critics point to his admiration for the strong individual and his anti-democratic attitudes, and they also link his utopian romanticising of nature to the Nazi *Blut und Boden* mysticism (Beyer 1975: 4; 180).

But great works of literature can hardly be reduced to a political formula. There are sides to Hamsun's work that would never fit into a simple explanation connected to his political views. The question has been raised how the writer of complex psychological portraits of unique individuals could subscribe to an ideology demanding total loyalty to the state and its cause. As the title of Robert Ferguson's biography (1987), *Enigma; the life of Knut Hamsun*, indicates, the life of this author will always remain a puzzle to the reading public.

History of literature: history of a nation

For a long time the history of Norwegian literature has been understood as a reflection of the history of Norway becoming a nation with an identity of its own. Each new period has been seen as a result of, or a reaction to, the previous one, the whole story contributing to the understanding of what it means to be Norwegian.

But there are other ways to understand the dynamics of history, especially through the 20th century. The realist tradition that was established by Henrik Ibsen and his contemporaries in the 1870s and 1880s has held a strong position in Norwegian literature ever since. For instance, a new

generation of realists appears at the beginning of the 20th century. In 1907
three of the most popular authors among the reading public through the
20th century appeared for the first time on the literary scene: Sigrid Und-
set (1882-1949), Olav Duun (1876-1939) and Johan Falkberget (1879-1967). They
are primarily known for their broad historical epics, detailed mimetic stories about people's lives in past times. They were followed by novelists
active in the 1930s who focus more on psychological explanations of individual development. Sigurd Hoel (1890-1960) and Helge Krog (1889-1962) represent a new combination of political radicalism and psychological in-
depth analysis.

Another radical generation of realists dominated the literary field in
the 1970s, emphasising political questions following the Marxist ideology
prevailing in the student uprising of 1968. Like the golden generation one
century earlier, they define the interesting topics to belong within the
political sphere; even love relationships carry political meaning in novels
such as *Kjærleikens ferjereiser* (*The ferry crossing*) (1974) by Edvard Hoem (1949-)
and *Gymnaslærer Pedersen* (1982) by Dag Solstad (1941-). The full title of the
latter is *Gymnaslærer Pedersens beretning om den store politiske vekkelsen som har
hjemsøkt vårt land* (High school teacher Pedersen's account on the great
political awakening that has afflicted our country), indicating how this
novel reflects over the socialist radicalism in the 1970ies in hindsight.

Dag Solstad belonged to a group of authors that was established
around the literary journal *Profil* in the 1960ies. From 1966 he was the editor together with the novelist Espen Haavardsholm and the poet Jan Erik
Vold. In the 1960ies they represented a generation of authors who were
interested in literary theory as well as literary form. Idealizing the great
European generation of modernists in the 1920ies, they were ready to
explore new ways of integrating literary form with content in order to
express the feeling of estrangement in modernity. To some extent this
more personal focus on role and identity returns after the political wave
of the 1970ies. Dag Solstads novels from the 1990ies typically focus on
middle-aged men's reflections over the modern condition. The plot typically circles around a stressful situation in novels such as *Genanse og verdighet* (1994), *Professor Andersens natt* (1996), *T. Singer* (1999). In *Shyness and
dignity* (*Genanse og verdighet*) the young students are seen from the point of
view of a school teacher who has been trying to teach Ibsen's plays to
young people for 25 years. The fact that his students find Ibsen boring, he
finds quite natural. After all, Ibsen is too complicated for 18 year olds, he

reflects. But driven to a point where his young students no longer tolerate this boredom, he realises that he is lost. His world has come to an end, and he has no idea how to move on.

Modernism in many phases

Parallell to these strong realist trends we can trace a modernist trajectory from the generation of the1890s onwards, with Knut Hamsun as the most outstanding representative. The last decades of the 20th century has seen a strengthening of this trend with a turn towards philosophical questions and phantasy, psychology and playful irony.

It is usually claimed that modernism arrived late in the history of Norwegian literature, and this is probably due to the strong position of mimetic realist writing. But it may be equally reasonable to regard the realists and the modernists as two competing trends, taking turns in dominating the scene. In the 20th century there are times when the two exist side by side, sometimes connected to different genres. For instance in the decades from the 1930s, we find novels in both traditions, though the realist trend may seem more dominant. The most obvious examples of modernist literature in the early 1900s we find in poetry.

Modernist poetry

The great writers of the realist era of the 19th century wrote mainly in the dramatic or epic genres. Ibsen wrote some poetry in his early years, but discarded most of it when he published his collected poems in 1871. In the generation from the1890s poetry came more to the fore. Though Hamsun only published one collection of poems, some of his most distinguished contemporaries, e.g. Sigbjørn Obstfelder, expressed alienated feelings about life mainly in the lyrical genre.

Tarjei Vesaas (1897-1970) is one of the most outstanding Norwegian writers of the 20th century. He published across a broad spectrum of genres: Novels, short-stories, drama and poetry. His novels cover the mimetic portrayals of rural life as well as symbolic and quite abstract allegories. Even in his prose, there is always a poetic style of writing, with few words and a characteristic short-breathed rhythm. Still it is first and foremost in his poetry that he undoubtedly belongs to the modernist tradition, drawing on symbols and painting existential landscapes.

Rolf Jacobsen (1907-1994) took the public by surprise when he published his first collection of poetry in 1933. His early poems point to a future world. They differed from the poetry of the previous decades in their modern form, with free verse, and focusing on modern 'unpoetic' topics such as industry and communication technologies. The title *Earth and Iron* (*Jord og jern*) gives a precise signal about Rolf Jacobsen's position between nature and technology, which became more obvious in his later poems. From the 1950s onwards, Jacobsen's fascination for technology enters more explicitly into conflict with his concern about nature, when he explores topics like environmental problems and nuclear weapons. Towards the end of his life Rolf Jacobsen included motifs concerning more personal relations in his poems. With his last collection *Night Open* (*Nattåpent*, 1985) he became the most popular lyricist in modern Norway.

Born at the same time, Olav H. Hauge (1908-1994) started writing much later, publishing his first collection of poems in 1946. Even later, in the 1960s he developed the poetic form that was to become his trademark: a condensed, economic manner of expression where nature and simple artefacts were allowed to tell their story without comment. Hauge lived in Hardanger on the west coast of Norway all his life, making a living from gardening and writing. In spite of being deeply rooted in his local environment, he was also very much internationally oriented. He read and translated British, French and German poetry, and also presented Chinese poetry to the reading public in Norway. Thus he is yet another example that in the Norwegian context some of the most interesting writers have united the local and the global, nature and culture in their writing.

Metareflection and poetics

As mentioned above, the politically oriented writers of the 1970ies changed to a more reflexive mood in the 1980ies. But the clearest renewal came from a new generation of writers who included a meta-perspective on writing and society as they set off to explore the late modern or post-modern condition. In contrast to the realist tradition they seem to question our possibilities to grasp 'reality' as such. And in contrast to previous modernists who mainly wrote poems and short stories, the writers of the 1980ies chose the broad format of the novel. Jan Kjærstad (1953-) published "A poetics for the 80ies" along with novels experimenting with identities, genres and narrative closure. In the 1990ies he followed up with a trilogy about Jonas Wergeland (*Forføreren*, 1993, *Erobreren*, 1996 and *Oppdageren*, 1999). The story about this modern media personality unfolds in parallel plot-lines seen from different perspectives. The result is a fragmented, yet rich description of the complex forming of identity in late modernity.

Among the new writers who appear on the scene in the 1990ies we find a continuation of the trends from the 80ies. But we also find a new atti-tude to the big philosophical questions posed in encounter with the loss of meaning that characterizes late modernity. When Erlend Loe (1969-) had his break-through with *Naiv.Super* in 1996, a new group of young readers found a style that reflected their life experiences (livsfølelse). This appar-ently simple story features a young man reluctant to grow up. The book appears as a collection of fragments, dominated by lists and reflections about his life here and now in a naive style corresponding to the first part of the title. But it also includes philosophical statements about the dimen-sion of time in the universe, forming a sort of collage of documents from Internet, modern advertising and music along with diary-like notes. This mix of high and low creates the humour and irony of the book, and presents a portrait of identity formation in a time when the value of authority, maturity and traditional 'bildung' is being questioned. In his later work Loe continues to write about the problems of men his own age. In *L* (1999) we follow a group of young men who are approaching 30, and find out it is about time to achieve something in life. In *Doppler* (2004) the protagonist is close to 40, and is still not ready to settle in modern materi-alist society.

Erlend Loe has his educational background in script writing for film, and has alternated between working with literature and film. He may rep-resent a new generation of cross-over writers who combine different forms of expression: literature, music and film.

At the turn of the millennium the major questions in literature are not concerned with building a national identity. Rather the questions of iden-tity formation are triggered by questions of how to find meaning in a glo-balised world of commercialisation, consumerism and media events.

Chapter 16

Children's Literature

By Elise Seip Tønnessen

In Norway – as well as in other European countries – we have seen a long-standing debate about the status of children's literature. Is it to be considered as art, possessing aesthetic qualities? Or does it rather belong to the field of education, playing its most important role in the upbringing of children, conveying good morals and cultural insights? These questions involve society's view of children as well as of the arts.

Children's literature has been known to be conservative. Traditionally it has mirrored the questions, tastes and activities of the writers' own childhoods. But since around 1970 children's literature in Norway has developed in parallel with general fiction. That can be seen in a wider variety of genres being published, and in experiments with form as well as themes previously not found suitable for children. We also find new narrative forms: A subjective view of the world mostly conveyed through an unreliable first person narrator, along with a more ambiguous literature without a finger pointing accusingly, and often offering an open ending with no clear message. In short we may claim with the Russian-Swedish scholar Maria Nicolajeva that children's literature is "becoming of age".

Bridging the gap

One explanation for the renewed interest in children's literature in Norway may be the improved conditions for authors in the field, financially as well as in terms of publicity. It is becoming common that authors publish across the age groups. Some authors question the separation of children's literature altogether, for instance Einar Økland, Tormod Haugen and Erlend Loe, who claim that they write *literature* without targeting one specific age group. The labels "children's literature", "young adult fiction" and so on, are primarily used by the publishers and the marketing system.

This kind of crossover is not entirely new. In the dawn of children's literature in Norway, Henrik Wergeland (1808-45) wrote poetry for children along with general fiction and non-fiction for other 'outsider' cultural groups like farmers and workers. A decade later Jørgen Moe (1813-82), the collector of folk tales, published the first stories narrated from a child's perspective (*I Brønden og i Kjærnet*, 1851).

Realism portraying modern problems

Throughout the 1970s new themes appeared in children's literature in the Scandinavian countries. Motifs that were previously considered to belong in adult literature alone entered the scene: political questions, sexual liberation, divorce and family problems, and drug abuse. Still the narrative form was not radically different from the realist tradition that has been dominant throughout the history of Norwegian literature. The problems explored were placed in a recognizable setting and solved in accordance with the logic of everyday life.

One exception is Tor Åge Bringsværd (1939-) who tended to combine the problems of modern life with fantasy literature. For instance in his story about "the blue people" and the sweet factory (*Det blå folket og karamellfabrikken*, 1974) the theme is pollution. The book portrays a society where the factory that produces sweets is a threat to the environment. The blue people would rather close their eyes and enjoy their sweets than wake up to reality. Tor Åge Bringsværd has published in different genres, and in the 1980s his fantastic stories were more in line with the general trend. From 1985 to 1995 he published a series of 12 picture books retelling the Old Norse myths about the rise and fall of the civilization populated by the Norse gods, human beings and trolls. He claims that each generation has to reconquer the old myths, and make them meaningful in their own contemporary context. His own contribution has been to cooperate with a new artist in every single book in the series of twelve. The result is a series where the images in all their variety connect the old stories to the life experience of readers today, for instance presenting Tor, the god of thunder, as a gang leader on a modern motor bike.

In Arne Samuelsen's illustrations for the story about Loke (1994), Tor, the god of thuder in Norse mythology, appears as a modern gang leader.

Tormod Haugen (1945-) is another initiator of the new trend in the 1980s. He mixes reality with dreamlike scenes, for example in *Zeppelin* (1976). The story is about Nina and the boy she calls Zeppelin, for want of another name (she finds the word written on his sneakers). The boy has run away to hide in a tree in Nina's garden. Together the children reflect on their relationship to their parents, who give them either too little or too much freedom. As the boy's situation gets more difficult, he withdraws into a mythological landscape of wolves, knights with swords and the dangerous web of a giant spider. Tormod Haugen was awarded the prestigious Hans Christian Andersen Medal in 1991. In later years his writing has turned to intertextual games with popular culture. *The Cry from the Jungle* (*Skriket fra jungelen*, 1989) has developed this post-modern style of writing to the full in a complex mix of genres. This book follows up a leitmotif in Haugen's work about children being overlooked or exploited by adults. An American psychologist captures unhappy children in order to reuse their dreams and imaginations in a machine that will make him able to control people's thoughts. The children escape into a jungle materializing from the children's fantasies.

These pioneers created new ways of writing for children in Norway, introducing the more fantastic, and also the surrealistic, the burlesque

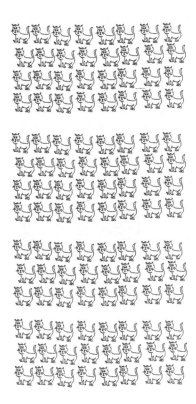

In his "cat sonette" Ragnar Hovland plays with new aesthetic forms.

and the poetic approach. In the tradition of new Norwegian (nynorsk) culture along the western coast of Norway, we saw a blossoming of humorous and playful experiments with form, for instance in Einar Økland's (1940-) poems and picture books. Ragnar Hovland's (1952-) contribution includes poems as well as picture books and novels. In his young adult fiction he tends to focus on how children deal with hopeless adults, with references to popular culture interwoven in the text. Rune Belsvik's (1956-) stories cover the whole range from fantasy stories for small children in his books about *Dustefjerten*, to young adult fiction exploring the development of teenage boys and their first approaches to sex.

In this context Jostein Gaarder started off as an outsider with his mix of didactic philosophical intent and fantastic literature in books such as *The Solitaire Mystery* (*Kabalmysteriet*, 1990) and *Sophie's World* (*Sofies verden*, 1991). Their unpredicted success started off a new era for the translation of Norwegian children's literature throughout the world.

Jostein Gaarder's novel Sophie's World *on the history of philosophy has been translated into 49 languages and has sold over 25 million copies. In 1995, it was the most sold novel in the world.*

At the same time we saw a new interest in picture books, and not only for the small children. Fam Ekman (1946-), active as an illustrator as well as a writer, was one of the pioneers in this development. Her first book is about little Jill and her fantastic journey into the world of art (*Hva skal vi gjøre med lille Jill*, 1976). The interplay between words and images became more complex when the two modes of expression were not necessarily telling the same story. This exchange is typical of the cooperation between Liv Marie Austrem (1947-) and Akin Düzakin (1961-), resulting in two books about a set of twins, one book from the perspective of the twin sister, the other focusing on the twin brother (*Tvillingbror*, 1995 and *Tvillingsøster*, 1997). Picture books have become interesting in new ways at a time when authors find methods of expression across the media, in writing as well as in music, images and film.

The new generation of writers in the 1990s develop this multimodal approach to children's literature even further. Writers such as Arne Berggren (1960-) and Harald Rosenløw Eeg (1970-) have made parallel careers in young adult fiction and in popular music. Rosenløw Eeg was awarded the Vesaas Prize for his debut novel *Glasskår* (*Fragments of Glass*, 1995). He has been known to write in a style that reproduces the rhythm and sound of young people's language. At the same time his books question established truths in society in new ways. For instance in the novel *Vrengt* (1999) he turns established views inside out (literally; *Inside out* is the translation of the title). A group of outsiders live together in the lofts of a shopping centre, all of them portraying forms of life that modern society has turned its back on. The novel leaves the reader with a pessimistic view of modern society, though not of the human race in general. The time when we expected a happy ending in books for children and the young seems to be long gone. The open ending as well as new forms of expression sum up the traits that most profoundly distinguish this generation of writers from the previous one.

Multimodal predecessors

A fruitful combination of books with other media is not entirely new. The 1950s are considered one of the glorious periods of children's literature in Norway. One obvious reason is that this decade fostered a generation of writers producing stories and lyrics across the media. During this peak in radio history, programming for children adopted regular forms with a "children's hour" (*Barnetimen*) for small children every morning, and a weekly programme for older children, or rather for the whole family, every Saturday afternoon. This was the cultural environment that fostered very popular writers for children, among whom the best known are Torbjørn Egner (1912-90), Alf Prøysen (1914-70) and Anne Cath. Vestly (1920-). Egner was known for his paintings, stage shows and songs as well as children's books and radio stories. For one thing, he introduced and retold A.A. Milne's stories about *Winnie the Pooh* to Norwegian radio listeners. Egner has also left his mark on the Norwegian school system with his Literature readers from 2nd to 9th grade, widely used for more than a generation. His multimedia work lives on in *Kardemomme by*, (Cardamum Town), situated in Kristiansand's zoo and amusement park. Alf Prøysen performed his songs and wrote short stories and plays for adults before he became a successful storyteller in the regular radio programmes for children. His stories about *Mrs. Pepperpot* (*Teskjekjerringa*) have achieved international acclaim. Anne Cath. Vestly started out as an actor, using this to advantage in her oral story telling on radio, and finally achieving great success with her books based on the radio stories. She writes about modern family life in the new suburbs that were built after World War II.

The textual universe presented to children in Norway is to an increasing extent becoming influenced by global trends and cross media publications. As we have seen, this may be used creatively to develop new aesthetics. On the other hand it may also create opportunities for commercialization and present a threat to the sense of Norwegian identity in children's books.

Chapter 17

Norwegian Art –
More than Munch

By Lisbet Skregelid

"SCREAM STOLEN FROM NORWAY MUSEUM". This and similar headlines reached the international news in August 2004. The most famous painting in Norway, *The Scream*, by the artist Edvard Munch, had been ripped off the museum wall along with another Munch painting, *Madonna*. Representing a common national heritage, the robbery caused a shock among Norwegians and also among art lovers around the world.

Norwegian art is more than Munch. This chapter gives a brief overview of Norwegian art, with a main emphasis on paintings. A selection of artworks and artists has been made, and thereby many have been left out. Many of the mentioned, and all the not mentioned Norwegian images and artworks can be explored in and outside museums and galleries, across Norway and abroad.

The First Images

The oldest images that we know of in Norway are rock carvings. The earliest carvings date to around 4200 BC. One of these sites was discovered in 1973 near the Alta fjord, located in the far north of Norway. At this UNESCO World Heritage site, more than 6,000 individual figures are carved into the landscape. The images depict people, animals, boats and weapons. Some carvings appear to show hunting scenes and others are considered to represent people holding traditional instruments such as "runebommen", the shamanic drum used in rituals by the Sami people. The carvings presumably played an important role in Norwegian culture. Also in the counties Østfold, Vestfold, Akershus, Buskerud, Nordland, Rogaland, Sogn og Fjorande, Sør Trøndelag and Nord Trøndelag rock carvings that date back to prehistoric times have been discovered.

The Viking Age, dating from the 8th to the 11th century, shows a wide variety of decorative objects used in daily life. The Vikings are known for woodcarving and fine personal ornaments in a decorative style similar to what is found in Celtic art. Most of the finest surviving examples of art from the Viking Age have been found in graves, especially jewellery and weapons. Viking images often portray man strongly connected to forces in nature. The Oseberg Ship, which can be seen in Oslo, is an excellent example of the decorative style of the Vikings. This style also influenced the ornamentation of the stave churches that were built all over the country during the Middle Ages. The Norwegian stave churches represent a distinct contribution to the history of European architecture because of their special wooden construction. Today, there are 29 remaining stave churches of a total of about 1 000. Several of the churches have been moved and preserved at new locations. One example is the church that was moved from Gol in the middle of Norway to The National Folk Museum at Bygdøy in Oslo.

In the Middle Ages, images and decoration in churches played an important role. The church altars were exquisitely decorated. Professional painters were also hired to decorate interior, furniture and objects in the private homes of the wealthy. From the 16th century, European art influenced the Norwegian painting style. The acanthus motive, a characteristic floral design deriving from Antiquity, was adopted in many different ways in Norwegian ornamentation. This can be seen in the tradition of rose painting, a peasant style of decoration, which became a well-established rural tradition.

The 19th century marked the beginning of a new era for the art of painting in Norway. At the turn of the century, portraits were extremely fashionable among prosperous Norwegians. Jacob Munch (1776-1839) and Matthias Stoltenberg (1799-1871) made a living from painting portraits of the rich and powerful. Professional painters were also engaged to make small, detailed paintings of different places in Norway. This style encouraged some artists to travel to Europe to receive a more professional and academic art education. The first one to head south was Johan Christian Dahl, also called the "Father of Norwegian painting".

National Romanticism – The First Norwegian Artists

Norway's newfound independence from Denmark in 1814 raised issues of national identity. During the 1830s and '40s, conscious effort was made by artists and intellectuals to define what it meant to be Norwegian. Painters searched for national identity by using their artistic skills.

Johan Christian Claussen Dahl (1778-1857) is considered to be the first Norwegian artist in the modern sense of the term. He was born in Bergen, and worked there as a decorative painter. His landscape paintings received recognition, and Dahl moved to Copenhagen in 1811 to receive a formal art education with the help of wealthy benefactors in his home town of Bergen. Following his years as an art student, Dahl moved to Germany and settled in Dresden. He was influenced by the German Romantic painter Caspar David Friedrich (1774-1840), and became a close friend of his. It was the dramatic confrontation with the landscape, and man's attempt to control nature, that interested Dahl. Magnificent Norwegian landscapes were the main motives in his production. Dahl continued to reside in Dresden, and went to Norway, especially the Western part of Norway, with his sketchbooks to study nature only five times. When painting landscapes such as *Stalheim* (1842) he had to rely on memories and his sketches in order to depict Norwegian nature. In his paintings of the Norwegian landscapes he wanted to find and give form to what was typical Norwegian. Dahl was not only the first Norwegian artist. He also contributed to the establishing of the Norwegian National Gallery, and was especially concerned with the preservation of his home country's outstanding national possessions – the stave churches.

For Norwegians, the painting *Brudeferden i Hardanger* (*The Bridal Voyage in Hardanger*) is automatically associated with the painter Adolph Tidemand (1814-1876), and his companion Hans Gude (1825-1903). This particular painting from 1848 has received iconic status as it reflects what many associate with Norway. Tidemand painted the bridal procession and Gude painted the landscape.

Tidemand was born in 1814, the year of the dissolution of the Danish-Norwegian union. He received private art lessons in his hometown of Mandal (in the very south of Norway), and his talent was soon recognized. At the age of 18 he moved to Copenhagen, and eventually he settled down in Düsseldorf, Germany. The art academy there enjoyed widespread international recognition, and Tidemand continued his studies there. Like Dahl, Tidemand was preoccupied by Norwegian motives. But whereas Dahl

Adolph Tidemand and Hans Gude: The Bridal Voyage in Hardanger, 1848.

depicts Norwegian nature, Tidemand shows us Norwegian culture. Tidemand was interested in Norwegian history, particularly after returning from a journey to Norway. After that, he often traveled to Norway. Today, Tidemand is regarded as the first Norwegian historic painter, and is best known for his depiction of Norwegian farm and street life.

Thomas Fearnley (1802-1842), Peder Balke (1804-1887), August Cappelen (1827-1852), Lars Hertevig (1830-1902) and Amaldus Nielsen (1838-1932) are other representatives of Norwegian Romanticism.

Realism, Naturalism and Neo-Romanticism

In the 1880s, many Norwegian artists went to Paris to explore French innovative art. Germany had become too conservative. The Norwegian artists were influenced by the new ways of painting represented by French artists such as Gustave Courbet (1819-1877) and Claude Monet (1840-1926).

Christian Krohg (1852-1925) was a Norwegian realist painter, author, journalist and lawyer. He was educated in Germany, but returned to Norway to work and live there most of his life. His stay in Paris from 1881-1882 was of great importance to him. In Paris, Krohg found inspiration in the realist painters such as Courbet, and chose his motives primarily from everyday life. He found the dirt in the city more poetic than fjords and mountains, and insisted that art should concentrate on life as it was lived and experienced by the individual human being. One of his most famous paintings, *Albertine i politilægens venteværelse* (*Albertine at The Police Doctor's Waiting Room*, 1885-87) shows a scene from Krohg's novel *Albertine*. The novel caused a scandal when it was published, and was confiscated by the police shortly after. Krohg based *Albertine* on a true story, and both the novel and the painting were very controversial in the 1880s. The painting shows us the situation when the young and poor seamstress Albertine is taken to the medical office at the police station to be registered as a prostitute. Krohg wanted his art to make a difference. In 1902, prostitution was declared illegal. In that way Krogh succeeded; his mission was to make art that influenced political issues. Krohg was a leading figure in Norwegian art in the transition from romanticism to naturalism. His social concern and his way of cropping motives like a snapshot influenced many of his contemporary artists. In 1883, Krohg contributed to the establishment of the Norwegian Autumn Exhibition, and he was the first professor director at The Norwegian Academy of Arts, founded in 1909. He also played an important role in a group of radical anarchist artists, called "Kristania-bohemen" (The Kristiania Bohemians). This active political group also involved Edvard Munch, who was instructed by Krohg in his early paintings. Krohg married one of the few women in this group, Oda Krohg (1860-1935). "The bohème princess", as she was called, was also a painter. She was a realist, but more influenced by the new impressionist style of painting. Especially in her landscapes one can see this.

Harriet Backer (1845-1932) and Fritz Thaulow (1847-1906) were also more influenced by the impressionist Monet than the realist Courbet. Their paintings are more concerned with form, colour and atmosphere, than political issues. Inspired by French *plein air* (outdoor) painting, Thaulow in particular became internationally orientated. Backer on the other hand is most known for painting colourful interior. For both of them, and for many of their contemporaries, it was not *what* one painted – but *how* one depicted a motif that was becoming more and more important. "L'art pour l'art", (art for art's sake) was a slogan used to affirm that art was valuable *as* art.

Two artists criticizing the romantic way of painting, especially the Düsseldorf style represented by Tidemand, were Erik Werenskiold (1855-1938) and Theodor Severin Kittelsen (1857-1914). Werenskiold chose his subjects from everyday life in the countryside. Norwegian landscapes should not be painted in Germany, he said. One had to know nature in order to give a credible representation of the scenery. Despite their realistic and natural-istic principles, Werenskiold and Kittelsen are best known for their illus-trations of fairytales and legends. Both of them were hired to illustrate traditional Norwegian fairytales collected by Asbjørnsen and Moe. Ever since then, their drawings have shown both children and adults what trolls and spirits, fairytale princesses and ash-lads really look like. Some images Kittelsen made for the book *Svartedauden* (*The Black Death*) have recently experienced their renaissance as some of the pictures in the book are used as album art by black metal bands. The images in the book show the scary figure "*Pesta*", *The Plague*, that killed between one third and two thirds of the European population during the 14th Century.

The era of realism and naturalism did not last long. The power and mystery in nature, Viking art and traditional Norwegian decoration inspired Norwegian artists as Norway was on its way of becoming totally independent from Denmark as well as Sweden. The landscapes painted by artists svch as Harald Sohlberg (1869-1935), represent the neo-romantic view to painting. Paintings should not only show nature, but people's, or the artist's, experience of nature. Paintings such as *Vinternatt i Rondane* (*Winter Night in Rondane*, 1914) are filled with symbolic content. The trees at different stages possibly indicate circle of life. Sohlberg claimed that the artist mind contain images, and will find these images in nature. Contem-poraries of Sohlberg included also artists such as Arne Kavli (1878-1970), Thorvald Erichsen (1868-1939), Halfdan Egdius (1877-1899) and Nikolai Astrup (1880-1928), who united the tendencies of the 1890s by developing the ambience of realism into a more abstract expression. This period also included Norway's probably most widely known artist Edvard Munch.

Edvard Munch

Edvard Munch (1863-1944) is regarded as one of the main figures of the artistic epoch known as Expressionism. He greatly influenced German expressionism in the early 20th century, and he is the most famous Norwe-gian artist internationally. The quote "I do not paint what I see, but what I saw" describes his approach to the making of art.

Munch was born in Hedmark and grew up in Oslo, then called Kristiania. His home was culturally stimulating, but: "Illness, madness and death were the black angles that kept watch over my cradle and they have followed me throughout my life", Munch said. The trauma caused by the deaths of his mother and sister by tuberculosis when Munch was a child, was reinforced by the religious mania of his father. In his art, Munch turned to these and other distressing memories again and again.

In 1879, Munch enrolled in a technical college to study engineering, but frequent illnesses interrupted his studies. Soon he became dedicated to art and left college to become a painter. He studied old masters and painted in a studio he shared with some friends. The Norwegian realist painter, Christian Krohg, instructed Munch in his work.

Munch travelled to Paris in 1885, and his work began to show the influence of the French impressionist style of painting. That year he started on the work that was to be his breakthrough *Det syke barn* (*The Sick Child*). In this painting he made a radical break with the realistic approach to the motif and introduced Modernism to Norwegian art. Haunted by the distressing memory of his young sister Sophie's deathbed, he strove to capture the tearful remembrance on canvas. The texture of the surface displays signs of a laborious, creative and painful process. When it was exhibited, he recorded: "No painting had aroused as much anger in Norway as this one". The contemporary critics responded with laughter and horror. With this provocative painting Munch had caused a scandal.

After this, his main works from the following years became less aggressive. Munch's association with the circle of radical anarchist artists, The Kristiania Bohemians, encouraged Munch to continue his mission: He wanted to present truthful close-ups of modern longings and agonies – he wanted to paint his own life.

In the autumn of 1889, Munch held a large separate exhibition in Kristiania. After this, he was awarded a state travel grant for three consecutive years. This led to regular visits to France and Germany, where his mature style developed under major influences by Vincent van Gogh (1853-1890), Paul Gauguin (1848-1903), Henri Toulouse Lautrec (1864-1901), the Art-Nouveau style and the Neo-Impressionists. In Berlin, Munch was invited to exhibit at the November exhibition. His paintings evoked bitter controversy at the show, and after one week the exhibition closed. The attention he was given encouraged Munch to develop his characteristic, and original, Synthetist aesthetic, as seen in *Skriket*, (*The Scream*), in which colour is the

Edvard Munch:
The Scream, 1893.

symbol-laden element. *The Scream* (1893) is Munch's most famous work. It is one of the pieces in a series titled *Livsfrisen* (*The Frieze of Life*), in which Munch explored the themes of life, love, fear, death and melancholy. *The Scream* has become an icon of our times, an image familiar to many who have never even heard of Munch himself. The whole landscape expresses a human emotion, in this case "inner hell" like anxiety, isolation and apocalypse. The screaming figure is stripped to its elements; a scull-like face, a twisted, agonized posture and the perspective is exaggerated. The colours convey waves of pain across the picture. The painting visualizes a real experience: "One evening I was walking along a path, the city was on one side and the fjord below. I felt tired and ill. I stopped and looked out over the fjord – the sun was setting, and the clouds turning blood-red. I sensed a scream passing through nature; it seemed to me that I heard the scream",

While in Berlin at the turn of the century, Munch experimented with a variety of new media, especially graphic work like woodcuts, in many instances reworking his older imagery. He was occupied with the loneliness, despair, and physical and mental agony that to him formed human life. In the autumn of 1908, increasingly heavy drinking and a destructive love affair, combined with Munch's ever-present anxiety became acute and he entered a mental clinic. The therapy Munch received in hospital changed him, and after returning to Norway he showed more interest in nature subjects, and his work became more colourful and less pessimistic. In 1911, Munch won a competition to paint a series of murals for the Great Hall in The University of Oslo. The main image portrays an emblematic sun and the rocky landscape of Kragerø, a little town by the sea in the county of Telemark.

Munch died in 1944, about a month after his 80th birthday. He left a large collection of pictures and biographical and literary notes to the City of Oslo, which built the Munch Museum in his honor. The museum houses the largest collection of his works. His works depicting "human beings that breathe and feel and love and suffer" are also represented in major museums and galleries in Norway and abroad.

The Vigeland Sculpture Park

Gustav Vigeland (1869-1943) was one of Munch's contemporaries. But while Munch painted human life, Vigeland gave form to people's lives by sculpturing them. Vigeland was born in Mandal, a coastal town in the very south of Norway, to a family of craftsmen and farmers. He had a special interest in handcraft, and he soon traveled to Oslo where he learned to carve wood. This encouraged him to become a professional sculptor. Vigeland also traveled abroad to study on his own and to learn more. The encounter with the French sculptor Auguste Rodin (1840-1917) and ancient and Renaissance artworks in Italy influenced his own sculpturing. His earlier works show that he was occupied with death and the relationship between man and woman. His first exhibitions in Norway received notable admiration. By the turn of the century, Vigeland was considered the most talented Norwegian sculptor. He received numerous commissions for statues and busts celebrating renowned notables.

In 1906, Vigeland planned a monumental fountain to be placed in front of the National Assembly, Stortinget. Because of some disagreement about the location, the project was postponed. In the meantime, Vigeland enlarged the project by adding several sculptures. The planned fountain

Gustav Vigeland: An Angry Young Boy
(Sinnataggen), *1925-1933.*

was never realized in the original site. Instead, it can now be admired in Vigeland's own sculpture park located in Oslo. This park is probably the most famous park in Norway and was created by Vigeland between the years 1907-1942. It all started when he was granted a new building nearby the park, when the city of Oslo decided to demolish his old home. He was also granted studio facilities for his sculpture work. In the following twenty years, Vigeland was devoted to the open sculpture exhibition in the park. The theme he worked with was 'The Human Condition.' Most of the statues in the park depict young and old people running, dancing, hugging, and so on. The main attraction in the park is *Monolitten* (*The Monolith*). The 14 meters tall column in the centre of the park is covered with entwined human bodies, and it is all carved from a single block of stone. Another well-known sculpture is that of An Angry Young Boy (*Sinnataggen*), located on the bridge of the park.

Vigeland lived and worked in his house by the park until his death in 1943. His home has become the Vigeland Museum, where visitors can see the works of art he donated to the City of Oslo, including the plaster models for the sculptures found in the park right outside.

Expressionism at the Beginning of The 20th Century

Munch, along with van Gogh and Gauguin, were of great inspiration to German expressionist movements that primarily aimed to express the artist's emotional experience. In France, an expressionist group was established with the painter Henri Matisse (1869-1954) as one of the leading figures. His decorative, colorful expressionist style and formal approach influenced a group of Norwegian artists who came to Paris to be tutored by their artistic hero. Henrik Sørensen (1882-1962) was prominent among these, as he interpreted his master in an individual manner. Matisse's basic idea was to stimulate each student's unique artistic character. Matisse also tutored Jean Heiberg (1884-1976), who adopted the expressionist style, but had a more controlled and academic approach to the canvas.

Ludvig Karsten (1876-1926), a third Norwegian student Matisse taught in his classes, became known to art critics as a late Impressionist. He was clearly under the influence of the more intense and colorful paintings by Matisse. Munch also inspired Karsten, and became a very good friend of his. Their friendship ended after a violent fight between the two in 1905. Despite of this dramatic event, Karsten continued to be one of the few of Munch's contemporary artists that Munch respected and approved of, and vice versa. Karsten was encouraged by Matisse to continue painting in his own personal colorful way. *Det blå kjøkken* (*The Blue Kitchen*) from 1913 is a fine example of Karsten's expressionistic approach to every day objects. Correct perspective is neglected. On the contrary, Karsten has created a powerful interpretation of the still life motif.

Sørensen, Heiberg and Karsten are all artists representing the beginning of Modernism in Norway. Modernism developed in the early 20th century as a reaction to all sorts of traditional art. The focus moved from motif to form, color and composition. For many artists, copying reality was not the main artistic occupation anymore. For some, like the expressionist, a modern approach meant more focus on real and direct feelings and color, but resemblance of nature. For others, it meant a complete detachment from reality and what could be seen with the eye. Abstract painting was on its way.

Abstract and Surrealist Painters

Thorvald Hellesen (1888-1937) was one of the first Norwegian abstract painters. During Word War I, he developed a decorative, abstract style influenced
by Fernand Legèr (1881-1955). Other students of Legèr in the 1920s were a
group of Norwegian women who contributed to a post-cubistic style of painting. This group included Charlotte Wankel (1888-1969), Ragnhild Kaarbø (1889-
1949) and Ragnhild Keyser (1889-1943). Despite the international orientation
and radical break with traditions, their works have not been much focused
on or approved of. Charlotte Wankel's *Maleri* (*The painting*) from 1925, is
strongly influenced by her teacher's utopian socialist ideas of human beings
and machines existing in harmony. In her paintings we often see people sim-
plified and transformed to geometrical figures. The forms seem to be superior to the colors. Wankel, her teacher and colleagues were inspired by the
artists Pablo Picasso (1881-1973) and Georges Braque (1882-1963) who with an
analytic and synthetic approach to painting, revolutionized art at the beginning of 1900s. The post-cubists were also influenced by Futurism, represented
by for example the Italian Umberto Boccioni (1882-1916) who wanted art to
represent speed, movement and rhythm, and glorified controversial aspects
like violence and war. Only to a moderate extent we see evidence of Futurism
in Norwegian art in the beginning of the 20th century.

Surrealism, which was an important artistic epoch in Europe at the
time, influenced only a few Norwegian artists. The Freudian ideas that
influenced a lot of international surrealist artist like Salvador Dali (1904-
1989) and Renè Magritte (1898-1967) were considered to be immoral and
primitive. However, there were exceptions. Kai Fjell (1907-1989), an autodidact artist, visualized in his work the intuitive and imaginative thoughts
he had during the process of paining. Arne Ekeland (1908-1994) was more
politically orientated. His aim was to liberate people politically and
socially, and make art that was in dialogue with contemporary society.

Social orientation - Decoration of Public Buildings

Painters that established themselves at the turn of the century include
Axel Revold (1887-1962), Per Krohg (1889-1965), and Alf Rolfsen (1895-1979).
Like many Norwegian artists, they were all educated in Paris by Matisse.
But these artists found painting purely for the sake of the art dissatisfying.
Per Krohg, son of Christian and Oda Krohg, developed a more political and

social approach to art than his teacher. During World War I, Per Krohg was a soldier fighting for the French. Like his father, Per Krohg continued to feel a responsibility towards society throughout his life as an artist. One way to perform in the social debate was to let more people experience their political message by decorating public buildings.

The large-scale mural painting method "al fresco", used by Italian Renaissance painters like Michelangelo Buonarroti (1475-1564) and Rafael Santi (1483-1520), was used to decorate public buildings and spaces. All the people of Norway were supposed to be given the opportunity to experience art. Within a mere two decades, an astonishing number of churches, schools, libraries and other public buildings were decorated. The motives we see in the murals are realistically orientated, and often show people working. Some say that the murals are lacking spontaneity and seem to be a bit static. Examples of mural paintings include Revold's decoration for the Bergen Stock Exchange (1918-1923), Krohg's murals at the Seamen's School in Oslo (1921-1924) and Rolfsen's decoration of the New Crematorium in Oslo (1932-1937). Revold, Krohg and Rolfsen are often referred to as "The Fresco Brothers." All of them contributed to the decorations in The Oslo City Hall.

Norwegian artists with a social concern during the interwar years included the painters Reidar Aulie (1904-1977), Willi Midelfart (1904-1975) and the weaver Hannah Ryggen (1894-1970). They were all politically orientated in their art and wanted people to wake up and realize what was going on around them.

Non-Figurative Painting

The experiences of World War II had only a brief impact on the work of Norwegian painters. The anxiety that characterized Norwegian art during the 1920s and 1930s was now replaced by the influence of abstract and non-figurative painting seen in American abstract expressionism. Expressions completely free of any boundaries were to dominate parts of Norwegian art. Despite strong opposition among the Norwegian public, abstract expressionism started to develop during the 1950s with the work of artists such as Ludvig Eikaas (1920-), Jakob Weidemann (1923-2001), Anna-Eva Bergman (1909-1987) and Inger Sitter (1929-).

The artists used the formal means of form, line, color and texture to create their non-figurative pieces of art. The "l'art pour l'art" attitude that

Inger Sitter: In the picture, 1964.

influenced the naturalists in the 1880s was now taken to new levels. Nature, a main inspiration source for the abstract expressionist, was hardly recognizable in the paintings. Nevertheless one can feel the presence of steep mountains, ice cold water, and moist forests, especially in Weidemann's abstract paintings.

Inger Sitter painted abstract paintings. Influenced by the American pop artist Robert Rauschenberg (1925-), she included the collage technique in her work. *In The Picture* (1964) is an example of a blend of painting and collage. She used a cutting from the English newspaper "The Observer". The words "In the picture" are visible in the newspaper clipping. Pieces of fabric are also included in the picture followed by blood red, white and blue paint. Sitter worked spontaneously and experimented in a way that provoked the Norwegian audience. Her abstract paintings were compared to children's scribbling and the slapdash painting of apes.

After 1960, some artists developed abstract painting even further. Gunnar S. Gundersen (1921-1983) used an original language of symbols within the framework of strict geometrical rules. Influenced by the constructive art of Hungarian Victor Vasarèly (1906-1997), he created compositions consisting of clear colors and sharp edged shapes. He stressed the importance of a paintings existence, not what it resembled. Arne Malmedal (1937-) developed the abstract, constructive style in his work by using a limited variety of colors and shapes.

Politically Orientated and Figurative Art

Not until 1965 did Norwegian painters terminate their close links with the German and French traditions. For decades, Paris had been the major inspiration. Now attention was drawn to other countries such as Britain and the United States. Strong impulses from American Pop art soon reached Norway. Pop art, a major visual artistic movement of the 20th century, was characterized by themes and techniques drawn from popular mass culture such as advertising and comic books. Artist like Per Kleiva (1933-), Willi Storn (1936-), Morten Krohg (1937-), and Anders Kjær (1940-) were inspired by the simple and figurative expression of Pop art represented by artist like Andy Warhol (1928-1987) and Roy Lichtenstein (1923-1997). They adopted the style in a more revolutionary and critical manner. The artists demonstrated their personal political views to the ongoing Vietnam War, to Third World issues, and various national issues such as the European Union referendum of 1972. The introduction of new techniques like silk-screen printing made this art form accessible to more people. Other graphic techniques like lithography, etching etc. were also welcomed both by the public and art communities. The 1970s are often referred to as "The Golden Age of Graphic Arts."

Kjartan Slettemark (1932-) is also known for his political work. In 1972 he used a passport with a fake photo with a portrait of himself and the American president Nixon. Using that passport he was actually able to enter the United States in 1972. He is also recognized for his artwork called *Av rapport fra Vietnam: Barn overskylles av brennende napalm. Deres hud brennes til svarte sår og de dør (From a Report on Vietnam: Children are Covered in Flaming Napalm. Their Skin is Burned into Black Wounds and They Die)*. During the summer of 1965, the USA had escalated the Vietnam War, with napalm bombings. Slettemark's response to this was to make an artwork containing a plastic assemblage with a blood-splattered miniature American flag between a pair of open red plastic lips. This artwork shocked the Norwegian cultural

Kjartan Slettemark:
From a Report on
Vietnam: Children are
Covered in Flaming
Napalm. Their Skin is
Burned into Black
Wounds and They Die,
1965.

and political scene. It overturned a whole set of traditions concerning free-dom of speech and art. Every day hordes of agitated people gathered in front of the artwork that was displayed outside the Parliament building. Many were convinced that this was not art and also wanted the picture banned because of its anti American message. After a week a provoked man demolished the artwork with an axe. Slettemark was so disappointed by this he decided to become a Swedish citizen. "I believe they would have poked my eyes out if I had stayed in Norway", he said. Slettemark is regarded to be the first artist in Norway working with performance art. Today, he works with all kinds of materials, focusing particularly on the installation of dolls made out of garbage. His current work lies at the inter-section between sculpture and installation art.

While many artists in the '60s and '70s continued their political devel-opment, other artists went more in the direction of figurative expression-ism. Håkon Bleken (1929-), Frans Widerberg (1934-), and Ørnulf Opdal (1944-) use symbolic language in their interpretations of the human being and the cosmos. Odd Nerdrum (1944-) is a figurative artist who paints in a classical manner. His pictures recall works by the Old Baroque Masters, particularly those of Michelangelo Caravaggio (1571-1610) and Rembrandt van Rijn (1606-1669). In his early works he raised questions concerning current society. Later, his work developed to get a highly characteristic appearance. Nerdrum has become a controversial artist, claiming that his art should be understood as kitsch rather than art. Nerdrum's art has gained international acclaim, especially in the USA.

Since the 1970s, focus on the actual technique of the painting has diminished and more attention has been paid to factors surrounding the picture. However, noteworthy figures sticking successfully to painting include among others Leonard Rickhard (1945-), Ida Lorentzen (1951-), Kjell Erik Killi Olsen (1952-), Anne Kathrine Dolven (1953-), Olav Christopher Jenssen (1954-), Kjell Nupen (1955-), and Håkon Gullvåg (1959-).

New Media – New Ideas

By the 1980s, Norwegian artists no longer followed a single line of influence and the decade was characterized by a large number of different forms and techniques. The period also saw the development of multimedia and installation art, and art based on ideas, also referred to as conceptual art.

Marianne Heske (1946-) is a representative of installation and conceptual art. She was also one of the first Norwegian artists to work with video. In 1980, her *Project Gjerdeløa* was exhibited in Paris at The Centre Georges Pompidou. A small, wooden barn from about 1630, originally situated in her native district Tafjord in the Western part of Norway, was taken apart and put together again in the exhibition building when it arrived in Paris. About 140 000 people saw *Gjerdeløa* when it was exhibited in Paris. Visitors to the exhibition could also watch different TV screens showing the process of dismantling and moving the barn from its original site, and people moving around the barn in the exhibition. *Gjerdeløa* was put back in its original place in Tafjord in 1981. With this project, Heske explored how we see an object in different settings. In Tafjord the barn was just a barn, in Paris inside the exhibition building it was considered as art. *Project Gjerdeløa* was realized 67 years after Marcel Duchamp (1887-1968) for the first time in 1913 placed a readymade in an art gallery. With the introduction of readymade and the conceptual approach he revolutionized the making and seeing of art.

Marianne Heske: Project Gjerdeløa, 1980-81. Installed in Centre Georges Pompidou in 1980 and reinstalled in Tafjord, 1981.

The art of Hilmar Fredriksen (1953-) has cut across the boundaries of artistic genres. In 1979, a strange looking work of art called *Kommunikasjonsstykke* (*Communication Piece*) was submitted to the annual Norwegian Autumn Exhibition. The artwork was an enclosed wooden box in the shape of a chair on baby carriage wheels. The artwork was rejected. Today, pieces of art like this using whatever media relevant to the artist's message is common in galleries and museums in Norway and abroad. The mixture of media is still what characterizes the works by Fredriksen, and artists like Per Inge Bjørlo (1952-) and Kurt Johannessen (1960-).

Contemporary Art

Norwegian art today is first and foremost characterized by vitality and variety. A large number of different forms and techniques exist side by side. Anything and everything goes. Realistic oil paintings and electronic works of art are exhibited in contemporary art galleries and museums. There is a noticeable interest in Norwegian contemporary art among artists, museum staff, promoters and collectors. A high level of activity, ambition and optimism also seems to draw international attention.

Ole Jørgen Ness (1961-) and Børre Sæthre (1967-) are artists that represent the blending of genres and media that characterize many contemporary artists. The use of new media like photography, video and electronic equipment has also emerged during the last few decades. For a long time photography was not accepted as art, but today it is an inevitable part of the art scene. From the 1990s, many artists saw the potential in using both straight and manipulated photography. Vibeke Tandberg (1967-) explores conventions of gender and identity in her self-portraits. By using computer manipulated photography she operates in the boundaries between the real and the possible. Mikkel McAlinden (1963-) plays with perspective showing us photographs that often appear more real than reality itself. Lotte Konow Lund (1967-) and Knut Åsdam (1968-) are artists working with a wide variety of media including video, another media used in contemporary art to a wide extent.

Some artists choose to address their art to a broader audience than those entering museums and galleries. Matias Faldbakken (1973-) and Gardar Eide Einarsson (1976-) collaborate on issues such as hidden structures of art and capital by moving their art out of the art institutions. Some of their art projects have drawn attention from the media because of

Bjarne Melgaard: New Love, Old Paint,
1996-1997. Part of installation located
at The National Museum of Art,
Architecture and Design. By courtesey
of Sørlandet Art Museum.

their unconventional character. In relation to the change of Bjørvika in Oslo from being a run down harbour area for the junkies to become a fancy Opera building, Faldbakken and Einarsson were invited to focus on the area in an exhibition in 2002. The artwork *Whoomp – it is* was a large, circular sculpture, with a white cover, similar to lounge furniture in a trendy club, that was placed under the motorway bridge. During the exhibition period, the artists made sure that a hole in the middle of the sculpture was always filled with Litago, a chocolate milk drink approved by children as well as drug addicts. With this artwork Faldbakken and Einarsson had made a meeting place for both new and old users of the area.

Morten Viskum (1965-) is a controversial artist who questions our relation to and use of animals and human beings within research. The ethical problems he was confronted with as a veterinary student has affected his making of art. His use of rats in formaldehyde on olive jars disgusted the shoppers and media, when the jars were placed on shelves in grocery stores throughout the country in 1995.

Bjarne Melgaard (1967-) is another artist that has provoked the Norwegian audience. However, he is considered one of Norway's most noted artists, and is sometimes referred to as "The New Munch". By drawing, painting, sculpturing, using video and making installation art in an imaginative and spontaneous manner, he explores themes like construction of identity, often connected to his own sexuality. In 2006, Melgaard exhibited his art in the London gallery *Pollock Fine Art* along with five fellow Norwegians and other international artists such as Andy Warhol. The exhibition was called "After Munch: Norwegian Contemporary Art" and demonstrated the artists' connections to and dialog with Munch. Despite the fact that Munch is the most known Norwegian artist internationally, and represents more or less a "one-person art movement," Norwegian artists have traditionally not had the courage to establish close relations to him and his work.

Norwegian artists have a historical tradition of traveling abroad, especially to Germany and France, for inspiration. Now the situation has changed. The younger generation of artists find Munch's expressive and symbolic art and extraordinary life relevant and inspiring, although some artists have a more critical and satirical approach to him. The London exhibition in 2006 confirms the international attention Norwegian contemporary art is given, and some Norwegian artists close links to Munch. However, Norwegian art is definitely more than Munch.

Chapter 18

Norway – Music and Musical Life

By Arvid O. Vollsnes

Through all the centuries of documented Norwegian music it has been obvious that there were strong connections to European cultural life. But from the 14th to the 19th century Norway was considered by other Europeans to be remote and belonging to the backwaters of Europe. Some daring travelers came in the Romantic era, and one of them wrote:

> "The fantastic pillars and arches of fairy folk-lore may still be descried in the deep secluded glens of Thelemarken, undefaced with stucco, not propped by unsightly modern buttress. The harp of popular minstrelsy – though it hangs mouldering and mildewed with infrequency of use, its strings unbraced for want of cunning hands that can tune and strike them as the Scalds of Eld – may still now and then be heard sending forth its simple music. Sometimes this assumes the shape of a soothing lullaby to the sleeping babe, or an artless ballad of love-lorn swains, or an arch satire on rustic doings and foibles. Sometimes it swells into a symphony descriptive of the descent of Odin; or, in somewhat less Pindaric, and more Dibdin strain, it recounts the deeds of the rollicking, death-despising Vikings; while, anon, its numbers rise and fall with mysterious cadence as it strives to give a local habitation and a name to the dimly seen forms and antic pranks of the hollow-backed Huldra crew." (From *The Oxonian in Thelemarken, or Notes of Travel in South-Western Norway in the Summers of 1856 and 1857*, written by Frederick Metcalfe, Lincoln College, Oxford.)

This was a typical Romantic way of describing a foreign culture. Romanticism encouraged young adventurous men not only to explore the exotic jungles and the southern seas, but also the exotic Europe. Norway was considered a country on the periphery where the inhabitants were still living in close contact with unspoiled nature. And their exotic music was a result of the majestic nature; mountains, glaciers, fjords and forests were sounding through their instruments and singing. This longing for authenticity was also crucial for the success of Norwegian music in the capitals of Europe with musicians like Ole Bull, Edvard Grieg and Johan Svendsen, who had their music background and education from Germany and Denmark.

The first signs – and the Viking Age

The first documents on musical activities are some 6000-year-old rock carvings and paintings of what is considered some musical activities, probably cult-connected. Some instruments have been found in archeological digs, but most instruments made of wood, bone or hides are perishable. However, some lurs (a kind of trumpets) have been found buried on the moors in the southwest of Norway, always in pairs mirroring each other. These are from the late Bronze Age, 1500–500 B.C. They are 1.5–2 m long, beautifully forged with an advanced technology for their times. They are decorated with symbols and may produce 10–12 tones. Probably these instruments were used in processions or other cult services.

Some straight, wooden lurs have been found, one in the Oseberg ship, the burial vessel of a lady from c. 830 AD. This was what is called the Viking Era, and several written documentations of music have survived from those days. The sagas have descriptions of various musical activities, also of courtly skald and leikar, poet and jester, providing stories and entertainment. Like his European counterpart a leikar could improvise a mocking song and be rewarded (or punished) for his skills. Some Arab merchants have given us accounts of meetings with Scandinavians in the Black Sea area. The Arabs describe the Nordic singing as "horrible" and "ugly" – perhaps because of different vocal ideals.

Around 1000 the Christian faith was gaining momentum with the help of missionaries and warrior kings. The most prominent was king Olav Haraldson, who was killed in a battle 1030 AD and later made a saint, St. Olav, because of the miracles associated with his relics at Nidaros Cathedral. This became the church in Northern Europe most visited by pilgrims, and because of its wealth and prominence, Nidaros (Trondheim) was in 1153 made the see for the archbishopric consisting of Northern Scandinavia, parts of Scotland, Ireland, Iceland and Greenland.

The church and the pilgrims brought new kinds of music, some of which was written down. Some new liturgical music in a distinct French and German style for the celebration of St. Olav was created, and the cathedral schools gave young men a basic education in singing and music. The men of the church were also the chroniclers of these times, and occasionally they would mention activities outside the church, including comments on the common people's musical activities, which are not always favorably mentioned.

The king and the kingdom were prospering and privileges were given to the Hanseatic League that had settled in Bergen in the 13th century. In 1388, however, Queen Margrethe I of Denmark became the sovereign as a result of an earlier marriage, and Norway (with its Western territories) was a Danish province till 1814. The Black Death 1349–50 killed more than half the population and threw the country into poverty. In adition, the Norwegian nobility became extinct. However, the church was still a mighty institution, and pilgrims kept on coming to Nidaros.

Reformation and Baroque – professional musicians

In 1536 the king decided that the Lutheran faith should be introduced, and he seized all churches and their valuables and land as his own property. In the beginning this Reformation did not affect the congregations of peripheral Norway, where they still sang the old hymns and used the Latin liturgy for some time. But with new Danish-educated priests and printed Bibles and hymnals, new church songs and chorals in the Danish language were introduced. This also affected the lay population; quite a few of the old hymns were later preserved as part of the Norwegian folk music repertory. The many hymns and the songs written by the priest Peter Dass (1647–1707) have also influenced popular music to this day.

In the 17th century we meet the first town musicians. The king in Copenhagen gave the privilege of playing music for money to one person in each city. This privileged master was to play a variety of instruments for various purposes, the trombone for processions, the fiddle for dances, the harpsichord for chamber music. He received a nominal fee for his official services in the town, otherwise people had to hire him if they wanted music performed by a professional. He might take apprentices and have subcontracts with local musicians who, for an annual fee, were allowed to earn some money through playing at betrothals, weddings and dances. Some of these privileged town musicians earned much money, and many a musician in the king's chapel in Copenhagen wanted and was rewarded with such a position, bringing with him modern European music and dances to the cities of Norway.

Two more professional groups of musicians were then emerging. The military garrisons used pipers and drummers, and with more prosperous cities, especially in the 18th century, more churches could afford an organ and an organist. In several cities private music societies were founded. They would form an orchestra consisting of the town musician and his apprentices and amateurs, who performed concerts and dramatic music – and played at the dances and balls. Some of these societies still exist today, the most prominent being "Musikselskabet Harmonien", founded in Bergen in 1765. It is still the parent organization of the large Bergen Philharmonic Orchestra, a fully national, state-supported orchestra. These music societies would also welcome traveling artists, both actors and musicians. They would stay in town for some weeks, playing with the music society's orchestra or solo, and would give lessons to people in town.

Only a few composers are known from the 18th century. *Georg von Bertouch* (1668–1743) was a general and head of the armed forces in Norway. He was born in what today is known as Belgium, was educated as a lawyer, with his thesis concerning copyright in opera – and was trained as a musician. After successful service for the king in Copenhagen he was promoted and sent to Norway. He wrote sonatas and cantatas in the Baroque manner. *Johan Henrik Freithoff* (1713–67) was the son of the town musician in Christiansand. He was a renowned violinist who traveled throughout Europe, the Middle East and North Africa. He loved Italian and French music and wrote violin sonatas and trio sonatas in a gallant style. He had a leading position at the court in Copenhagen and served as a violinist in the king's chapel.

In Trondheim *Johann Daniel Berlin* (1714–87), of German descent, not only was the town musician, organist, composer and music theorist, but also architect, head of the fire brigade and water supplies, inventor and meteorologist. It is impressive that he also found time to compose sinfonias and concertos in a Gallant style bordering on Classicism. His son *Johan Henrik*

Berlin (1741–1807) was an organist who composed cantatas, sonatas and some sinfonias in a more Classical style known from several European countries.

In the 18th century foreign trade was increased considerably, with Norway exporting fish, seafood and pelts. Europe had a great need for timber and metals from the mining industries established near the ores. This created more communication with people and ideas – and music – from Central Europe, the Netherlands and England. Young men went to Copenhagen to the university and returned as civil servants or clergy. A real university was not established in Norway till 1811.

A national awakening

The young Norwegian intellectuals returning home around 1800 were enthusiastic about the new ideas of enlightenment and the political slogans of the French revolution. They wanted a free Norwegian country, and in the political chaos after the Napoleonic wars, they seized the opportunity to form an independent state and wrote a new constitution in the spring of 1814. But the larger European nations forged a union with Sweden in the fall through the Kiel treaty. Norway got a Swedish king but kept its constitution and self-rule on internal matters.

This short intermezzo of freedom strengthened the quest for a national culture that was fully Norwegian, which the young intellectuals considered important to the whole population of only 885 000 inhabitants. The scholars and writers wanted to put a blanket over the 400 years of cultural slumber under Danish rule. They would turn towards the sagas and chronicles of the medieval ages, which in their eyes represented the peak of national culture. They translated the sagas into modern language and produced new history books with emphasis on the daring Vikings.

Norwegian folk music was used as the basis of variations and potpourris, first by visiting foreign performers like Abbé Vogler and German immigrants, but also gradually by the Norwegians themselves. The first national composer to do so was Waldemar Thrane (1790–1828) in his singspiel *Fjeldeventyret* (1824). The famous violin virtuoso and composer Ole Bull (1810–80) often used folk music in his music. He was a showman, dazzling audiences all over Europe and in the US with his daring virtuoso playing and his charismatic appearance. He was an eager champion of everything nationally Norwegian. He started the first theatre with

Norwegian, not Danish, as the language on the stage, and frequently gave concerts, together with folk music fiddlers playing the Hardanger fiddle and dancers in national costumes.

Norway had no academy of music or conservatory, so the young people often went abroad to study music. In the first part of the 19th century a number of young men and women went to Paris to learn, among them the pianist and composer Thomas D. A. Tellefsen (1823–74), a student and friend of Chopin's who settled in Paris. But after 1840 Leipzig with its new conservatory became more important, and Halfdan Kjerulf (1815–68), Edvard Grieg (1843–1907) and Johan Svendsen (1840–1911) studied there. Kjerulf, called the father of the Norwegian *lied* (romantic song), wrote more than 100 songs. He also composed charming piano pieces and arranged several folk tunes for the piano. Pianos were found in many bourgeois homes, and songs and pieces for the piano were in demand.

Norwegian Folk Music

Normally one would think of Norwegian folk music as the music that was orally transmitted and belonged to most people's everyday life. There are few sources for music and dance in the rural areas before c. 1840 when a systematic collecting of folk art was started. First the focus was on religious folk tunes, i.e. with text connected to the Christian belief. But other vocal music was also included, epic ballads, songs about trolls and fairy tale characters. These were mostly sung as entertainment. The soothing lullabies and cattle calls had specified functions in their everyday life, and some songs were specially designed to accompany pulling a heavy boat ashore or other hard manual or repetitive labour.

But some of the preserved vocal tunes were meant for dancing, which was actually the major area of instrumental folk music. There are scores of fiddles (violins), Jew's harps and recorders preserved, instruments common to all of Europe. The willow flute was a seasonal but important instrument in May/June. But many Hardanger fiddles and Norwegian dulcimers – characteristic national instruments – are preserved. A Hardanger fiddle looks like and is played like an ordinary violin, but it has four or five sympathetic strings under the fingerboard, strings sounding softly when the upper strings are struck. The Norwegian dulcimer has one melody string, which is played over a fretted board while some drone strings tuned in a major triad are struck. The strings are plucked with a plectrum, often a feather shaft.

For over a century writers have made a binary division of the instrumental folk music: districts and regions using the Hardanger fiddle vs. districts using an ordinary violin for dance music. The Hardanger fiddle was in vogue in the central parts of southern Norway: from Hardanger, Voss, Sogn over the mountains to Hallingdal, Valdres and south through Telemark and Setesdal. This was, however, an inaccurate division, and with the increasing exchange of musical material this is today even more dubious.

Dance music is dependent on the local dances, who is dancing and how the steps are performed. A dancing tune is called a *slått*, stemming from the verb *slå*, which means to beat; the slåtts are "beaten" from the instrument. Some dances are in triple meter (*springar, springdans, pols*), some in duple meter (*halling, gangar*). Most dances are for groups of pairs, female and male together, but halling is most often a male solo dance in which the man is showing off his agility, force and creativity.

The repertory of the old fiddlers also consisted of "listening slåtts", programmatic music depicting nature and herd life. Taking Ole Bull as a model, many fiddlers gave concerts in theatres and concert halls or at fairs. They realized programmatic music was popular and composed a number of new pieces with virtuoso elements. Late in the 19th century a score of fiddlers went to the USA to earn a living in the Norwegian settlements, and a Norwegian fiddle tradition still exists with an interesting repertory somewhat distinct from the Norwegian one.

Especially in eastern Norway the old folk dances met with "round dances" (polka, mazurka, rheinlender) coming from Germany and Sweden around 1860 together with the accordion. Conservative fiddlers and dancers scorned the new dances and the new instrument which could not play the "blue" notes like a fiddle or a singer. But today both round dances and instrument are integrated in the folk music.

The blue notes are important in traditional music from most parts of the country. If we extract a scale from a slått, we will find some of the well-known, old church modes (ecclesiastical modes). But the intervals are not tempered and made equal when sung or played on many instruments. In a major scale the third might be performed somewhat flattened without turning into a minor third. The seventh would also be flattened, making a softer leading tone. The fourth, however, might be raised, and this may be one of the reasons why a number of slåtts are characterized as "Lydian".

The folk music organizations (mostly established around 1900) have managed to preserve many traditions. However, music and musical life are not static; the last four decades have brought major changes, not least in the concept of folk music. It is not restricted to the rural areas and enclaves in the larger cities. Today the young musicians are multicultural, and their close contact with jazz, classical music, rock, pop and hip-hop brings new elements to the folk music arenas. They are arranging traditional slåtts in untraditional ways, maybe for a band consisting of Hardanger fiddle, a viola, guitar, bass, synth, percussion and vocal, which would be considered "impure" some decades ago.

Collecting Folk Music

Having the desire to form a nation is not enough. You must have evidence of the excellence of its culture as well. In the first part of the 19th century eager scholars worked to collect Norwegian folk art, folk poetry and fairy tales. The physical objects were put into museums, while the fairy tales and poems were published in both scholarly and popular collections. Some of these collections have a few melodies preserved as well. But the most systematic collection of folk music was done by L.M. Lindeman (1812–87), who was an organist and composer. He wanted to introduce religious folk tunes in the churches and got a grant from the government to do so. The grant was then expanded to include all kinds of folk music, so every summer after 1848 Lindeman would walk through remote valleys to write down "old" and "authentic" music. His manuscripts are impressive sources for the music he heard. He wrote down not only the melodies and texts but also peculiarities in tonality, manner of performance and background.

Lindeman wanted the music brought back to "the people", i.e. he would put them into use again. The people who could do this were those who could read or play the printed notes. So his collections are arrangements of the folk tunes for the piano, or voice and piano. These collections were later sources for further arrangements of new compositions by Kjerulf, Grieg, Svendsen and others.

Collecting folk music has continued up till now, and the major collections are now done with audio or video equipment. A large part of the collections are preserved in the Norwegian Folk Music Collection at the University of

Oslo and the National Library. The last 100 years have brought an interest in regional styles, and regional archives have also been founded.

Edvard Grieg – national romanticism and radical music

Edvard Grieg achieved international renown during his lifetime. The English loved Grieg's artistic refinement and his piano concerto. The French were enthralled by his harmonies – but many French turned their back on him because of his uncompromising standpoint in the Dreyfus affair in 1900. The Germans and the Americans regarded Grieg as the composer who succeeded in capturing the mystical and utopian qualities of a small nation that was untouched by the modern world, that still retained something of its original character, its unspoiled mountains, fjords and waterfalls. Then there were all the various myths and sagas inspired by the forces of nature: the huge, powerful trolls and giants, the alluring wood spirits and *fossegrim* (a violin-playing being believed to dwell beneath waterfalls), the elves and little people in the forests, and the headless ghost who appears to sailors as a harbinger of death. Edvard Grieg was considered to be a national Norwegian composer, which would turn out to be an advantage.

Edvard Grieg was an independent thinker who defied prevailing trends and was critical of established views. Born in Bergen, he was the son of a well-to-do merchant of Scottish and Danish descent. Bergen, a centre of trade in the Hanseatic period, traditionally had strong ties with Germany, as well as with Britain, and an international atmosphere permeated the town.

Grieg was sent to the conservatory in Leipzig at the age of 15 for a traditional German music education. He was homesick for Bergen at first, but found solace in his landlord's assurance that "it is the same sun, the same moon and the same Lord God watching over you here as in Bergen." Grieg found his years in Leipzig (1858–62) interesting and rewarding, and was particularly intrigued by the music of Chopin, Mendelssohn, Schumann and Wagner. However, later in life he criticized the teaching at the conservatory, particularly the fact that no attempt was made to bring out the individuality and distinctive talent of the students. Nonetheless, it is clear that his studies had an important bearing on his mastery of the art of composition.

As a young man, Grieg also spent a number of years in Copenhagen, where he met the Norwegian composer Rikard Nordraak (1842–66), who repeatedly stressed how important it was that Norwegians find their own,

Edvard Grieg (1843-1907) was a Norwegian composer and pianist who composed in the Romantic period.

national Norwegian platform. Thirty years later, Grieg himself wrote, "I didn't want to be merely Norwegian, much less chauvinistically Norwegian; I just wanted to be myself. I wanted to find expression for the best that was within me, which was something a thousand miles away from Leipzig and its atmosphere. But that this 'best' consisted in love for my homeland and an appreciation of the great melancholic scenery of western Norway – that I would not have realized, had I not, through Nordraak, been led to self-examination."

During his years in Copenhagen, Grieg composed a number of piano pieces and songs, including the well-known "I Love But Thee", his gift to his cousin, soprano Nina Hagerup, when they became engaged to be married. In the autumn of 1865, Grieg went to Germany to hold a series of concerts. From there he went on to Italy, where he was captivated by the atmosphere, the light and the people. Grieg performed his own works in Italy as well, and met Henrik Ibsen (1828–1906) in Rome.

In 1866 Grieg moved to Christiania (Oslo), which was to serve as his home base for almost ten years. There he composed, conducted (sharing a position with Johan Svendsen) and taught until finally, in June 1867, he could afford to marry Nina. Grieg considered Christiania provincial; there were too many cliques for his taste, and the audiences, who were more interested in the gossip and social trappings of the concerts than in the music itself, showed little appreciation of the new currents in European music. His most well known work, *Piano Concerto in A Minor*, was composed during this period, in the summer of 1868. When Grieg persuaded Franz Liszt to sight-read the concerto in Rome in 1870, the enthusiasm of the great virtuoso knew no bounds.

In 1874 the Storting, the Norwegian parliament, granted an honorary income to Grieg and Svendsen, enabling Grieg to give up his demanding position as conductor and many of his students. Not long after this, Grieg began to compose music for Henrik Ibsen's play *Peer Gynt*, a project that was to demand a great deal of his time and creative energy. In many ways, the new production of *Peer Gynt* in 1876 was a different play, a musical drama. The two suites from the incidental music (composed in 1888 and 1892) are among the most frequently recorded works in the world.

Grieg's collaboration with the poet Bjørnstjerne Bjørnson (1832–1910) and Ibsen brought him into contact with some of the most romantic of all Norwegian literature, the sagas, folk tales and legends. However, Grieg also had a deep love of nature. He liked nothing better than hiking in the mountains around Bergen and up from Sogn and through Jotunheimen. There, in the domain of the trolls, he found challenging peaks, which afforded him splendid vistas, shimmering, iridescent glaciers and tranquil plateaus, where he became acquainted with the Norwegian folk culture.

Grieg adapted folk tunes, and composed songs and violin sonatas. But he also developed his own distinctive form of tone poem, the lyric pieces for piano. These 66 pieces soon became very popular in homes and drawing rooms all over Europe, but they were also frequently used in teaching and were included in the concert programs of pianists of all ages and levels of proficiency. The publishing company C.F. Peters, with whom Grieg had signed a contract, welcomed each new volume, printing them in large editions. Many of the lyric pieces were also published in pirate editions and included in various anthologies, particularly in the USA; thus they reached a wide public. However, these pieces have earned Grieg an undeserved reputation as a "miniaturist", a composer who was unable to compose in the larger forms.

His music was so popular that he was invited to give concerts in the various capitals of Europe, winning great acclaim. Grieg conducted, played his own works and accompanied Nina, who sang his songs, along with several violinists, who played his violin sonatas. The tours were their chief source of income. Grieg was to continue these concert tours throughout Europe until the very end of his life. He continued to enjoy success, and became friends with a number of well-known composers and musicians such as Brahms, Dvorak, Tchaikovsky and Brodsky. Moreover, Grieg was awarded many orders and other honors as well as honorary doctorates that gained him extensive press coverage.

The Griegs lived for years in hotels and rented flats. Finally in 1885 they were able to move into their own, newly erected house, Troldhaugen, south of Bergen. This distinctive house is built on a secluded hilltop with a magnificent view over the bay. It was to be a true home for the two artists, where they could seek peace and quiet between their numerous, exhausting concert tours. Today the house is a museum, and an elegant concert hall has been built in a small valley right beside it.

It is interesting to observe the radical effect Grieg's encounter with new trends in Europe was to have on his attitudes and musical development towards the end of his life. He continued to regard himself as very Norwegian and hoped that Norway would break out of the union with Sweden. But at the same time, he arranged the first major international music festival in Bergen (1898), where he opened the door to ideas from Europe and invited the *Concertgebouw* orchestra from Amsterdam to participate. He wrote some of his finest romances based on texts by A.O. Vinje and Arne Garborg, both of whom wrote their poetry in *nynorsk*, or New Norwegian, which is based on the dialects spoken in the rural areas. This was regarded as extremely radical and was in keeping with Grieg's determination to emphasize anything that would help to strengthen a feeling of national cohesion and give people a sense of identity by demonstrating their roots. He also composed three of his major works, *Nineteen Norwegian Folk Songs* (opus 66), *Norwegian Peasant Dances* (opus 72), both for piano, and *Four Psalms* (opus 74) for mixed choir and baritone solo, which are arrangements of Norwegian folk songs, with an almost modernist way of treating the folk tunes.

However, he had become more open-minded; he had become a kind of Norwegian European. Grieg himself claimed, "I am no longer so exclusively Norwegian in my music as I once was. In my more recent works, I have sought a broader, more universal view of my own individuality, a view influenced by the great currents of history and cosmopolitan trends ... We should not live by the ideals of our youth. I have no faith in the old rubbish about the ideals of youth. In that case, there would be no development."

This open-mindedness also had a political side. He was a stern critic of the French verdict on Captain Dreyfus, an unfair trial, and he was a proponent for Norway's independence, which did not come till 1905. These ideals are also reflected in Grieg's music, and they may be the reason why he became an ideal for many other composers. He was a source of inspiration for Claude Debussy and Maurice Ravel in France, and Béla Bartók and George Enescu in eastern Europe. Composers from all the Nordic countries sought him out: Johan Svendsen, Christian Sinding, Johan Halvorsen, Carl Nielsen and Jean Sibelius; and Frederick Delius and Percy Grainger came from Britain. The composer from the far north had something to offer them all, composers and musicians, professionals and amateurs alike.

Grieg was particularly innovative in his treatment of melody and harmony. By using modes common both to Norwegian folk music and to old church music, he created a completely unique type of melodic line. His rhythms are also frequently derived from Norwegian folk music, particularly the unusual rhythmic patterns and phrasing of the various dances.

Grieg was particularly sensitive to subtle harmonic nuances, which he employed in individual chords and longer passages. In some respects, he anticipated the use of tone colors that have become the hallmark of the French Impressionists. He frequently combined this with elegant contrapuntal melodies in the inner voices, creating an elegant tapestry of sound. Not only was Grieg an outstanding pianist with a great sensitivity to a wide range of pianistic possibilities, but also his mastery of nuances is apparent even in his works for large orchestras.

Grieg has rightly been called a master of miniature forms, while his large-scale works have been undeservedly underestimated. He had his own personal solutions to the problems posed by the larger forms, as can be seen in the symphony, the piano concerto, the variation work *Ballade*, the string quartets and the sonatas. Here, too, Grieg emerges as a modernist in terms of form. The traditional, restrictive solutions employed in classical German Romanticism did not suit his mode of expression. Thus he felt a need to depart from established compositional practices. Perhaps this is the reason young people today are rediscovering Grieg's cyclical works and interpreting them in a totally new way.

Johan Svendsen – the symphonic master

From the 1840s we see a steady increase in the number of professional musicians and composers and there is a tendency towards institutionalization. A number of short-lived orchestras appear, and the steady use of orchestras in the theatres (including operas) also brought more symphony concerts. But the great movement from those years on was the male choir. Starting among the students it spread to other groups: artisans, clerks and workers. Every composer wrote for male choirs. Later in the century mixed choirs were spreading rapidly, also contributing to the philharmonic choirs. The choir movement subscribed to a national ideology, permeating the movement and the music. Through the choirs' appearances at national celebrations and political events the national consciousness was strengthened. Also, through their great festivals serving as important cultural events, the music and texts became a reminder of the slow struggle towards freedom for the country.

Johan Svendsen was just a young lad when he was a military musician, played in the theatres and sang in a male choir. He was rewarded with a grant from the Swedish-Norwegian king and was able to study at the Leipzig conservatory before earning his living as a violinist in Paris and in Bayreuth, where he stayed almost a year with Richard Wagner. In these formative years he composed some of his finest orchestral music, like his first symphony and his concertos for violin and violoncello. He shared the position as conductor of the *Musikforeningen* orchestra in the Norwegian capital with Grieg for a number of years, and during these years he composed his second symphony, his world-famous *Romance* for violin and orchestra and the four Norwegian rhapsodies. Svendsen combines in his music a highly sophisticated orchestral technique with a classic European romantic style in form and counterpoint. Some of his melodies and rhythms bear an unmistakable "Norwegian" stamp. Through lack of proper editions of his scores his music was for years neglected (with the exception of his *Romance* for the violin). But new recordings have reestablished Svendsen's reputation and put him beside the most prominent European symphonists of the late 19th century.

Svendsen accepted the position as head conductor of the Royal Theatre and Chapel in Copenhagen in 1884. Later he was offered the position as conductor at the Metropolitan Opera in New York, but he politely declined. He had heard the orchestra when visiting his first wife's family in New York, but his Danish orchestra sounded better and was more amiable, so he stayed on in Copenhagen.

In Grieg's shadow

Towards the end of the century some composers were noted for not following the paths of Grieg and Svendsen. Agathe Backer Grøndahl (1847–1907) (she was also a famous pianist) wrote Romantic piano music and songs, Johan Selmer (1844–1910) was our first programmatic composer, and Christian Sinding (1856–1941) won his fame abroad through both chamber music and symphonic works. Gerhard Schjelderup (1859–1933) premiered most of his operas in Germany. Johan Halvorsen (1864–1935) spent most of his life conducting and writing theatre music, but he also gave the world some magnificent concert music.

By the end of the 19th century music in the church was improved, not least through the conservatory that was established in 1883 in Kristiania (Oslo) primarily to educate more organists. For years the only public musical educational institutions had been in the bands of the military services. After their compulsory service the young men returned to their homes to form bands and perform in their home community. In the last decades of the century the traditional band music repertory gradually was expanded through adding fashionable foreign dances. Wind bands have played an important role in the musical life in small communities up to this date.

It is difficult to assess the importance of Edvard Grieg both at home and abroad. To most Norwegians he was *the* Composer, and the style of some of his music became synonymous with *Norwegian*. Grieg's aim was to have both a foundation in one's own country and at the same time have an open mind towards the international world and new musical trends. But despite his open-mindedness and his generosity, Grieg's stature made it difficult for the young Norwegian composers making their debut around World War I to walk out of his vast shadow and find a place of their own in the sun.

Among those who made it, two different strategies were chosen: some looked towards Europe and the new aesthetics and modern styles emerging from Paris and Berlin, often with an anti-Romantic attitude. Others wanted to nourish the national tendencies in Grieg's music and even make the folk music and its "inherent manifestation of Norwegian nature and the spirit of the people" (common expressions at those times) a new and somewhat different basis for their music. This dichotomy created a heated debate, which lasted for a long time, and even towards the end of the 20th century some faint echoes were heard. But amidst all this flak we find composers who ideologically, at least verbally, belonged to one camp but had their stylistic preferences in the other.

Norway still had a small population (2.8 million in 1930) and had finally in 1905 won its independence. People still needed national symbols and icons to take pride in, especially as they felt that European and American popular dances, entertainment music and film music were invading some of the old arenas at the expense of the prevailing national music (albeit imports in the first place), and that gramophone and radio to a too large extent promoted newfangled dances and jazz. Some reactionary groups were tainted with the fear of everything foreign and some even with traits of racism. Some voices were, however, raised against isolationism and provincialism, and luckily they were heard. The traditional folk music, which earlier had been considered to be worthy of a broad dissemination through the schools and used at important events, became marginalized and "sent back" to the rural areas and ghettos in the larger cities again.

Both in Bergen and in Oslo the symphony orchestras were reorganized in 1919, which gave more energy to already vital concert activities on a commercial market. This was the "age of the thousand lady singers", who together with numerous pianists were giving recitals through the season. Many larger theatres were staging the occasional opera among the bread- winning operettas, and the amateur choirs loved to perform the large oratorios.

But even so, music education was either conducted on a private basis or in a conservatory that primarily was a school for organists. Many young people wanting a music education went abroad to study, and both Paris and Berlin were popular. But the majority of them returned to Norway with a confirmation of their conservative beliefs and an inclination towards the Romantic music – and often without any understanding of the new radical music. Several music critics in Norway were also conservative and proving their bias and ignorance through their writings. A common expression was "musical communism" for any modern music, something you had to fear. Abusive words were not uncommon, and the most cited excerpt from a newspaper critic concerns Fartein Valen's tonal orchestral song *Ave Maria*, at its premier performance in 1923. This traditional Latin prayer was "blasphemous, meaningless sounds lurking like jellyfish in muddy waters; the whole thing was embarrassing, distasteful and ridiculous…". Some critics hinted at conspiracy and gave needle pricks like "Is this composer also adhering to the Association of the melody less composers?" – or describing "the hoax of the untalented internationalists".

The heated debate on modernism also included physical arguments. A journalist who had ridiculed a conservative composer was knocked down during the intermission in a symphony concert. And a couple of years later, the open-minded chairman received a black eye during a board meeting in the composers' association.

To simplify the issue we tend to say that the 1920s were the experimental years, jazzy and urban, while the 1930s were colored by the recession and a more somber national movement. The music of leading European composers like Stravinsky, Prokofiev, Schönberg and Honegger was rarely performed. But it was in the 1920s the leading radical composers of their generation established themselves. Fartein Valen (1887–1952) published his first radical atonal music, though his most famous works were composed in the 1930s and 1940s (Churchyard by the Sea, Violin Concerto, Symphonies). For many years his name was synonymous with radical Norwegian music, and his impact as an ideal for younger Scandinavian composers was great. His atonal music was heatedly debated in the press around 1930–33. It was loved by an ardent group of admirers, which created a more positive climate for his works in the concert halls than for other contemporary radical music.

In the 1920s Ludvig Irgens-Jensen (1894–1969) performed his free tonal and almost atonal songs and his more traditional Tema con variazioni (orchestra) before writing his more classical Passacaglia, the most performed new Norwegian orchestral piece after Grieg in the first half of the century. His large "Dramatic symphony" Heimferd ("Home Coming"), almost like an oratorio with choir and soloists on a text about the saint, King Olav, was considered the most prominent of national music – despite its contemporary European style. It is interesting to note that Irgens-Jensen's music was considered modern between the wars even though some of the more nationally inclined composers have music with a much harsher and radical harmonic style. During World War II Irgens-Jensen's music (spread without the composer's name on it) set to patriotic poems was considered crucial to the formation of an added spiritual resistance.

Harald Sæverud (1897–1992) was also connected with the musical resistance. He had his first symphony premiered in Berlin in the early 1920s, having learnt by meeting music both from the modern Germany and eastern Europe. Later some of his orchestral music, including his anti-Romantic music for Henrik Ibsen's drama *Peer Gynt*, together with some of his best piano music, shows a truly original composer.

David Monrad Johansen (1888–1974) presented radical French tendencies in his early works and was at the same time spokesman for the national movement both in his writings and in his oratorio like *Voluspå* ("The Prophecy of the Seeress"), with a text from the old Norse literature. But he was open and receptive towards some European and Norwegian radical music, and he shied away from the most ultra national movement. Later in the 1930s he found a new path in a mixture of his old style and German and French neo-classicism.

These composers developed their individual styles and became leading figures. And together with the younger Eivind Groven (1901–77) and Geirr Tveitt (1908–81) they have all often been performed and have won recognition abroad. The latter two both had an aesthetic foundation in Norwegian folk-art and stylistic roots in its folk music but adhered to European tendencies.

But there is also another group of composers with fewer performances abroad, who also merit recognition and whose music may be heard on CDs. Pauline Hall (1890–1969) was for many years the leading lady of Norwegian music as a composer, a critic and an organizer. She detested and criticized strongly dilettantism and superficial national composers. One of her famous proclamations was against some national infighting. She paraphrased a saying by Grieg on his own music, which he characterized as "reeking of cow pies". In the debate at the time, she sarcastically said, "It is not enough that the music should reek like a cowshed, but the manure must also have the smell from the correct county's cows."

Pauline Hall's interest in French music is obvious in her orchestral *Verlaine Suite*, with some respectful dues paid to Debussy and Ravel. But her generous musicianship and her humor and wit may be heard in her neo-classical *Suite for Winds* (quintet) from 1945. Impressionism was scarce in Norway, but besides Pauline Hall's early works some fine specimens are also found in the music of Alf Hurum (1882–1972). He left Norway in 1924 to found and conduct the Honolulu Symphony Orchestra, but after 1930 he spent most of his time in Hawaii devoting his life to painting.

The young Bjarne Brustad (1895–1978) also had a brief affair with impressionistic music, but he is more like a Norwegian Béla Bartók. His violin concertos and his *Rhapsody for Violin and Orchestra* are major variations on the style we meet in his popular chamber music. His *Fairy Tales Suite* for violin solo and his *Capricii* for violin and viola are among the finest chamber works from the 1930s and found in the repertory of the great stars.

Olav Kielland (1901–85) was a successful conductor who also struggled to find some extra days to compose. It is problematic to compare a composer's personality with his music, but here we may find a high degree of correspondence. The music is vigorous, direct and somewhat edgy, as we hear in his best orchestral piece, *Concerto grosso norvegese*.

Following another path from Norwegian national music C.G. Sparre Olsen (1903–84) was more soft-spoken. He was a lyricist with a special gift for melody and colorful harmonies. Unfortunately few of his larger works are available in modern recordings, but his chamber music, songs and piano works are liked by a large audience. Groven, Tveitt, Kielland and Olsen take a positive creative path in their music. Not being content with arranging or recomposing folk music, they found a way of utilizing some folk music elements and putting them as integral elements in symphonic frames.

Some composers have the misfortune to be remembered solely for one composition. This was the case for Harald Lie (1902–42), whose orchestral song *Skinnvengbrev* ("Bat Letter", text by Aslaug Vaa) was recorded by Kirsten Flagstad and so lived on. Starting late on his musical career and being ill during his last years, Lie's list of works is short, but some of his symphonic music is to be found on a CD.

Olsen and Lie were among Fartein Valen's students, as was Klaus Egge (1906–79). He was a dominant personality both as a writer, chairman of the Norwegian Composers' Association for 27 years and composer. His first compositions show an extension of the national movement with his piano sonata on the melodies from the ancient *Draumkvedet* ("The Dream-lay") as the peak of these years. But he chose a neo-classical path in the late 1930s, and after his wind quintet he developed a new kind of free tonality based upon certain elements from Norwegian folk music. His first symphony and his second piano concerto were composed during World War II, but premiered when the occupation came to an end.

Those composers mentioned here are just a few who were respected and had some success during their lifetime. Norwegian orchestras and musicians programmed substantial parts of the new compositions being created before 1950. Irgens-Jensen and Monrad Johansen were the composers who had the largest number of performances of larger works abroad before World War II, and their music was noted in leading circles both in Europe and in the USA. This is somewhat remarkable, considering Norway is a small country. Monrad Johansen had some of his music published in Germany, but Irgens-Jensen did not have a publisher till 1934, a Norwegian company with a limited distribution.

After the war Valen, Sæverud, Egge and to some extent Tveitt also had the fortune of having their work frequently performed abroad and earning commissions from foreign symphonic societies. The composers of the inter-war years were the first to be recorded on the new LP records during the 1950s, and through performances by leading musicians and conductors their music was for a while still heard and appreciated both in the concert halls and on the radio.

Look to Europe – the post-war generation

During the German occupation of Norway 1940–45 most cultural exposés were used for propaganda, but the resistance movement put a ban on most public performances. The rulers implemented censorship on all public performances, the programming was to be approved by the Nazis. But they could not stop church services and church choirs, so the churches became important concert arenas. Closed associations formed their choirs and arranged performances for their members and "friends", and chamber music societies held their meetings in private homes.

The Oslo Philharmonic Orchestra was important to the rulers, but a number of the orchestra's musicians would become "sick" when they were to play at official arrangements. In the fall of 1944 the orchestra defied the nazi rule and stopped all activities as there was "a lack of oil and coal to heat the concert hall" Aula of the Oslo University.

But in the euphoric weeks of May 1945 the orchestra was reassembled and invited to perform when King Haakon returned from British exile in June. On this occasion more than 7000 singers performed choral music for the king, including new songs that were composed and performed in secrecy during the war.

Some musicians and composers had collaborated with the oppressors, and the new music establishment boycotted these. Some of these composers were eager nationalists, and this kind of music was then discredited among the young composers. They had to look for new and international ideals, not in Germany but in France where the leading lady, Nadia Boulanger, was teaching and promoting the neoclassical aesthetics and the French style of clarity in music to American and European students.

In Norway the soft-spoken and reticent Fartein Valen became the ideal for the young generation, even though he did not teach much after the war. A second generation of modernists was established during the 1950s with composers like Knut Nystedt (1915–), Maj Sønstevold (1917–96) and Gunnar Sønstevold (1912–91), Øistein Sommerfeldt (1919–94), Johan Kvandal (1919–99), Finn Mortensen (1922–83), Egil Hovland (1924–) and Arne Nordheim (1931–). Some of the old polarization between the modernist and the folklore inspired composers was still obvious, but without the acerbic comments and the hard antagonism in the public discussion. In this modernist trend it is interesting to observe that Nystedt and Hovland were instrumental in revitalizing and reforming the church music by using J.S. Bach and older church music, also as models for the liturgical practice, and at the same time composing new church music in a modern expressive style.

But there was a gradual change of focus during the 1960s. The new, younger generation wanted a place for themselves, and to achieve this, they had to get rid of the old generation and their "moth-eaten" national music. They did not denounce specific works or persons, but in vigorously claiming more room for new music, a score of older music had to be left out, often without any aesthetic evaluation. The older composers were ousted out of office, and sorely neglected when music for major performances and recordings was chosen. This dramatic shift in policy led to a further diminished knowledge of the older music, especially by the older generation, those making their debut before World War II. Also younger producers in the radio station (only one channel) tended to ignore this generation through lack of knowledge and in the belief that the belittling of this music by the young radicals was "outdated". This self-centered and one-eyed policy created a schism between not only composers but also a musical audience who could not understand why their older, much loved national music disappeared.

There is a stylistic diversity among leading composers like Kåre Kolberg (1936–), Alfred Janson (1937–), Ketil Hvoslef (1939–) and Trygve Madsen (1940–) and also in their individual styles during their active years. The almost dogmatic modern tendencies from the German "Darmstadt School" and serialism was not met with enthusiasm in Norway. The new expressive, modern music from Poland, however, was well received among the young composers, as was the Polish electronic music, Arne Nordheim produced his major electronic compositions in Warsaw. Gradually a "new simplicity" with a new tonality made some of the modern music more palatable for a wider audience.

Cultural Policies

We can hardly speak of a homogeneous music community in Norway. Actually there are several parallel music communities where the various genres thrive side by side. Some of the activities in these communities are guided by commercial principles. Others are nonprofit undertakings, having nothing whatsoever to do with money. However, by far the majority of these activities function according to a kind of mixed economic model, with the direct or indirect participation of public institutions.

Although composers and performers are often those who attract the most attention in our musical landscape, some important general trends are to be found in Norwegian thought, education and cultural policy. In the course of the 1970s and 1980s, the Government and the Storting (the Norwegian national assembly) adopted a number of new cultural objectives. Most of these are set out in a series of White Papers on cultural policy, which were intended to provide an overall assessment of the objectives and conditions of art in a modern society. These White Papers introduced a broader concept of culture into the planning process. Sport and amateur activities were at first implicitly included in this concept, as well as the dissemination of art to as many people as possible. The concept of "cultural democracy" became a catchword. More attention was focused on popular music forms and the role played by voluntary organizations, and regional cultural development and decentralization – even in the planning and decision-making stages – became goals in themselves. The role of artists in the community was more broadly defined, also in terms of financial support. Participation by the individual citizen was regarded as beneficial in itself, and importance was attached to developing the individual's aptitudes and abilities, all without favoring any particular genre or music form.

Roughly speaking, this cultural responsibility is shared between the municipalities, the counties/regions and the State, depending on the functions to be fulfilled. The State is in charge of opera, the symphony orchestras, higher education in music, certain archives and special funding for various festivals and organizations, including amateur organizations. For

The Oslo Opera House was opened in April 2008.

example, the oldest existing symphony orchestra in Europe, the Bergen Philharmonic Orchestra, was a private organization (the music society "Harmonien") for 215 years. After 1980 it is fully financed by public funds.

Opera was performed at infrequent intervals in some Norwegian cities in the 20th century, often financed by theatres and private enthusiasts. The Norwegian Opera and Ballet was established in 1958 and is fully funded by the government, with their main stage in Oslo but also with responsibilities as a touring company. The new opera house in Oslo was finished in 2008, a beautiful building on the sea front with the very best facilities for opera and ballet. The government also supports smaller opera companies in other cities, companies that may have one single production every year. Some opera composers are also performed abroad: Edvard Fliflet Bræin (1924–1976), Antonio Bibalo (1922–2008) and Gisle Kverndokk (1967–) are the most recognized during the last few decades.

From the 1960s a conscious effort has been made in Norway to incorporate music education into all kinds of educational institutions, ranging from kindergarten and municipal music schools, through upper secondary and up to conservatory, university and academy level. We are now beginning to see the results: a new generation of outstanding young Norwegian artists is appearing on concert podiums around the world. Young pianists like Leif Ove Andsnes and Håvard Gimse, violon cellist Truls Mørk, trumpeter Ole Edvard Antonsen and violinist Henning Kraggerud appear as soloists with leading orchestras. But the most famous of performers is probably still the opera singer Kirsten Flagstad (1895–1962), whose recordings are constantly selling well. At the same time, the quality of our ensembles, symphony orchestras and opera has improved steadily.

Two state institutions also deserve special mention. The first of these is the Norwegian Cultural Council, an independent body that administers a state cultural fund set up to preserve valuable culture and to promote innovative activities, pilot projects and experimental endeavors. The Cultural Council also supports record series, which serve as a kind of anthology of Norwegian music. The second is the Norwegian Concert Institute (Rikskonsertene), a state concert institution that also fulfils an important educational role. Every year the Norwegian Concert Institute contributes to 10,000 concerts throughout the country, either directly by arranging tours or indirectly by giving grants to local arrangers.

Another important aspect of Norwegian music is the widespread amateur activity, which is now fairly well organized. This includes all kinds of choirs, orchestras, ensembles, symphonic bands, brass bands, etc. Many of these collaborate closely with local music schools and the professional musicians to be found in the area.

Sámi Music

Roughly 60,000 people are registered as Sámi people in Norway, and they have had their own parliament since 1989, a forum that has made Sámi culture and language a major topic. Traditional Sámi music in Northern Europe is called *joik*, an often reiterated, short vocal piece, orally transmitted or improvised. A joik might be a characterization of a person, a landscape, a stone or a puppy playing. It may be wordless or have a short text. The musical rhythm will normally follow the text closely, and the melody will be based on variations on a pentatonic structure and have a limited ambitus.

From around 1970 Sámi artists have been more conscious of their heritage and included elements of joik in symphonic and chamber music (as did Jon Persen, b. 1941). Joik has also been the basis for some folk groups accompanied by a rock band, and the artist Mari Boine (1956–) has via folk-rock entered the world music scene with strong elements from joik. The Finnish-Swedish-Norwegian multi artist Nils-Aslak Valkeapää (1943–2001) composed larger works based on his own text and joik-like melodies, works that reached a wide audience and paved the way for his receiving an honorary prize from the Nordic Council.

Sámi joiks have been collected and published in all the countries having a Sámi population. In Norway the major collection is to be found in Tromsø University Museum.

Jazz

In the 1920s and 1930s jazz was almost synonymous with dance music. But visits by leading American and French jazz musicians changed this, with people listening to jazz or going to concerts. During World War II jazz had to go underground, often camouflaged as "sewing clubs" where the "embroidering" was done by saxophone or piano.

I the 1950s big bands were cherished, but most players were amateurs or musicians in the theatres, like the trumpeter Rowland Greenberg (1920–94) and saxophonist Bjarne Nerem (1923–91) and the pianist Einar Iversen (1930–). But in the 1960s a more professional attitude was spreading, together with a more experimental trend, which created a musical diversity both on a national and local level, not least through the first international jazz festivals. In these and the following years Norway produced a number of great jazz artists who have won international renown, such as singer Karin Krog (1937–), percussionist Jon Christensen (1943–), saxophonist Jan Garbarek (1947–), bassist Arild Andersen (1945 –), singer Radka Toneff (1952–82), pianists Ketil Bjørnstad (1952–) and Jon Balke (1955–). It is typical that most of them are not only performers but also arrangers and composers, and they have changed the public's concept of what jazz is today

It is also characteristic to see crossovers from jazz and into jazz. Terje Rypdal (1947–) won fame as a guitarist in jazz and rock and composed in these genres as well as opera and symphonies. Jazz meets folk music, from Norway, eastern Europe or far away "exotic" countries, and something new is created. But the basic element of improvisation is clearly heard in the music of trumpeter Nils Petter Molvær (1960–) and Bugge Wesseltoft (1964–), even in music to accompany a movie. In recent years several young jazz groups have also played material typical of the rock scene and the electronica circuit. But traditional improvised jazz is still played, and two piano trios, led by Tord Gustavsen and Helge Lien respectively, have had successes with their recordings and festival appearances abroad. In general critics seem to notice a "clean and fresh sound" in Norwegian jazz, which may be the result of the painstaking efforts to produce these recordings in the best studios with the best equipment, and transforming this sound to live performances.

Norwegian Jazz Archives has been established for the purpose of collecting recordings and other material related to this art form.

Rock

The rock scene seems to follow the general trends in Europe. There are, however, a couple of peculiarities, which are noted as such. The black metal music was a kind of youthful protest against their view of a "dull" and established society. Some of the groups have chosen a harsh expression with a strong beat and sound, and some have chosen heathenism, Satanism or worshipping the old Norse gods as their trademarks. It may seem that the context is more important than the music itself.

The electronic development has also created a super sensitive soundscape. Some of the young DJs have experimented with quite simple equipment and produce exquisite sounds over and around a very pronounced dance beat. This happened as a non-commercial challenge initially, but some of the best DJs are now hired as producers for commercial pop stars from the USA and Europe.

Diversification of music

The young DJs got their inspiration from the electronic music produced by people like Arne Nordheim in technically sophisticated and complicated electronic studios from the 1960s onwards. Nordheim, with his international fame, was an inspiration also for the young "art music" composers. But they had in addition a great teacher in Finn Mortensen, who was appointed the first professor at the State Academy of Music, established in 1973. The generation making their debut as composers around 1970 consists of composers like Magne Hegdal (1944–), Terje Bjørklund (1945–), Ragnar Søderlind (1945–), Olav Anton Thommesen (1946–), Lasse Thoresen (1949–) and Synne Skouen (1950–). It is hard to find a common denominator among these fine composers; their styles vary, also for the individual composer. Music drama might be common for most of them, but while some write full-length operas, others only write short experimental scenes to explore the possibilities of the voice without any stage or props.

The following generation, with composers like Magnar Åm (1952–), Cecilie Ore (1954–), Håkon Berge (1954–), Rolf Wallin (1957–), Ståle Kleiberg (1958–), Nils Henrik Asheim (1960–) and Asbjørn Schaathun (1961–), are as mixed as the preceding one. But they may be more occupied with musicianship and music from earlier decades, experiencing more with expressiveness and storytelling also in their instrumental music.

Part 4

Facts about Norway

Chapter 19

Statistics and Comparisons

By Silve-Linn and Lars Aase

Geography

Norway consists of the mainland, the archipelago of Svalbard and the island of Jan Mayen. The Antarctic islands; Bouvet Island, Peter I Island and Queen Maud Land, are dependencies of Norway but not part of the Kingdom of Norway. The mainland of Norway can be compared in size to Vietnam or the state of New Mexico, and has 2 542 kilometers total land borders. Norway is divided into 19 counties and 434 municipalities.

Total area (incl. lakes)	384 802 km²
Mainland	323 782 km²
Svalbard	61 020 km²
Jan Mayen	377 km²

Source: Statistics Norway 2008

Norway's terrain is glaciated and consists mostly of high plateaus and rugged mountains. The country is divided by fertile valleys and scattered plains. The coastline is deeply indented with fjords and bays, with approximately 50 000 islands situated along the coast.

Coastline without fjords and bays:	2 650 km
Continental coastline:	25 148 km
Including islands:	83 281 km

Source: Statistics Norway

Land use compared. Percentage of total land area, 2005-2006				
Country	Arable land	Pasture	Forest area	Nationally protected area
Norway	3	-	38.2	6.8
Denmark	64	8	12.7	11.1
France	38	18	31.6	13.3
Germany	34	14	30.2	31.5
United Kingdom	26	46	11.6	30.1
Italy	38	16	23.3	19.0
United States	19	26	32.6	25.1
China	16	43	-	-

Sources: Food and Agriculture Organization of the United Nations, Arable land and pasture
OECD Environmental Compendium, Forest area and nationally protected area

Climate

Compared to other areas on the same latitude; such as Alaska, Greenland or Siberia, Norway has a very mild and pleasant climate. In the county of Nordland, which includes the city of Bodø and the Lofoten islands, the mean temperature is an average 25°C/77 F higher than areas on the same latitude in Canada and Russia. The reason is the North Atlantic Current, also known as the Gulf Stream.

Along the coast there is a lot of precipitation; summers are cool and winters mild. Inland areas have less precipitation and more variation as far as temperatures are concerned. Summers are warmer and winters colder than in the coastal areas. The mean temperatures during the winter months are usually above freezing along the entire coast from Vest-Agder county to Lofoten in Nordland. The inland areas, regardless of latitude, have very low mean temperatures in the winter. The Finnmark plateau is the coldest area with a mean monthly temperature of -15°C/5 F in the winter. In the summertime, the warmest areas are in the southeast and the southern coast of Norway. Skudenes in Rogaland county on the west coast has the highest annual temperature of 7.7°C/45.9 F. The west coast also has one of the highest normal annual precipitations in Europe, in the area from Hardanger Fjord to Møre county.

Norway is divided by the Arctic Circle at 66° 33'. In the areas north of the Arctic Circle, the sun stays below horizon level during the winter months and in the summertime; the sun is above the horizon 24 hours a day. On the mainland, the first day of midnight sun is usually May 13th at Nordkapp, the North Cape. The midnight sun then spreads southwards until June 4th when it arrives in Bodø. The following weeks seem like an endless summer day before the sun starts to go below the horizon again towards the end of July. On Svalbard the midnight sun begins on April 20th and lasts until August 20th. All midnight sun dates vary by approximately 24 hours each year.

Flora and fauna

There are between 230 000 and 270 000 known and registered plants in the world, but the actual number is estimated to be much higher. Approximately 2 630 of these are found in Norway. Half of these are native to Norway, while the rest have originated elsewhere. 593 of these foreign species are now considered and integral part of Norwegian plant life. 110 of these are spreading and might have a considerable effect on the native flora.

Although genuinely untouched wilderness hardly exists in Norway anymore, its geographical qualities cause a large variety of natural habitats. Large predators in Norway include brown bear, wolves, lynx and wolverine. Until the mid-1900s there were large populations of these animals in Norway, but by the middle of the 20th century wolves and bears had almost been exterminated as a result of excessive hunting. In the 1970s, all large predators were protected by law. Today, the populations of lynx and wolverines are considered viable. The population of wolves has reached its political target, although that number is subject to intense debates between farmers, politicians and environmentalists. It is estimated that a total of approximately 1 000 bears reside in Scandinavia, and the last registration of bear population in Norway estimated a total of 35-55 bears. This registration was conducted in 2003, but a 2006 report based on DNA findings from 6 northern Norwegian counties found material from 71 different individuals. A similar project based on material from southern counties will be conducted in 2007, and a new estimate of the Norwegian bear population should follow.

80 per cent of the population in Norway says they want wolves in the country, but most of them want to live well away from where the wolves live

Large predators		
Species	*Specimens*	*Date*
Wolf	19-26	01.03.2008
Brown bear	126	16.4.2008
Wolverine	362 (+/- 39)	01.10.2007
Lynx	409-439	01.06.2007

Source: Directorate for Nature Management 2008

Other wild mammals include wild reindeer in the mountains of southern Norway, red fox, arctic fox, moose, and deer. The arctic fox is endangered; only 50 adult species are estimated alive today and might become extinct. Around 200 000 domesticated reindeer are found in Finnmark, the north-ernmost county. Polar bears are only found on Svalbard, where the last estimate suggested a population of approximately 2 000 animals.

Biodiversity		
	Mammal species, number. 2004	*Mammal species, threatened. 2006*
Norway	83	10
Denmark	81	4
France	148	16
Germany	126	10
United Kingdom	103	10
Italy	132	12
United States	468	41
China	502	84

Source: EarthTrends 2008

The International Union for Conservation of Nature and Natural Resources publishes its red list of plants and animals that are threatened by extinction or sizeable reduction every year. There are approximately 40 000 known species in Norway, of which 18 482 are evaluated for the list. The Norwegian Red list contains 3 886 species, or 21% of the evaluated species.

Life in the waters

Common fish species for commercial use include salmon, trout, cod, haddock, pollock, saithe, tusk, ling, mackerel, herring, redfish and halibut. Of all registered fish in Norwegian waters, 257 have been registered in marine waters and 32 in freshwater.

Of the 75 whale species in the world, about twenty species frequent Norwegian waters. Hunting minke whale is legal, but under quota restriction. In 2003, the minke whale harvesting quota 711. This was an increase compared to the 2001 quota of 549. In 2007, the quota is 1 052 specimens – a basis quota of 955, and an additional 97 that were not killed in 2006. The International Whaling Commission estimated the total minke whale population in the northeastern part of the Atlantic Ocean and the waters around Jan Mayen at around 107 000 specimens.

The coastline of Norway is also home to several seal species; the common seal, grey seal, ringed seal, and harp seal. The most common species are subject to hunting. In 2004, the Norwegian government stated its intention of regulating population growth in coastal seals to reduce damage to the fisheries and local communities. The Parliament, Stortinget, amended the fisheries legislation and allowed foreign nationals to participate in hunting seals.

Population

Total:

- 4 769 736 (01.07.2008)

Life expectancy, 2007:

- Males: 78.2 years
- Females: 82.7 years

Infant mortality rate, per 1 000 live births, 2007:

- Boys: 3.2
- Girls: 2.9

Births in 2007:

- Number of births: 58 500
- Mother's average age: 28.1
- Percentage of children born to married parents: 45 %
- Percentage of children born to unmarried, cohabitant parents: 44 %
- Percentage of children born to single mothers: 11 %

Source: Statistics Norway 2008

Life expectancy at birth, 2005	
Sweden	80.5
Norway	79.8
France	80.2
Italy	80.3
Germany	79.1
Greece	78.9
United Kingdom	79
United States	77.9
Cuba	77.7
Latvia	72
Swaziland	40.9

Source: UN Human Development Report 2007

Most populous cities, 2008	
Oslo	560 484
Bergen	247 746
Trondheim	165 191
Stavanger	119 586
Kristiansand	78 919
Fredrikstad	71 976

Source: Statistics Norway 2008

The number of inhabitants in urban settlements increased by about 67 400 during 2007. Since 2000, the four largest cities comprise 55% of the national population growth. As of January 1st 2008, 79% of the total population was registered as living in urban settlements. These settlements occupy 2 333 square kilometers of Norway's total area.

Urban population, percentage of total population, 2005	
Norway	77
Russia	73
Finland	61
Austria	66
South Africa	59
Italy	68
United States	81
China	40
Israel	92

Source: 2007 World Development Indicators

Immigrant population

The immigrants in Norway come from 213 different countries. In 1920, the immigrant population in Norway comprised 2.8% of the total population. In 2007, about 9.7% of the total population has some kind of immigrant background. Around half of the members of this group was born abroad with neither parents nor grandparents born in Norway, and 79 000 persons were born in Norway to foreign-born parents. These persons are regarded as the total immigrant population, numbering approximately 460 000 in 2008. In 2007, Norway had the highest net immigration ever peaking at 40 000 – 16 000 more than in 2006. By January 1st 2007, there were 125 1491 refugees in Norway, the majority of which came from Iraq and Somalia.

Foreign-born populations in Europe, percentage of total population, 2005	
Denmark	7.2
France	10.7
Germany	12.3
Italy	4.3
Sweden	12.4
United Kingdom	8.6
Norway	7.4
Total EU, EEA, Switzerland	8.9

Source: *Migration Policy Institute 2008*

Immigrant population in Norway, 2008	
First generation immigrants	380 644
Born in Norway with foreign-born parents	78 970
Persons with immigrant background	716 967
Foreign citizens	266 260

Source: *Statistics Norway 2008*

Answers to three questions on relation to immigrants, percentage of total respondents, 2007			
"Would you feel uncomfortable if..."	Yes	No	Don't know
"...You or someone in your closest family had an immigrant as domestic help"	10	89	1
"...Your new neighbour was an immigrant"	8	91	1
"...You had a son or daughter that wanted to marry an immigrant"	32	64	4

Source: *Statistics Norway 2008*

Ethnic minorities

Norway is the home of an ethnic minority group called the Sàpmi, or the Sàmi population. The Sàmi language is one of Norway's two official languages. The Sàmi live all over Norway, but the most concentrated Sàmi settlements are located north of the Arctic Circle. The estimated total of the Sàmi population in Norway varies from 40 to 100 000, but there is no statistical evidence available to provide a definite number. Statistics Norway suggests a total Sàmi population of 40 000, but intermarriage and other issues make it difficult to estimate a specific number. 12 650 persons are registered on the Sàmi electoral list. In 2007, there are 2 820 persons registered as associated with domesticated reindeer herding, 1 150 children attending Sàmi childcare, and 990 children in primary schools with Sàmi as the language of education. There is a general consensus that the largest portion of the Sàmi population, possibly around 70%, resides in Norway, even though the Sàmi habitat includes areas in Sweden, Finland and Russia.

The following numbers are based on estimates, as no statistics of ethnic origin are kept. The figures are imprecise and reflect the number of people who claim affiliation to the minority group, and not necessarily those having fluent command of the language. For instance, it is estimated that approximately 25 000 people in Norway speak the Sàmi language, although the total ethnic minority group possibly number three times as many.

National minorities in Norway, estimated population.	
Sami	50 000-100 000
Kven	10 000-15 000
Jews	1 500-2 000
Forest Finns	A few hundred
Romani (Travellers)	2 000-3 000
Roma (Gypsies)	300-400

Sources: Ministry of Culture and Church Affairs, European Charter for Regional or Minority Languages Report, April 2005. Nordic Sami Institute 2008. Statistics Norway 2008.

Crime

On January 1st 2006, a total of 3 355 persons were serving sentences in prison. 6 per cent were females. During the course of 2006, more than 11 900 new imprisonments were registered.

Offences reported to the police, 2007	
Type of offence	*Number*
Total	398 199
Offences for profit	180 337
Traffic offences	68 748
Offences of narcotics	40 755
Other offences	44 903
Offences of violence	25 702
Damage to property	23 354
Economic offences	7 137
Sexual offences	3 802
Environment offences	2 592
Work environment offences	869

Source: Statistics Norway 2008

Recreation and culture

Almost nine out of ten Norwegians watch television every day. On average, a Norwegian watches television two hours and 28 minutes every day. In ten years, the share of daily radio listeners has decreased from 66 to 54%. In 1997, 13% of the population had internet access in their homes. In 2007, 79% now have Internet access at home and two out of three Norwegians use the Internet every day. Three out of four read newspapers every day, with a higher representation among persons with higher education. This is a 10% decrease from 1991.

The number of people attending popular music concerts has been the cultural activity with the highest increase, from 31% in 1991 to a record high of 47% in 2004. Going to the cinema is the most popular cultural event; almost seven out of ten Norwegians have seen at least one movie at the cinema in the last twelve months. Sporting events have the highest frequency of visitors. Women and children aged 9-15 have the highest annual frequency of use of cultural arrangements, whereas men attend sporting events much more frequently and go to more popular music concerts.

Percentage of population participating in cultural activities a year, ages 9-79, 2004	
Cultural activity	Percentage
Cinema	68
Sporting event	55
Public library	54
Theatre (plays, musicals, etc.)	49
Art exhibition	42
Museum	42
Concerts, popular music	35
Concerts, classical music	35
Ballet, dance performances	12
Opera	5
Religious or philosophical gathering	40

Source: Statistics Norway 2008

Alcoholic beer consumption, 2004	
Country	Litres per person
Ireland	108.0
Germany	115.9
Austria	108.6
United Kingdom	100.8
Denmark	90.1
Netherlands	77.9
Norway	55.0
France	33.4
Italy	29.6

Source: The Brewers of Europe Statistics 2008

A crowd of people at a football (soccer) match. Football is the most popular sport in Norway attracting an increasing number of spectators

Education

Structure of the Norwegian school system		
Level	Duration, years	Age
Primary school	7	6-13
Lower secondary school	3	13-16
Upper secondary school	3	16-19

All public education in Norway is free of charge. During the school year of 2007/2008, a total of 616 388 students were enrolled in primary and lower secondary education at a total of 3 160 institutions. 192 168 were enrolled in upper secondary schools. On October 1st 2007, 219 464 students were enrolled at universities and colleges. One out of four Norwegians have completed a higher education, and 60 per cent of all students enrolled in higher education are women. However, the proportion of men who have completed a postgraduate degree is almost double to that of women. 32% of all Norwegians aged 19-24 are enrolled at a college or university. During 2007/2008, 11 201 Norwegian students were studying abroad. The United Kingdom and Denmark were the most popular places to study.

Total government funds spent on education, NOK million, 2005		
Level	2000	2005
Pre-primary and primary	32 412	45 753
Upper secondary	17 944	22 651
Universities and colleges	19 918	27 728
Education not definable by level	4 106	7 327
Subsidiary services to education	166	1 730
Other	4 615	2 717
Total	79 162	107 916

Source: Statistics Norway 2007

The PISA survey - 2006

The OECD Programme for International Student Assessment (PISA) is a survey of the knowledge and skills of 15-year-olds in 57 countries. In 2006, the focus was on science, but the assessment also included findings on reading and mathematics. Here are the 20 best countries – and the ranking of Norway.

SCIENCE	READING	MATHEMATICS
1. Finland	South-Korea	Taiwan
2. Hong Kong	Finland	Finland
3. Canada	Hong Kong	Hong Kong
4. Taiwan	Canada	South Korea
5. Estonia	New Zealand	Netherlands
6. Japan	Ireland	Switzerland
7. New Zealand	Australia	Canada
8. Australia	Liechtenstein	Macao
9. Netherlands	Poland	Liechtenstein
10. Liechtenstein	Sweden	Japan
11. South Korea	Netherlands	New Zealand
12. Slovenia	Belgium	Belgium
13. Germany	Estonia	Australia
14. Great Britain	Switzerland	Estonia
15. Czech Republic	Japan	Denmark
16. Switzerland	Taiwan	Czech Republic
17. Macao	Great Britain	Iceland
18. Austria	Germany	Austria
19. Belgium	Denmark	Germany
20. Ireland	Slovenia	Slovenia
---	---	---
33. Norway	25. Norway	29. Norway

Childcare

At the end of 2007, 249 815 children aged 1-5 attended kindergarten. This was a 4 per cent increase from 2006, and includes 84% of all children in this age group. 69% of all children aged 1-2 were enrolled in kindergarten, and almost 94% of all children aged 3-5. Almost 199 221 children attended kindergarten full time, defined as 41 hours or more. There are about 6 600 kindergartens in Norway, 200 more than the previous year. There are 134 400 children in public and 115 500 in private kindergartens. 76 100 people were employed in kindergartens, of which 8 percent were male.

Source: Statistics Norway 2008

Religion

In January 2008, 82% of all Norwegians were registered members of the Church of Norway. 73.5% of all newborn children were baptized, and 67% of all 15-year olds chose to be confirmed in the Church of Norway. In 2007, 403 909 people were registered in religious of philosophical communities outside the Church of Norway. 225 507 were registered members of Christian communities. Islamic communities had approximately 79 000 members, the same number of people who were registered in life stance communities such as the Norwegian Humanist Association. The Roman Catholic Church has 51 502 members, and the Pentecostal congregations have 40 398 members.

Source: Statistics Norway 2008

Environment

Norway is relatively poor in minerals but has rich natural resources in crude oil, natural gas, fish, and forests. Although not a member, Norway's environmental policies are highly influenced by the European Union. The Department of the Environment suggests that 80-90% of Norway's environmental policies are influenced by the policies of the European Union. From 1994 to 2002, 152 environmental bills were implemented in Norwegian legislature.

Norway signed the Kyoto Protocol and is committed to reducing the greenhouse gas emissions to no more than 1% higher than the 1990 level in the period of 2008-2012. From 1990-2007, Norway's greenhouse gas emissions rose by 11%. In 2007, emissions rose to 2.7% higher than the year before. After two years of decline, the opening of two large plants in 2007 made the year the one with highest emissions ever. 168 countries have ratified the Kyoto protocol, and Norway is among the 36 industrialized countries that have committed to a national quota of CO_2 emissions in the period 2008-2012. The projected CO_2 emissions for Norway during this period are higher than the quota. Norway has about the same distance to meet the Kyoto target as the Netherlands. Denmark, France, Italy, Spain and Ireland still have far to go; whereas Sweden, Germany and the United Kingdom have reached the target.

At the conference on Bali in 2007 Norway presented their plans on spending 3 billions NOK yearly, the next three years, on work against deforestation. These plans were agreed upon by both the government and the opposition.

Energy and the environment, 2005				
	Energy production, million tons	Net imports, million tons	CO2 emissions, million tons	Electric consumption. TWh
Norway	233.7	- 200.44	37	116.22
Denmark	31.3	- 10.52	47.51	36.09
France	136.89	143.30	388.38	483.23
Germany	134.50	214.47	813.48	586.41
United Kingdom	204.3	32.26	529.89	376.63
Italy	27.63	159.33	454	332.23
United States	1630.68	734.87	5816.96	4046.6
China	1 641		5 101	2 363
World	11 468		27 136	16 695

Source: International Energy Agency, Key World Energy Statistics 2007

Tourist attractions

Most popular tourist attractions, by paying visitors, May 1st to August 31st 2006:

1   Holmenkollen Ski Arena, Oslo

2   Bryggen, The Hanseatic Museum, Bergen

3   Kristiansand Zoo and Amusement Park, Kristiansand

4   Tusenfryd Amusement Park, Ås/Oslo

5   Flåm Railway, Flåm

6   Hadeland Glassworks, Jevnaker

7   Fløibanen Funicular, Bergen

8   The Fortress Town, Fredrikstad

9   The Viking Ship Museum, Oslo

10   Hunderfossen Family Park, Lillehammer

In a survey of the most popular World Heritage Sites, Norway's western fjords emerged as the winner. These include the dramatic Geirangerfjord,

More than one million tourists from all over the world visit The Holmenkollen Ski Arena in Oslo every year. The best ski jumpers in the world meet here every winter to compete. During the Winter Olympic Games in 1952, more than 140.000 people watched the ski jumping. This is an Olympic spectator record.

the world's longest fjord Sognefjorden, and the UNESCO World Heritage Site Nærøyfjorden. Other popular tourist destinations include the Lofoten Islands, the North Cape, Vigeland Sculpture Park, Urnes Stave Church, The Arctic Circle Centre, Jotunheimen mountain plateau, and the Norwegian coastline seen from the sea aboard the Norwegian Coastal Express, also known as Hurtigruten.

More information: www.visitnorway.com

Politics

Norway is a constitutional monarchy with a parliamentary system of government. The present government was appointed on October 17th, 2005. Jens Stoltenberg is the prime minister, leading a majority government represented by the Labour Party, the Socialist Left Party, and the Centre Party.

325

Formally, the current governments two "Big Issues" are a binding climate policy and commitment to the Millennium Development Goals. On a more pragmatic scale, the issue the average Norwegian might think of as the government's "Big Issue" is its election promise to provide all children admission to kindergarten by the end of 2007.

More information: www.government.no

On June 17th 2008 the Storting ratified the Marriage Act for heterosexuals and homosexuals. This act included amendments of the Marriage Act (allowing couples of the same sex to enter marriage), the Adoption Act (married couples are now allowed to be evaluated as prospective adoptive parents), the Act on Biotechnology (lesbian spouses and cohabitants can now get the same access to medical assisted reproduction) and the Children Act (giving children conceived by medically assisted reproduction the same legally protection as those born in heterosexual relationships).

Political structure in Stortinget (Parliament), 2005-09	
Party	*Seats*
The Labour Party	61
The Conservative Party	23
The Progress Party	38
The Socialist Left Party	15
The Christian Democratic Party	11
The Centre Party	11
The Liberals	10
Total	169

Ministries
Office of the Prime Minister
Ministry of Agriculture and Food
Ministry of Children and Equality
Ministry of Culture and Church Affairs
Ministry of Defence
Ministry of Education and Research
Ministry of Finance
Ministry of Fisheries and Coastal Affairs
Ministry of Foreign Affairs
Ministry of Government Administration and Reform
Ministry of Health and Care Services
Ministry of Justice and the Police
Ministry of Local Government and Regional Development
Ministry of Petroleum and Energy
Ministry of Labour and Social Inclusion
Ministry of Trade and Industry
Ministry of Transport and Communications
Ministry of the Environment

Selected international agreements and treaties
CE: Council of Europe
EEA: European Economic Area
EFTA: European Free Trade Association
UN: United Nations
ICJ: International Court of Justice (Haag)
IMF: International Monetary Fund
NC: Nordic Council
NATO: North Atlantic Treaty Organization
OECD: Organization for Economic Cooperation and Development
OSCE: Organization for Security and Cooperation in Europe
BSSSC: Baltic Sea States Subregional Co-operation

Norway is not a member of the Organization for Petroleum Exporting Countries, nor is it a member of the European Union. The Norwegian people voted against EU membership in popular elections in 1972 and 1994.

Priorities in public spending (% of GDP)			
Country	Public expenditure on health (2004)	Public expenditure on education (2002-05*)	Military expenditure (2005)
Norway	8.1	7.7	1.7
Germany	8.2	4.6	1.4
United States	6.9	5.9	4.1
United Kingdom	7.0	5.4	2.7
Italy	6.5	4.7	1.9
France	8.2	5.9	2.5
Spain	5.7	4.3	1.1

Source: Human Development Report 2007/2008
*Data refer to the most recent year available

Economy and resources

The Norwegian economy is to a large extent dependent on non-renewable resources: Oil and natural gas. The Norwegian Government Petroleum Fund was established in 1990 and the first allocation to the Fund was made five years later. Its purpose is to safeguard future considerations, such as pensions and healthcare. By the end of 2004, the Petroleum Fund reached 1 000 billion NOK, or 72% of the gross domestic product. The accumulated balance of the Petroleum Fund itself cannot be withdrawn. The surplus from the interest is used to cover the non-oil budget deficit. The Ministry of Finance through the Bank of Norway is responsible for determining the investment areas for the Fund. The Norwegian parliament, Stortinget, decides how the money is to be spent.

GDP per capita, purchasing power parity in US Dollars		
Country	2002	2005
Norway	36 600	41 420
United States	35 750	41 890
Germany	27 100	29 461
Italy	26 430	28 529
United Kingdom	26 150	33 238
Sweden	26 050	32 525
Spain	21 460	27 169
Portugal	18 280	20 410
Latvia	9 210	13 646

Source: UN Human Development Report 2007/2008

Rich and poor states, 1820	
Country	Income per head in 1990 USD
United Kingdom	1 756
Netherlands	1 561
United States	1 287
Denmark	1 225
Germany	1 112
Norway	1 004
Japan	704
China	523

Source: John Kay, Culture and Prosperity, 2004

Official development assistance, 2005	
Country	*Percentage of gross net income*
Norway	0.94
Netherlands	0.82
Denmark	0.81
France	0.47
United Kingdom	0.47
Germany	0.36
United States	0.22

Source: UN Human Development Report 2007/2008

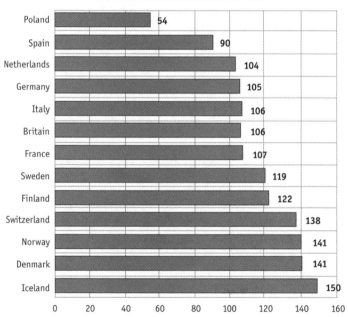

Relative price level for Actual Individual Consumption in selected countries. 2005. EU25=100

- Poland: 54
- Spain: 90
- Netherlands: 104
- Germany: 105
- Italy: 106
- Britain: 106
- France: 107
- Sweden: 119
- Finland: 122
- Switzerland: 138
- Norway: 141
- Denmark: 141
- Iceland: 150

Source: Statistics Norway 2006

Price level indices. 15 Euros=100, 2001				
Country	Food and non-alcoholic beverages	Alcoholic beverages and tobacco	Health	Education
Norway	132	241	130	123
United Kingdom	108	185	108	118
Germany	101	85	117	133
France	108	96	90	86
Italy	98	84	102	92
Spain	81	65	77	71
Netherlands	96	90	91	94
Denmark	130	136	129	130

Value of exports and imports of goods and services. Percentage of GDP, 2005		
Country	Imports	Exports
Norway	28	45
United Kingdom	30	26
Germany	35	40
Netherlands	63	71
France	27	26
Sweden	41	49
China	32	37
United States	15	10

Source: UN Human Development Report 2007/2008

Norway: Exports of principal commodities, 2006	
Commodity	*NOK Million*
Total	668 949
Petroleum, petroleum products and related materials	362 976
Gas, natural and manufactured	164 401
Non-ferrous metals	51 949
Fish	34 667
Machines and transport equipment	66 291

Source: Statistics Norway

Inequality in income or expenditure, 2007		
Country	*Share of income or consumption, poorest 20%, per cent*	*Share of income or consumption, richest 20 %, per cent*
Czech Republic	10.3	35.9
Norway	9.6	37.2
Germany	8.5	36.9
Denmark	8.3	35.8
France	7.2	40.2
Italy	6.5	42.0
Russia	6.1	46.6
United Kingdom	6.1	44.0
United States	5.4	45.8

Source: Human Development Report 2007/2008

The Global Competitiveness Report 2007-2008.	
The rankings are calculated from both publicly available data and the Executive Opinion Survey, a comprehensive annual survey conducted by the World Economic Forum together with its network of Partner Institutes (leading research institutes and business organizations) in the countries covered by the Report. This year, over 11,000 business leaders were polled in a record 131 countries.	
1.	USA
2.	Switzerland
3.	Denmark
4.	Sweden
5.	Germany
6.	Finland
7.	Singapore
8.	Japan
9.	Great Britain
10.	Netherland
11.	South-Korea
12.	Hong Kong
13.	Canada
14.	Taiwan
15.	Austria
16.	Norway
17.	Israel
18.	France
19.	Australia
20.	Belgium
34.	China

Kilde: World Economic Forum

Employment

During 2008, the Norwegian work force totalled 72.8% of the population between 16 and 74 years of age. 70.9% were employed and 2.5% registered unemployed. The large number of employed persons is mainly due to the high frequency of women in the work force. Almost seven out of ten women were employed. 42% of these women were employed part time, compared with 12% of the men. 30 years ago, less than half of the female population held jobs outside the home.

Employment in the three main sectors
Perent of total employment. 1980, 1990 and 2000

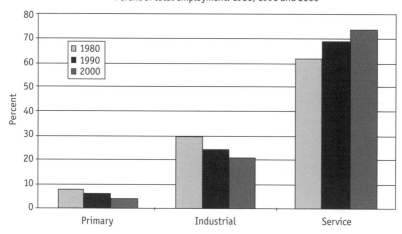

Employed persons 16-74 years, 2008	
Total	2 497 000
Health and social services	485 000
Domestic trade, hotels, restaurants	428 000
Manufacturing	283 000
Real estate, finance, business activities	340 000
Education	222 000
Public administration and defence	158 000
Transport and communication	158 000
Construction	182 000
Agriculture and forestry	56 000

Source: Statistics Norway

Immigrants and employment. Percentage employed, 2007		
Region	First generation immigrants	Norwegian born to foreign born parents
Total	63.3	58.4
Nordic countries	74.5	74.1
Non-EU Eastern Europe	61.9	61.7
New EU countries in Eastern Europe	75.9	67.9
Africa	49.0	49.6
North America and Oceania	64.2	64.9
Asia	56.3	56.1

Source: Statistics Norway

Gender

The Department of Children and Equality is responsible for official gender related issues in Norway. In May 2005, the Parliament approved a government proposal to join all administration offices regarding discrimination. This new institution was established January 1st. 2006, and is called the New Equality and Anti-Discrimination Ombud. Its purposes include enforcing the various Norwegian anti-discrimination acts and prohibitions, investigating possible breaches of these laws, dealing with complaints, making sure the UN gender and discrimination related conventions are implemented in Norwegian law and public governance, as well as actively promoting equality and develop new knowledge through documentation and monitoring. The establishment of the Ombud has been criticized for overstretching its purposes and for lacking a more efficient and balanced distribution of power. The criticism has also included complaints that ethnic discrimination and gender related inequality are separate issues that need to be dealt with separately.

Another public institution to improve equality between sexes is the Norwegian Equal Pay Commission. It was appointed June 16th, 2006. There has been no systematic reduction of the gender pay gap difference since 1985. In 2005, women employed in the private sector have an average wage of 84% to that of the male employees. In the public sector, the same percentage is at 87%. The Equal Pay Commission is appointed to investigate what can be done to narrow the wage gap, and submitted its recommendations in May 2008. They found that the pay gap is not caused by age or length of education, but rather by the traditional gender divided labor market. Some of the suggestions they make to close this gap include a wage rise in the public sector, a more equal share of the maternity leave, and a project witch is to support companies who appoint women for managing positions.

Gender pay gap difference between average gross hourly earnings of male and female employees, 2006	
Countries	Difference as a percentage of male gross earnings
Germany	22
United Kingdom	21
Denmark	17
Norway	16
Sweden	16
EU-25	15
France	11
Italy	9

Source: Eurostat Yearbook 2008

Women's political participation			
Countries	Year women received right to vote	Year first woman elected (E) or appointed (A) to parliament	Year women received right to stand for election
Norway	1913	1911 (A)	1907, 1913
Sweden	1919, 1921	1921 (E)	1919, 1921
United States	1920, 1965	1917 (E)	1788
United Kingdom	1918, 1928	1918 (E)	1918, 1928
France	1944	1945 (E)	1944
Italy	1945	1946 (E)	1945
China	1949	1954 (E)	1949

Source: UN Human Development Report 2007/2008

Female unemployment rate, as percentage of male rate, 2006	
Countries	Percentage of male rate
United Kingdom	86
Norway	94
United States	100
Sweden	103
Germany	119
Denmark	136
Italy	165
Greece	243

Source: Human Development Report 2007/2008

Female legislators, senior officials and managers. Percentage of total, 2005. Women's share of positions defined according to the International Standard Classification of Occupations; ISCO-88	
Countries	Percentage of total
United States	42
Russia	38
Germany	37
United Kingdom	34
Italy	32
Norway	30
Sweden	30

Source: Human Development Report 2007/2008

Chronology

10 000 BC:	The last ice age ends
8 000 BC:	Settlements along the Norwegian coast
4 000 BC:	Animals are domesticated and grain cultivated
500 BC:	Weapons and tools in iron
793 AD:	The first Viking attack, on the Lindisfarne monastery in north-east England
800-900:	Norwegian settlements on the British Isles
850-1000:	Norwegian settlements on Greenland, Iceland and the Faroe Islands
880-900:	King Harald Haarfagre ("Fairhair") starts the first phase of the political unification by establishing a kingdom along the western coast of Norway
950-1050:	Christianity introduced in Norway
1066:	Norwegian Vikings are defeated at the Battle of Stamford Bridge near York, England
1134:	The Civil Wars begin. Start of the second phase of political unification of Norway
1152-53:	The national assembly in Trondheim establishes the first Norwegian archbishopric, and regulates the relationship between the church and the king, and the church and society
1349:	The Black Death reaches Norway, killing perhaps 50 per cent of the people
1380-1814:	Danish-Norwegian union (Sweden was part of the union until 1523).
1536-1537:	Lutheran Reformation
1739:	The 1739 School Ordinance was passed
1741-1790:	Public poverty assistance program is established
1771-1824:	Hans Nielsen Hauge. A religious reformer.
1814:	The Peace of Kiel assigns Norway to Sweden. Norwegian uprising; a national assembly in Eidsvoll passes a constitution on Norway May 17. The war with Sweden ends with a personal union with the kingdom of Sweden (a common king)

1814-1905:	Union with Sweden
1814-94:	Søren Jaabæk. Political reformer.
1828-1906:	Henrik Ibsen. Poet and dramatist.
1848-1851:	The Thrane movement. A popular protest
1854:	First Norwegian railway from Christiania (Oslo) to Eidsvoll
1859-1952:	Knut Hamsun. Novelist.
1861-1930:	Fritjof Nansen. Explorer.
1872-1928:	Roald Amundsen. Explorer.
1884:	Responsible parliamentary government is established. Political parties emerge: Liberals (Venstre) and Conservatives (Høyre)
1885-1905:	Conflict over foreign policy (trade consulates) with Sweden.
1887:	Norwegian Labour Party established
1897-1987:	Einar Gerhardsen. Labour Party leader and prime minister.
1905:	Union with Sweden dissolved by the Storting
1913:	Universal suffrage for women
1914:	The First World War. Norway is neutral
1914-2002:	Thor Heyerdal. Explorer.
1940: April 9:	German attack on Norway. Five years of occupation. The royal family and the government flee to England. National Socialist Party: the only party permitted
1945:	May 8: Liberation Day
1949:	Norway becomes a member of NATO
1952:	The Olympic winter games are held in Oslo
1957:	Law guarantees the public right of access to the countryside
1960:	Norway is one of the founding members of the European Free Trade Association (EFTA)
1969:	Oil is found in the North Sea
1972:	The Norwegian people say no to membership of the EEC
1978:	The Norwegian Gender Equality Act adopted
1989:	The first Sámi Parliament (Sámediggi)
1994:	The Norwegian people say no to membership of the EU
1994:	The Olympic winter games are held at Lillehammer
1995:	Sophie's World by Jostein Gaarder is the number one bestselling novel in the world

Further reading

Akselberg, Gunnstein: *Bergen – an International Meeting Place and a Linguistic Melting pot*, Bergen: Nordica Bergensia, no. 26, 2002.

Almaas, Ingerid Helsing: *Norway – a Guide to Recent Architechture*, Batsford, 2002.

Andersen, Bjørn G.: *Ice Age Norway – Landscapes Formed by Ice Age Glaciers*, Oslo: Universitetsforlaget, 2000.

Barr, Susan: *Norway – a Consistent Polar Nation?*, Oslo: Kolofon, 2003.

Bezmer, Jeff et.als: *Language Teaching and Learning in a Multicultural Context – Case Studies from Primary Education in the Netherlands and Norway*, Oslo: Novus, 2004.

Blindheim, Martin: *Gothic Painted Wooden Sculpture in Norway 1220-1350*, Messel forlag, 2004.

Brimi, Arne og Ardis Kaspersen: *Norwegian National Recipes – an Inspiring Journey in the Culinary History of Norway*, Oslo: Norsk fakta forlag, 2000.

Bruland, Kristine (ed.): *Essays on Industrialization in France, Norway and Spain*, Oslo: Unipub, 2005.

Bryne, Arvid and Jean Aase: *They Painted Norway: Glimpses of Norwegian Nature and Norwegian Artists*, Oslo: Andresen&Butenschøn, 2004.

Danielsen, Rolf et.als: *Norway: A History from the Vikings to Our Own Times*, Oslo: Scandinavian University Press, 1995.

Grinde, Nils: *A History of Norwegian Music*. Lincoln:University of Nebraska Press 1991.

Grinde, Olav: *Fjord Norway*, Kom forlag, 2000.

Gullestad, Marianne: *Kitchen-table Society – a Case Study of the Family Life and Friendships of Young Working-class Mothers in Urban Norway*, Oslo: Universitetsforlaget, 2001.

Hagelund, Anniken: *The Importance of Being Decent – Political Discourse on Immigration in Norway 1970-2002*, Oslo: Unipax, 2004.

Hermansen, Pål: *Panorama Norway – a Love-letter to the Beauty and Drama of the Norwegian Landscape*, Natur- og kulturforlaget, 2004.

Hohler, Erla Bergendahl: *Norwegian Stave Church Sculpture* (2 vols), Oslo: Universitetsforlaget, 1999.

Kautto, Mikko et.als.: *Nordic Welfare States in the European Context*, Routledge, 2001.

Nordvik, Harald and Tove Bull (eds.): *Norway: Portrait of a Nation*, Oslo: Dinamo, 2004.

Sejersted, Francis: "A Theory of Economic and Technological Development in Norway in the Nineteenth Century", in *Scandinavian Economic History Review & Economy and History*, vol. XL, no.1, 1992.

Statistical Yearbook of Norway, Oslo: Statistisk sentralbyrå, 2004.

Stensersen, Øivind and Ivar Libæk: *History of Norway – From the Ice Age to Today*, Oslo: Dinamo, 2003.

The Curriculum for the 10-year Compulsory School in Norway, Oslo: Norsk læremiddelsenter, 1999.

Vikør, Lars: *The Nordic Languages. Their Status and Interrelations*, Oslo: Novus, 1995.

Vollsnes, Arvid O.: *Norges musikkhistorie*, vol. 1-5. Oslo: Aschehoug 1999-2001.

References

Chapter 1: In Search of Norwegian Values:

Døving, Runar: "Matpakka. Den store norske fortellingen om familien og nasjonen", in *Din: Religionsvitenskapelig Tidsskrift*, no. 1, 1999, pp. 4-12.
Eidsvåg, Inge: "Den norske folkesjelen – finnes den?", in *På Norske Vinger*, no. 5, 1994, p.12.
Furre, Berge: "Ikkje alt som tel, kan teljast", in *Bedre Skole*, no. 4, 2004, pp. 48-55.
Lysklett, Olav B., Kari Emilsen og Trond Løge Hagen: "Hva kjennetegner natur- og friluftsbarnehager?", in *Barnehagefolk*, no.4, 2003, pp. 79-85.

Chapter 3: Why is Norway a Wealthy Country?

Bruland, Kristine: "Skills, Learning and the International Diffusion of Technology: A Perspective on Scandinavian Industrialization", in Maxine Berg and Kristine Bruland (eds): *Technological Revolution in Europe. Historical Perspectives*, Cheltenham UK/NorthhamptonUS, 1998.
Danielsen, Rolf, Ståle Dyrvik, Tore Grønlie, Knut Helle and Edgar Hovland: *Norway: A History from the Vikings to Our Own Times*, Oslo: Scandinavian University Press, 1995.
Furre, Berge: *Norsk historie 1914-2000. Industrisamfunnet – frå vokstervisse til framtidstvil*, Oslo: 2000.
Hodne, Fritz and Ola Honningdal Grytten: *Norsk økonomi i det 19. århundre*, Bergen: Tano, 2000.
Hodne, Fritz and Ola Honningdal Grytten: *Norsk økonomi i det 20. århundre*, Bergen: Tano, 2002.
Hovland, Edgar and Helge Wallum Nordvik: "Det industrielle gjennombrudd i Norge 1840-1914 med samtidens og ettertidens øyne", in Bjørn Basberg, Helge W. Nordvik and Gudmund Stang (eds.): *I det lange løp. Essays i økonomisk historie tilegnet Fritz Hodne*, Bergen 1997.
Sejersted, Francis: "A Theory of Economic and Technological Development in Norway in the Nineteenth Century", in *Scandinavian Economic History Review & Economy and History*, vol. XL, no.1, 1992.
Senghaas, Dieter: *The European Experience. A Historical Critique of Development Theory*, Leamington Spa 1985.

Chapter 4: Religion in Norway: A Bird's Eye View

Eidhamar, Levi G.: *Religioner og livssyn*, Kristiansand: Høyskoleforlaget, 2004.

Heimskringla. Snorres kongesagaer, 6th edition, Oslo: Gyldendal, 2003.

Jakobsen, Knut A.(ed.): *Verdensreligioner i Norge*, Oslo: Universitetsforlaget, 2001.

Oftestad, B (et.als): *Norsk kirkehistorie*, Oslo: Universitetsforlaget, 1993.

Repstad, Pål: *Religiøst liv i det moderne Norge. Et sosiologisk kart*, Kristiansand: Høyskoleforlaget, 2000.

Repstad, Pål: *Dype, stille, sterke, milde: Religiøs makt i dagens Norge*, Oslo: Gyldendal Norsk Forlag, 2002.

Sødal, Helje Kringlebotn (ed.): *Kristendommen II. Tro og tradisjon*, Kristiansand: Høyskoleforlaget, 2004.

Chapter 6: The Norwegian Welfare State

Birkelund, G.E. and T.Petersen: "Det norske likestillingsparadokset: Kjønn og arbeid i velferdssamfunnet", in I.Frønes and L.Kjølsrød (eds.), *Det norske samfunn*, Oslo: Gyldendal, 2003.

Furuholmen, C. and J. Magnussen: *Health Care Systems in Transition: Norway*, Copenhagen: WHO Regional Office for Europe, 2000.

Hagen, K. and I.Lødemel: "Fattigdom og sosial eksklusjon", in I. Frønes and L. Kjølsrød (eds.), *Det norske samfunn*, Oslo: Gyldendal, 2003.

Hatland, A., S. Kuhnle, and T.I.Romøren: *Den norske velferdsstaten*, Oslo: Gyldendal, 2001.

SHD: "The Health and Social Affairs Sector in Norway – An Overview", in The Norwegian Ministry of Health and Social Affairs web-site: http://odin.dep.no/hd/engelsk/publ/veiledninger/bn.html , 2004.

SOS: "The Norwegian Social Insurance Scheme 2004", in The Norwegian Ministry of Social Affairs web-site: http://odin.dep.no/filarkiv/205375/Brosjyre_engelsk_-_2004.pdf

Chapter 7: Education in Norway: Its History, Basis and Practice

Blichfeldt, J. F.: *Lærer for livet? Grunnskolelærerens arbeidsmiljø*. Oslo, Universitetsforlaget, 1985.

Charlton, K.: *Education in Renaissance England*. London; Routledge and Keagan Paul

Coleman, J. (1968): "The Concept of Equality of Educational Opportunity." *Harvard Educational Review*, vol 38. No 1. pp. 7 - 22, 1965.

Dokka, H. J.: *Reformarbeid i Norsk skole: 1950-årene - 1980*. Oslo, NKS-forlaget, 1981.

Dokka, H. J.: *Fra allmueskole til folkeskole: Studier i den Norske folkeskoles historie i det 19. hundreåret*. Oslo, Universitetsforlaget, 1967.

Helgheim, J.: *Allmugeskolen paa bygdene*. Oslo, H. Aschehoug & co, 1980.

Husén, T.: *Social Background and Educational Career*. Paris, OECD, 1972.

K.U.D.: *Normalplan for landsfolkeskolen*. Oslo, H. Aschehoug & Co, 1947.

K.U.D.: *Mønsterplan for Grunnskolen*. Oslo, H. Aschehoug & Co, 1974.

K.U.D.: *Mønsterplan for Grunnskolen*. Oslo, H. Aschehoug & Co, 1987.

Levin, H.: "The Dilemmas of Comprehencive School Reform in Western Europe", *Comparative Review*, 1976.

Myhre, R.: *Den Norske skoles utvikling: Idé og virkelighet*. Oslo, Fabritius forlag, 1967.

Rust, V. D.: *The Democratic Tradition and the Evolution of Schooling in Norway*. New York, Greenwood Press, 1989.

Skard, S.: *Classical Tradition in Norway*. Oslo, Universitetsforlaget, 1980.

Statisktisk sentralbyrå: *Historisk statistikk*, 1988.

Stenhouse, L.: *An Introduction to Curriculum Research and Development*. London, Heinemann, 1987.

Stette, Ø. (red.): *Opplæringsloven med forskrifter*. Oslo, Pedlex Norsk skoleinformasjon, 2001.

Sysiharju, A.-L.: "Primary Education and Secondary Schools" in F. Wisti et al. (eds): *Nordic Democracy: Ideas, Issues, and Institutions in Politics, Economy, Education and Culture Affairs of Denmark, Finland, Iceland, Norway and Sweden*. København, Det Danske selskab, 1981.

Tveit, K.: "Lesekunne og undervisning før folkeskolevesenet". I *Nordisk kulturhistoria*. Jyväskylä, 1981.

U.F.D. http://www.dep.no/ufd/engelsk/education/014081-120036/dok-bn.html

U.F.D.: *Læreplanverket for den 10-årige grunnskolen*. Oslo, Nasjonalt læremiddelsenter, 1997.

Wergeland, N.: *Christiansands beskrivelse*. Oslo, Universitetsforlaget, 1963.

http://www.utdanningsdirektoratet.no/templates/udir/TM_Artikkel.aspx?id=2376 (kunnskapsløftet)

http://udir.no/upload/larerplaner/Fastsatte_lareplaner_for_Kunnskapsloeftet/Samiske/kunnskapsloftet_samisk_oversikt_070308.pdf

Chapter 10: Is Norway an Egalitarian Country?

Bourdieu, Pierre: *Distinction: a Social Critique of the Judgement of Taste*, London: Routledge & Kegan Paul, 1984.

Gullestad, Marianne: *Livsstil og likhet*, Oslo: Universitetsforlaget, 1985.

Halvorsen, Knut: "Marginalisering, sosial tilhørighet og verdifellesskap", in *Avslutningskonferansen Velferd og samfunn 20.-21. april 1999. Foredragene*, Oslo: Norges forskningsråd, pp. 225-232, 1999.

Halvorsen, Knut: *Sosialpolitikken i globalt og komparativt perspektiv*, Oslo: Tano Aschehoug, 1999.

Hellevik, Ottar: *Nordmenn og det gode liv. Norsk monitor 1985-1995*, Oslo: Universitetsforlaget, 1996.

Knudsen, Knud: *Har det blitt mer eller mindre likhet?*, Paper presented at The Reseach Council of Norway's Conference on Welfare Research, October 2004. www.program.forskningsradet.no/vfo/nyhet/nyhet481.php3.

Martinussen, Willy: "Fellesskapsverdier står sterkere enn antatt", in *Samfunnsspeilet*, vol. 13, no. 4, pp. 5-11, 1999

Martinussen, Willy and Anders Todal Jensen (eds.): *Velferdsstaten i våre hjerter*, Oslo: Ad Notam Gyldendal, 1994.

Stjernø, Steinar: *Adjø solidaritet?* Paper presented at The Reseach Council of Norway's Conference on Welfare Research, October 2004. www.program.forskningsradet.no/vfo/nyhet/nyhet481.php3.

Chapter 11: Minorities: Past and Present

Gullestad, Marianne: *Den norske sett med nye øyne. Kritisk analyse av norsk innvandringsdebatt*, Oslo: Universitetsforlaget, 2002.

Seeberg, Marie Louise: *Dealing with Difference: Two Classrooms, Two Countries: A Comparative Study of Norwegian and Dutch Processes of Alterity and Identity, Drawn from Three Points of View*, Nova Rapport, no.18, 2003

www.samediggi.no

http://odin.dep.no/krd/english

Chapter 12: Trends in the Development of Childhood

Ariès, Philippe: *Centuries of Childhood. A Social History of Family Life*, New York: Vintage Books, 1962.

Egner, Torbjørn: *When the Robbers Came to Cardamom Town*, Oslo: Cappelen, 1994.

Frønes, Ivar: *Moderne barndom*, Oslo: Cappelen, 2003.

Håland, Kristine: *Den sosiale mobiltelefonen: ein kvalitativ og kvantitativ studie av ungdom mellom 16 og 18 år sin bruk og oppfatningar av mobiltelefonen*, University of Bergen, 2003.

Juul, Jesper: *Ditt kompetente barn – på vei mot et nytt verdigrunnlag for familien*, Oslo: Pedagogisk forum, 1996.

Nilsen, Ann Christin E.: *Negotiating Children's Work: A Comparative Study of Children's Work in Norway and Zimbabwe*, University of Bergen, 2002.

Reynolds, Pamela: *Dance Civet Cat. Child Labour in the Zambezi Valley*, Harare: Baobab Books, 1991.

Serpell, Robert: "Cultural Models of Childhood in Indigenous Socialization and Formal Schooling in Zambia", in C. Hwang, M.E. Lamb and I.E.Siegel, *Images of Childhood*, New Jersey: Lawrence Erlbaum Associates, 1996.

U.F.D. *Læreplanverket for den 10.årige grunnskolen*. Oslo: Nasjonalt læremiddelsenter, 1997

UNESCO: *World Culture Report*, Unesco Publishing, 1999

World Values Survey, www.worldvaluessurvey.org/

Ytrehus, Siri: *Fattige barn i Norge. Hvem er de og hvor bor de?*, Oslo: Fafo- rapport 445, 2004.

Chapter 13: The Norwegian Language – Democracy in Practice?

Bourdiev, P.: Distinction. *A social critique of the Judgement of Taste*, London, 1984.
Bourdiev, P.: *Language and Symbolic Power*, Cambridge, 1991.
Jahr, Ernst Håkon: *Innhogg i nyere norsk språkhistorie*, Oslo: Novus, 1992.
Johansson, Stig and Anne-Line Graedle: *Rocka, hipt og snacksy. Om engelsk i norsk språk og samfun*, Kristiansand: Høyskoleforlaget, 1997.
Mæhlum, Brit, Gunnstein Akselberg, Unn Røyneland and Helge Sandøy: *Innføring i sosiolingvistikk*. Oslo: Cappelen, 2003.
Omdal, Helge and Lars Vikør: *Språknormer i Norge*. Oslo: Cappelen, 2002.
Omdal, Helge and Rune Røstad (eds.): *Krefter og motkrefter i språknormeringa. Om språknormer i teori og praksis*. Forskningsserien nr. 33. Høgskolen i Agder. Kristiansand: Høyskoleforlaget, 2003.
Sandøy, Helge: *Lånte fjører eller bunad*, Oslo: Cappelen, 2000.
Torp, Arne and Lars Vikør: *Hovuddrag i norsk språkhistorie*, Oslo: Ad Notam Gyldendal, 1996.
Vikør, Lars: *Språkplanlegging. Prinsipp og praksis*, Oslo: Novus, 1994.
Vikør, Lars: *The Nordic Languages. Their Status and Interrelations*. Oslo: Novus, 1995.
www.samediggi.no

Chapter 14: Norwegian Myths and Tales

http://www.gyldendal.no/toraage/artikler/mytologi.html
Bringsværd, Tor Åge and Johanne Marie Hansen-Krone: Gud og troll i samme kropp [God and troll in the same body], 1991.
Munch, Peter Andreas: Norse mythology: Legends of Gods and Heroes. http://www.vaidilute.com/books/munch/munch-contents.html, 1926.
Willumsen, Liv Helene: "Regine Normann - Nordlandets Forfatterinne", http://www.boe.kommune.no/side.asp?S=74. Bø kommune i Vesterålen. Sist oppdatert 10.04.2007, 2007.
http://www.cyberhymnal.org/bio/l/a/n/landstad_mb.htm

Chapter 15: Trends in Norwegian Literature: Ibsen, Hamsun and Beyond

Andersen, Per Thomas: *Norsk litteraturhistorie*. Oslo: Universitetsforlaget, 2001.
Beyer, Edvard: *Norges litteraturhistorie*. Oslo: Cappelen, 1975.
Bull, Francis; Fredrik Paasche; A.H. Winsnes og Philip Houm: *Norsk litteraturhistorie*. Oslo: Aschehoug, 1961.
Ferguson, Robert: *Enigma : the life of Knut Hamsun*. London : Hutchinson, 1987.
Fidjestøl, Bjarne; Peter Kirkegaard; Sigurd Aa Aarnes; Asbjørn Aarseth; Leif Longum og Idar Stegane: *Norsk litteratur i tusen år*. Oslo: LNU/Cappelen, 1996.
http://www.ibsen.net
http://www.hamsun.no/nettressurser.html

Chapter 16: Children's Literature

Birkeland, Tone, Gunvor Risa and Karin Beate Vold: *Norsk barnelitteraturhistorie*, Oslo: Samlaget, 1997.

Nikolajeva, Maria: *Children's Literature Comes of Age: Toward a New Aesthetic*, New York: Garland, 1996.

Rottem, Øystein: *Norges litteraturhistorie. Vår egen tid 1980-98*, Oslo: Cappelen, 1998.

Vold, Karin Beate: "Norwegian Children's Literature: Word Games, Earnestness – Diversity of Genre and Experiment in Form", http://odin.dep.no/odin/english/norway/history/032001-990014/dok-bn.html, 2000.

http://www.barnelitteratur.no/

Chapter 17: Norwegian Art

Absolute Arts (2006, June 30) "After Munch: Norwegian Contemporary Art?". Located at the web on the 22nd of August 2008: http://absolutearts.com/artsnews/2006/06/30/34012.html

BBC (2004, August 22) "Scream stolen from Norway museum?". UK: BBC News. Located at the web on the 22nd of August 2008: http://news.bbc.co.uk/2/hi/europe/3588282.stm

Bryne, Arvid: *They painted Norway*, Andersen & Butenschøn AS, 2004

Eckoff, Audun: "Kommunikasjonsstykke/Communication Piece" I: Eckcoff, Audun, Karin Hellandsjø, Randi Lium, Erlend Høyersten: *Hilmar Fredriksen*. Bergen: Bergen Kunstmuseum, 2006.

Kofoed, Holger og Bjerke, Øyvind Storm: Tidens øye. *En innføring i norsk malerkunst*. Oslo: J.M. Stenersens Forlag A/S, 2001.

Kofoed, Holger: *Modernismen i kunsthistorien fra 1870 til 1990-årene*. Oslo: Gyldendal Norsk Forlag A/S, 2004.

O`Neill, Amanda: *The Life and Works of Edvard Munch*. Bristol: Parragon Book Service Ltd, 1996.

Petterson, Jan Åke: *Kjartan Slettemark Permanent Haugart 2004-2006*, Haugar Vestfold Kunstmuseum, 2006.

Stang, Ragna: *Edvard Munch: mennesket og kunstneren*. Stabekk: Den Norske Bokklubben, 1989.

Sørlandet Art Museum (2006) *The Permanent Collection*. Kristiansand: Sørlandet Art Museum.

Chapter 18: Norway – Music and Musical Life

Grinde, Nils: *A History of Norwegian Music*. Lincoln:University of Nebraska Press, 1991

http://www.mic.no/english

http://www.norway.org.uk/culture/music/

http://www.norway.org/culture/music/

http://www.jazzbasen.no/index_eng.html

Notes on contributors

Maagerø, Eva:	Associate Professor, Lingustics, Vestfold University College
Simonsen, Birte:	Assistant Professor, Education, Agder University
Andreas Aase:	Assistant Professor, World History, Agder University
Lars Aase:	University Student, History, Agder University College
Silve-Linn Aase:	University Student, History, University of Oslo
Olav A. Abrahamsen:	Associate Professor, History, Agder University
Olav Helge Angell:	Associate Professor, Sociology, Diakonhjemmet University College
Kjetil Børhaug:	Associate Professor, Political Science, Bergen University College
Arvid Hansen:	Assistant Professor, Education, Agder University
Levi Geir Eidhamar:	Associate Professor, Religion, Agder University
Knut Mykland (1920-2005)	Professor, History, University of Bergen
Ann Christin E. Nilsen:	Sociologist. Norwegian Social Research (NOVA)
Pål Repstad:	Professor, Sociology of Religion, Agder University
Lisbet Skregelid:	Research Fellow/Assistant Professor, Art, Agder University
Helje Kringlebotn Sødal:	Associate Professor, Religion, Agder University
Elise Seip Tønnessen:	Associate Professor, Literature, Agder University
Arvid O. Vollsnes:	Professor, Music, University of Oslo

Photo Credits

s. 204:	Sverre A. Børretzen, AKTUELL/Scanpix
s. 205:	Berit Keilen, Scanpix
s. 210:	Sverre A. Børretzen, AKTUELL/Scanpix
s. 214:	F. Bau
s. 217:	Scanpix
s. 240 (r.):	Scanpix
s. 240 (l.):	© Austrian Archives/CORBIS/Scanpix
s. 253:	Arne Samuelsen
s. 255:	Magnar Kirknes, Scanpix
s. 261:	Oil on canvas. Photo: Bjørn Thunæs, Scanpix, BONO
s. 265:	Munchmuseet, BONO
s. 267:	Bronze sculpture. Photo: Bjørn Sigurdsøn, Scanpix, BONO
s. 271:	Acrylic and collage on canvas. Photo: Morten Thorkildsen. The National Museum of Art, Architecture and Design, BONO
s. 273:	Assemblage and oil on canvas. Photo: Morten Thorkildsen. The National Museum of Art, Architecture and Design, BONO
s. 275:	Photo: Marianne Heske
s. 277:	Mixed media. Sørlandet Art Museum. The National Museum of Art, Architecture and Design, BONO
s. 288:	Scanpix
s. 301:	Jan Tomas Espedal, Scanpix
s. 311:	Arne Nævra, Scanpix
s. 320:	Erik Johansen, Scanpix
s. 325:	Jan Greve, Scanpix